IMPLIED CONSENT AND SEXUAL ASSAULT

IMPLIED CONSENT AND SEXUAL ASSAULT

Intimate Relationships, Autonomy, and Voice

MICHAEL PLAXTON

McGill-Queen's University Press
Montreal & Kingston | London | Chicago

ISBN 978-0-7735-4619-6 (cloth)
ISBN 978-0-7735-4620-2 (paper)
ISBN 978-0-7735-9792-1 (ePDF)
ISBN 978-0-7735-9793-8 (ePUB)

Legal deposit fourth quarter 2015
Bibliothèque nationale du Québec

Printed in Canada on acid-free paper that is 100% ancient forest free (100% post-consumer recycled), processed chlorine free.

This book has been published with the help of a grant from the Canadian Federation for the Humanities and Social Sciences, through the Awards to Scholarly Publications Program, using funds provided by the Social Sciences and Humanities Research Council of Canada. Funding has also been provided by the University of Saskatchewan Publications Fund.

McGill-Queen's University Press acknowledges the support of the Canada Council for the Arts for our publishing program. We also acknowledge the financial support of the Government of Canada through the Canada Book Fund for our publishing activities.

Library and Archives Canada Cataloguing in Publication

Plaxton, Michael, 1975–, author
Implied consent and sexual assault : intimate relationships, autonomy, and voice /
Michael Plaxton.

Includes bibliographical references and index.
Issued in print and electronic formats.
ISBN 978-0-7735-4619-6 (bound).–ISBN 978-0-7735-4620-2 (paperback).–
ISBN 978-0-7735-9792-1 (ePDF).–ISBN 978-0-7735-9793-8 (ePUB)

1. Sexual consent – Canada.   2. Rape – Law and legislation – Canada.   3. Sex crimes – Law and legislation – Canada.   4. Women – Legal status, laws, etc. – Canada.
5. Man-woman relationships – Canada.   I. Title.

KE8928.P63 2015   345.71'0253   C2015-905626-8
KF9325.P63 2015   C2015-905627-6

Set in 10.25/14 Warnock Pro with Trade Gothic LT Std
Book design & typesetting by Garet Markvoort, zijn digital

CONTENTS

ACKNOWLEDGMENTS

This book would not be here but for the patience and kind indulgence of friends and colleagues, both at the University of Saskatchewan and elsewhere. I am indebted to Rosemary Cairns-Way, Clare Chambers, Kyle Kirkup, and Tim Quigley for looking over drafts of chapters. Two anonymous peer reviewers had generous things to say about this work and offered some valuable advice for improving it. Many thanks. Patricia Marino showed boundless kindness toward a complete stranger, provided extensive and detailed comments on the manuscript, and gave me some (much-needed) encouragement. She is the very model of collegiality. Carolyn Yates provided stalwart copyediting, saving me from much embarrassment. I am grateful to Lisa Clark for motivating me to undertake this project in the first place. Special thanks to Carissima Mathen and Dwight Newman, both of whom have had to endure endless conversations and soliloquies on implied consent. They read over drafts and provided insightful feedback and consistent encouragement from the very beginning.

Finally, Katrina has given me unwavering love and support. As she would say, she has my back. My appreciation is beyond measure.

IMPLIED CONSENT AND SEXUAL ASSAULT

INTRODUCTION

The Project

Can or should the doctrine of implied consent have any place in Canadian sexual assault law? Since the Supreme Court of Canada's landmark ruling in *R. v. Ewanchuk*,[1] lawyers and legal academics have proceeded on the basis that this question is a non-starter – on both legal and moral grounds.[2] As a legal question, it is (rightly) assumed that the Supreme Court settled it and, more importantly (but more contentiously), that there was no basis for reaching a different conclusion. Recognizing the doctrine of implied consent in the sexual assault context, it is widely thought, would necessarily be incompatible with women's equality rights, would effectively resuscitate the marital rape exception (or something like it), and could not be reconciled with the developments that have occurred in sexual assault law over the last thirty years. As a moral question, it is widely assumed that reviving the doctrine of implied consent would be incompatible with treating women as ends in themselves.

In this book, I challenge both assumptions. We can recognize a doctrine of implied consent – albeit one modified in certain important respects – without taking issue with any of the reforms or animating aims of contemporary sexual assault law. Properly understood and suitably adapted, the doctrine may be seen not only as consistent with the equality rights of women and the moral imperative to treat them as ends in themselves, but also as advancing and promoting those objectives. It does so, I argue, by recognizing that women should have a meaningful voice in determining the norms that govern their intimate relationships[3] and sexual lives.

Making this argument requires us to revisit a number of the central pillars of Canadian sexual assault law. What did the 1983 and 1992 legislative reforms to the law of rape and sexual assault really set out to achieve? What does it mean to respect women's sexual autonomy? When does sexual touching amount to treatment of another as a mere instrument of gratification? Under what circumstances does someone engage in the wrong of stereotyping? In fashioning criminal prohibitions, how significant is context?

I argue that the offence of sexual assault targets a particular kind of wrong – that of sexual instrumentalization. With respect to some intimate relationships, those defined by respect and mutuality, the sexual norms accepted by the parties deserve limited deference by the criminal law. This is true because – and to the extent that – those norms reflect an exercise of sexual agency by all parties to the relationship, who are entitled within limits to decide for themselves how physically and sexually available they should be to each other, and in what ways. Where mutuality exists, concerns about voice, wishful thinking, and stereotypes are necessarily lessened. This is especially true insofar as the kind of sexual touching authorized by the parties veers away from the intrusive and penetrative and toward the more trifling and transitory. Finally, the criminal law can reanimate the doctrine of implied consent (with appropriate modifications), recognizing the importance of sexual agency and autonomy, without placing women at additional risk of sexual violence. This can be done through the use of legal presumptions.

Right at the outset, it is worth making clear some of the arguments I do not make, and a few of the premises I do not rely upon.

First, I do not rest my argument on a balancing of rights – i.e., of women's right to equality and sexual integrity and criminal defendants' right to certain substantive and procedural protections. I focus entirely on what a commitment to women's sexual agency and autonomy, understood in its relational sense, entails. Nor do I direct that inquiry merely at tracking its limits – that is, by way of saying that women are not entitled to this or that protection. On the contrary, my point is that sexual autonomy is more fulsome than cases like *Ewanchuk* and *R. v. J.A.* might give us reason to suppose, and that women are not well served when the offence of sexual assault is taken to preclude implied consent. At its core, the doctrine of implied consent enhances women's autonomy. Or so I argue.

Second, I do not reject claims by various criminal law and sexual assault scholars that the substantive law must sometimes be context insensitive or overbroad for the sake of achieving important policy goals. For the sake of argument, I am prepared to accept that criminal offences must sometimes be defined in such a way that they catch people who are not strictly engaging in the wrongs they were intended to target. My argument rests on the comparatively modest claim that overbreadth should be a last resort, and that we can often avoid the perils of context sensitivity without defining criminal wrongs in an overbroad fashion. Quite simply, the law gives us a wider array of tools than proponents of criminal overbreadth sometimes acknowledge.

Third, I do not make the absurd suggestion that all or most intimate relationships (including marriages) are defined by mutuality, or that they are private arrangements beyond the legitimate scope of legal oversight or regulation. It is the criminal law's legitimate business to protect people from each other – including from intimate partners. At least sometimes, the law can and should intercede even when doing so is contrary to the wishes of the people it protects. For the purposes of this book, in other words, I am prepared to accept a limited form of state paternalism. My point of departure, however, is that there are limits on how far the law should preclude people from living certain ways of life, even when they are informed by social norms we regard as pernicious. I embrace, then, a qualified form of political liberalism – as well as a qualified version of sex positivity.[4]

Fourth, I do not claim that a doctrine of implied consent is needed to stop an epidemic of criminal prosecutions of men accused of sexually assaulting their intimate partners. So far as I know, Crown prosecutors have, by and large, not pursued charges in the kinds of cases that concern me – if, indeed, such cases ever come to their attention in the first place. The problem with overbreadth in this context, I argue, is not that men and women are prosecuted and convicted for blameless sexual conduct – it is that their conduct is labelled as criminally wrongful whether or not they are prosecuted. This argument rests on what is known in criminal law theory circles as "the expressive function of the criminal law," the idea that its primary function is not punitive but educative.

Finally, I do not presume that there is anything fundamentally wrong or misguided about Canadian sexual assault law or its animating ideas and aims. In many or most cases, the existing law yields correct conclusions about whether wrongful sexual touching has taken place. The law as it stands can be seen as an attempt to give women a meaningful voice in determining whether and how they are to be touched sexually, by whom, and under what circumstances. A properly modified and constrained doctrine of implied consent does not challenge the direction of the law, but pushes it further.

In reaching that conclusion, I draw upon a number of orthodox criminal law theorists. I am most strongly influenced, however, by several contemporary feminist thinkers. The most notable is Martha Nussbaum, whose analysis of objectification remains, in my view, the most sophisticated on offer. But feminist work of the 1970s and 1980s, as well as more recent work by Jennifer Nedelsky, Elaine Craig, Clare Chambers, Sally Haslanger, and Rae Langton, also guides my understanding of the wrong that the offence of sexual assault is intended to target.

The Core of Sexual Assault: *Flaviano*, *Ewanchuk*, and *J.A.*

Canadian sexual assault law is very good at explaining what is wrong with most kinds of wrongful sexual touching. Fifteen years after *Ewanchuk*, its core holdings have become common knowledge among criminal lawyers and legal academics. We know that, in determining whether a complainant consented to sexual touching, we must look exclusively to her[5] subjective state of mind rather than any ostensibly objective meaning of her conduct.[6] We also know that consent cannot be given in advance; we must look to the complainant's subjective state of mind at the time the sexual touching took place.[7] The defendant, to have had an honest but mistaken belief in consent, could not have inferred it from the complainant's silence, acquiescence, or passivity.[8] Such an inference would amount to recklessness or wilful blindness – culpable states of mind.[9] Finally, we know why consent matters, why we should emphasize the complainant's subjective state of mind in deciding whether the actus reus of the offence is made out, and why the signals the complainant gives to the defendant, rather than the defendant's (perhaps wishful) state of mind, should determine whether the defence of honest but mistaken belief is available: proceeding in this way protects individuals' sexual integrity and autonomy.[10]

For the most part, my argument does not draw extensively upon case authorities – it is more philosophical or analytical than doctrinal in nature. It is, however, worth observing that the legal propositions I have just mentioned will lead to appropriate results in the vast majority of cases that reach the courts. Take, as a powerful recent example, *R. v. Flaviano*.[11] The complainant was seventeen years old and lived in a rented duplex with her mother and stepfather. She knew the defendant as her family's landlord but in no other capacity – only as "a regular old person."[12] He knocked on the door. When she answered, he said he wanted to examine the gas meter. She let him in, and told him there was also a problem with the dishwasher. He checked the meter and the dishwasher, and proceeded to make idle conversation. This did not bother the complainant, who thought the defendant was just "being friendly," like "the usual old person who could be trusted."[13] But the conversation took a violent turn:

> When the [defendant] ran out of small talk, he "started getting really awkward." [The complainant] expected he might just leave, but instead he asked, "Can you do me a favour? ... But it has to be a secret between me and you." She said, "Yeah." He said, "Can you give me a blow job?" [The complainant] said, "No." She was caught off guard. She never thought he would be that kind of guy, where he would ask someone her age. She was stuttering and "really sort of scared." She said, "No, I don't think I want to do that."[14]

The defendant persisted: "[D]on't you have a boyfriend that you do this kind of stuff for?" he asked.[15] "I won't tell anybody and you won't tell anybody ... So you can't get in trouble and I won't get in trouble."[16] According to the complainant, "[h]is body language straightened out, like a peacock, while he continued to say 'do me this one favour.'"[17] He offered her money.[18] The complainant "had the feeling she was going to get hurt, because the [defendant's] tone of voice was aggressive. He was inching toward her and she didn't know what to do. She was frightened and scared."[19] She led the defendant to the only exit, hoping he would leave.[20] But he didn't. Instead, he locked the door.[21] Terrified, she went downstairs to her room. The defendant followed. There, he took out his penis, saying, "just do me this one favour."[22] "Numb," the complainant complied.[23] The defendant proceeded to sexually penetrate the complainant.[24] When he left, he threatened her: "You can't tell anybody about this ... I know where you live and I know where you stay. I know this is your bedroom ... I have a key to the house and I have people."[25]

The very fact that this case proceeded all the way to the Supreme Court is jarring. The issue ostensibly was whether the defendant could have had an honest but mistaken belief in consent. Even the defendant, in his written submissions to the court, pointed to no affirmative act suggesting the complainant was interested in his advances – before, that is, she became so terrified and worn down by his persistence that she complied.[26] Under the circumstances, her behaviour could not be construed as anything other than ambiguous. As for the silence with which she responded to the defendant's final demands – well, *he* had silenced her. He made it abundantly clear that nothing she said would make any difference; that he would harass and threaten her until she acceded. Her silence, far from excusing his conduct, illustrated and underscored his domination over her. Small wonder, then, that the Supreme Court dismissed the appeal in a single paragraph, finding "no evidence that the accused had taken any reasonable steps to ascertain [consent] following [the complainant's] initial rejection of the [accused's] sexual advances."[27]

There are startling parallels between *Flaviano* and *Ewanchuk*.[28] After briefly meeting for the first time only the day before, Brian Ewanchuk telephoned the complainant's apartment to ask if she was interested in a job selling his woodwork.[29] She said she was. They met in the parking lot of a local shopping mall, and had a "very business-like, polite" conversation in the defendant's van.[30] He suggested that they go inside his trailer so the complainant could see his work. She agreed.[31] They entered the trailer. The complainant believed the defendant locked the door behind them. She was afraid.[32]

Once inside, the defendant and complainant sat next to one another on the floor while she examined a portfolio of his work. After a short while, "the conversation turned to more personal matters."[33] The defendant touched the complainant's hand, arms, and shoulder.[34] He asked her for a massage, so she rubbed his shoulders. He then asked if he could massage her. She agreed, and he massaged her shoulders and arms. At this point, the defendant "attempted to initiate more intimate contact," and manoeuvred his hands around the complainant's stomach and underneath her breasts. She forced his hands away, and said "no." He stopped.[35] When the defendant tried to continue his "non-sexual" massaging, the complainant again said "no." Again, he stopped.[36]

The defendant asked the complainant to turn around. He massaged her feet, then started to move his hands toward her inner thigh and pelvic region.[37] As Major J. put it: "The complainant did not want him to touch her in this way, but said nothing as she said she was afraid that any resistance would prompt the accused to become violent. Although the accused never used or threatened any force, the complainant testified that she did not want to 'egg [him] on.'"[38]

The defendant laid on top of the complainant and ground his pelvis against her.[39] According to the complainant, he told her "he could get [her] so horny so that [she] would want it so bad, and he wouldn't give it to [her] because he had self-control."[40] The complainant, who had done nothing to physically encourage the defendant – and, indeed, who had expressly rejected his sexual advances – asked him to stop.[41] Again, he did: "The accused again told the complainant not to be afraid, and asked her if she trusted that he wouldn't hurt her. In her words, the complainant said, 'Yes, I trust that you won't hurt me.' On the stand she stated that she was afraid throughout, and only responded to the accused in this way because she was fearful that a negative answer would provoke him to use force."[42]

Almost immediately, the defendant again positioned himself on top of the complainant, grinding against her. He placed his hands inside her shorts, then undid his own, exposing his penis.[43] The complainant, once again, said "no." The defendant gave her one hundred dollars, ostensibly for the massage.[44] He asked her not to say anything about it to anyone. The complainant said that she needed to leave. The defendant opened the door and, after a brief conversation outside the trailer, the complainant left.[45]

In *Ewanchuk*, too, one is struck by the utter futility of the complainant's voice. Like *Flaviano*, fifteen years later, *Ewanchuk* was a case in which the defendant treated every rebuff and protestation as nothing more than an invitation to try again. Again, the complainant was psychologically and emotionally bludgeoned into compliance.

But the cases share another similarity – in both, the defendant and complainant were essentially strangers to one another. The relationship between the defendant and the complainant in *Flaviano*, to the extent it was a relationship at all, was not even that of landlord and tenant. To her, he was simply an "old person." There was nothing on which he could have based a belief that she was sexually interested in or available to him – beyond, that is, the purely wishful thinking that a young woman by herself must be open to sexual advances from any man. Indeed, the comments reported by the Crown Respondent in its factum are telling – on one occasion, the defendant acts as though a sexual tryst with him would be no different to the complainant than an encounter with her boyfriend; on another, he equates it to an impersonal commercialized transaction he might have with a prostitute. His remarks emphasize the anonymity of the complainant to the defendant – her fungibility – but also the fact that, so far as he was concerned, she could have no serious reason not to engage in sexual activity with him. She might have passing fancies or whims, but no serious plans or commitments and no reasons conceivably weighty enough to justify withholding what he wanted from her. In the defendant's narcissistic fantasy, he was the only genuine agent.

We might make similar observations about *Ewanchuk*. Again, the defendant and the complainant were virtual strangers. The complainant saw the defendant as nothing more than a prospective employer. He, in turn, knew nothing about her. Yet he presumed, in the face of her clear rejection, that she was sexually interested in him and that she wanted him to make her desire him. And, in the end, he handed her money – again, as if it was an impersonal sexual transaction between a prostitute and a client.

To point out this dimension of anonymity and commodification is not to say that there is necessarily anything wrong with anonymous sexual encounters, whether commercial or not. It is only to say that we are not entitled to presume that every person we meet is waiting to engage in one with us, and that every protestation and rebuff amounts to coquettishness. To an important extent, both *Flaviano* and *Ewanchuk* stand for the proposition that voices matter; that we must engage with others as real people with lives independent of our fantasies, whose words reflect plans and values that have an existence independent of us, and not as actors in a pantomime whose words we must register only so we can manoeuvre around them. Since voices matter, we have a responsibility to ask whether and how we can engage sexually with each other – to take "reasonable steps" in ascertaining consent. Having a meaningful voice is an important part of what it means to have sexual autonomy.

Canadian sexual assault law is very good at explaining what is wrong with the conduct of a Brian Ewanchuk or a Vittorio Flaviano. What about when we move away from cases in which the complainant is attacked by a stranger or acquaintance to cases in which the defendant is the complainant's partner or spouse? To a point, it can explain those, too. Consider a case like *R. v. V. (R.)*, in which the defendant was the complainant's husband.[46] The defendant sexually penetrated the complainant without her consent, and claimed later that he honestly and mistakenly believed that she consented. There was no anonymity in this relationship – quite the contrary. Yet the Ontario Court of Appeal denied that their relationship made any difference to the reasonableness of his sexual touching.

That was a relationship, however, in which the complainant and defendant had ceased to have sexual contact with each other. They slept in separate beds and, on recent prior occasions when the defendant attempted to initiate sexual touching, the complainant showed no interest. The defendant, then, could not have inferred the complainant's sexual interest from anything she had said or done. He implicitly proceeded on the basis of her marital status alone, projecting onto her his fantasies of what a wife – any wife – must want her husband to do, rather than paying attention to what she actually said and did. Her voice, and her sexual autonomy, was taken no more seriously than that of the complainants in *Ewanchuk* and *Flaviano*.

Consider, too, a case like *J.A.*[47] The complainant and defendant had been "long-time partner[s]."[48] With her consent, the defendant choked the complainant into unconsciousness.[49] According to her evidence, she and the defendant had engaged in erotic asphyxiation before.[50] While unconscious, the defendant tied the complainant's hands behind her back and inserted a dildo into her anus.[51] She gave conflicting testimony as to whether this was the first time he had done this,[52] but did not suggest this was a regular or accepted sexual practice in their relationship. Shortly after the complainant awoke, the defendant removed the dildo and the couple had vaginal intercourse.[53]

The central issue in the case was whether it was possible for the complainant to give advance consent to the sexual touching that took place while she was unconscious. The Supreme Court said no, and found the defendant guilty of sexual assault. This case is quite different from *Flaviano*, *Ewanchuk*, and *V. (R.)* – those arguably turned less on actual consent than on the defence of honest but mistaken belief in consent. But in a crucial sense, *J.A.* shares things with the others. First and foremost, the complainant once unconscious was unable to express any preferences one way or the other – to exercise her voice – about the sexual activity in question. That, in turn, made it all too easy for the defendant to project his own fantasies about what the complainant "would" want. If anything, the fact that an issue was made of the complainant's advance "consent" to anal penetration with a dildo on a single prior occasion underscores just why there was a real danger of wishful thinking: her preparedness, while in a state of intoxication, to engage in a particular kind of sexual experimentation on a single prior occasion did not make it reasonable for the defendant to suppose that she wanted that sort of highly intrusive, penetrative sexual activity again.

The Penumbra of Sexual Assault

Even if we say, for the sake of argument, that the defendant's conduct toward the complainant in *J.A.* was informed by the sexual preferences and desires she had expressed in the past, we can still see ample room for concerns that are, at bottom, the same as those animating the decisions in *Ewanchuk*, *Flaviano*, *V. (R.)*, and others. They are concerns with voice and autonomy; wishful thinking and the way (male) desires are often structured by norms of masculinity, possessiveness, and domination; and the stereotyping of women as naturally predisposed to passivity and submission. Contemporary sexual assault law in Canada makes a great deal of sense in light of these worries.

We run into a problem, though, once our attention shifts toward situations in which the sexual touching in question occurs not only in the context of an intimate relationship, but where it is relatively non-intrusive, and where the norms of that relationship – as understood by both parties – permit a degree of sexual access. In at least some of those cases, we may hesitate to conclude that the touching reflects a lack of appreciation for anyone's voice. The norms structuring that relationship may be such that both parties have had, and continue to have, a more or less equal say in determining whether and how they may engage sexually, now and in the future. Furthermore, there may be no question of either party being unable to present a meaningful objection to the touching, to steer it in new directions, or to, as it were, ratify it after the fact. The touching itself may be relatively trivial. It may be a kiss or an unexpected embrace.

We should not kid ourselves into thinking these instances of touching are somehow less sexual, and we should not assume they are harmless or are somehow too personal and private to warrant the criminal law's attention. But nor should we gloss over the fact that, for many individuals, a degree of physical openness in their intimate relationships is not only expected but legitimate and desirable. The question I address in this book is whether the present law of sexual assault in Canada can or should accommodate that point.

Ewanchuk and Implied Consent

In *Ewanchuk*, the Supreme Court rejected the doctrine of "implied consent" in the context of sexual assault law.[54] That conclusion was thought to follow directly from the core propositions I mentioned earlier: that we must look exclusively to the complainant's subjective state of mind in determining whether she consented,[55] and that we must look to her state of mind at the time the touching occurred.[56] This point was emphasized in the court's decision in *J.A.*[57] McLachlin C.J., writing for the majority, remarked:

> The only relevant period of time for the complainant's consent is while the touching is occurring ... The complainant's views towards the touching before or after are not directly relevant. An offence has not occurred if the complainant consents at the time but later changes her mind (absent grounds for vitiating consent). Conversely, the *actus reus* has been committed if the complainant was not consenting in her mind while the touching took place, even if she expressed her consent before or after the fact.[58]

She continued: "[T]here is no substitute for the complainant's actual consent to the sexual activity at the time it occurred. It is not open to the defendant to argue that the complainant's consent was implied by the circumstances, or by the relationship between the accused and the complainant."[59] Moreover, the majority observed, it is not open to the defendant to say that he lacked the mens rea for sexual assault because he thought the complainant was generally in a state of mind receptive to any sort of sexual touching. Following *Ewanchuk*, McLachlin C.J. observed that the defence of honest but mistaken belief in consent will apply only where the defendant took "reasonable steps to ascertain consent, and [believed] that the complainant communicated her consent *to engage in the sexual activity in question*."[60]

In light of *Ewanchuk* and *J.A.*, there is now a real question as to whether we must characterize the many kinds of casual sexual touching in which long-term couples engage with each other as sexual assaults. There is nothing unusual about people in intimate relationships giving each other unexpected kisses, bites, hugs, caresses, or gropes. Sometimes these are given to test the other's interest in more intimate sexual touching. Sometimes they are offered in a spirit of playfulness, affection, and fun – not at the other's expense, but as something to be shared together. Many have a sense that these are – or at least can be – blameless.

Yet it is no longer clear that this sort of sexually tinged play is permissible in light of sections 265 and 273.1 of the Criminal Code.[61] In the absence of a doctrine of implied consent, a defendant could not claim any special right of sexual access by virtue of the kind of relationship he had with the recipient of the touching.[62] He must, instead, argue that there was subjective consent or an honest belief in subjective consent to the touching at the time it occurred. But in many cases, any such suggestion would be, at best, artificial. At worst, it would be disingenuous or a flat-out lie. If A sneaks up behind his long-time intimate partner, B, to kiss her on the neck when she is not expecting it, or gives her thigh a quick and unexpected squeeze under the table in a restaurant, it is not obvious that there is, or can be, any kind of subjective consent. Certainly, there is no subjective consent before the touching has taken place, though that fact is insignificant in itself anyway.[63] More importantly, it is not clear that B has an opportunity to consent to the touching even while it is happening: by the time she can register it, it is over. To speak of B subjectively consenting to the sexual touching while it is happening, then, would be entirely artificial.

Nor could A say, before engaging in the touching, that he honestly believed that B had signalled her subjective consent to it at that time. Indeed, A may have intended to surprise B with a playful and spontaneous expression of intimacy or closeness – to show he authentically cares about B when she isn't watching and when there is no immediate expectation that he manifest affection in some way. A might hope B will be pleased with these expressions of affection – that she will be delighted, amused, aroused, or flattered. There is, however, no guarantee of that. She may be engrossed in other tasks, and find a kiss on the back of the neck an irritating distraction. She may find a display of affection, in a public setting, somewhat déclassé. She may, for whatever reason, simply not be in the mood to receive an expression of affection in good humour. And she is entitled to react in these ways. We may be disappointed or hurt when and if the attentions we give a partner meet with less enthusiasm than we would like, but we could not justly complain. In trying to play with or express feelings of closeness to a partner, we take a (possibly conscious) risk of being rebuffed. At the same time, being in an intimate relationship means, if only to some men and women, giving and receiving spontaneous displays of tenderness and affection. That being the case, we must surely entertain the possibility that touching each other in this way need not amount to a sexual assault.

Indeed, individuals in intimate relationships frequently take risks that can go much further than those in the above examples. As counsel in *J.A.* pointed out, it would not be so unusual to kiss a partner while he or she sleeps.[64] We may, in fact, touch a sleeping intimate partner in a much more sexualized way. Because these instances of sexual touching are more intrusive, we may hesitate to categorically say that they are wholly unproblematic. But the idea that *all* of these kinds of behaviour – which happen every day in ostensibly healthy, intimate relationships[65] – must amount to sexual assault strikes many individuals as deeply counter-intuitive.

That it may be counter-intuitive is not determinative of anything: objectification is arguably so rife in our culture that hierarchical, oppressive modes of treatment can be mistaken for signs of healthy intimacy. Feminist analysis is important, in part, because it exposes the role of social norms in structuring our understanding of what intimacy *is*.[66]

Nevertheless, the fact that many people regard the kinds of sexual behaviour I have described as harmless or even praiseworthy cannot be instantly dismissed as a case of distorted preference.[67] Even adaptive preferences are still preferences that must be taken seriously.[68]

In *J.A.*, McLachlin C.J. responded to this criticism in the following terms:

> Running through the arguments in favour of carving out particular circumstances as exceptions to the conscious consent paradigm of the Criminal Code is the suggestion that the strict approach Parliament has adopted toward consent in the context of sexual assault has no place in relationships of mutual trust, like marriage. However, accepting this view would run counter to Parliament's clear rejection of defences to sexual assault based on the nature of the relationship. The Criminal Code does not establish a different inquiry into consent depending on the relationship between the accused and the complainant. Their relationship may be evidence for both the *actus reus* and the *mens rea*, but it does not change the nature of the inquiry into whether the complainant consented, as conceived by the Criminal Code.[69]

She continued with the observation that "[t]his concept of consent produces just results in the vast majority of cases."[70] Furthermore, she noted, it is the role of Parliament, and not the courts, to decide when consent is necessary to license sexual touching, and what such consent entails. "In the absence of a constitutional challenge," McLachlin C.J. concluded, "the appropriate body to alter the law on consent in relation to sexual assault is Parliament, should it deem this necessary."[71]

The majority in *J.A.* is surely right that it falls to Parliament to decide what sorts of conduct amount to criminal wrongs.[72] The interesting question – the one which, the majority pointedly observed, was not asked in *J.A.* – is whether people, when engaging in the sexually playful conduct with their partners I have described above, commit the wrong that Parliament intended to target by creating the offence of sexual assault. If not, there is some reason to think that the offence is overbroad – possibly in the constitutional sense, but more significantly as a matter of political morality and criminal law theory.

Subjectivity and Autonomy

There are two prominent running themes in this book. The most important – and the most elusive – is that mere reference to subjectivity in discussions of consent, though it will ordinarily suffice in cases like *Flaviano, Ewanchuk,* and *J.A.*, is inadequate when we try to make sense of the intuition that the sexual norms governing intimate relationships should have legal significance. When we interact with one another on an anonymous basis, or in the context of a relationship in which there is no legitimate expectation of sexual touching, we typically have no reason to look for anything other than a discrete consenting state of mind at the precise moment the touching takes place.[73] That narrow inquiry makes less sense, however, in the context of some intimate relationships. We still need to look to the complainant's subjective state of mind, but our concern should be with more than an isolated mental event. We should, in addition, consider the complainant's plans and wider normative commitments, in order to see the significance of the sexual touching for her. There is a need to appeal to a deeper level of subjectivity.

This is closely related to my emphasis in this book on relational autonomy or agency. Typically, we act as though an individual has autonomy only insofar as she can control whether and how others interact physically with her. On that view, autonomy is essentially all or nothing: either we control physical or sexual access to our own bodies, or we don't. If we lack control, we lack autonomy – period. This way of understanding autonomy lends itself to an analysis that focuses on each moment as the site of a discrete decision in which control is either present or absent.

The difficulty is that this approach does not acknowledge the moral difference between having control stripped away (through force, social pressure, oppression, or deception) and ceding control. It treats control as something inalienable, even by the person herself. That is a problem because people frequently want to be in a position in which they lack control over others' physical or sexual access to them. This does not entail the radical conclusion that the law should permit individuals to alienate control over their physical and sexual integrity for all time and in all ways – to, say, sell themselves into slavery. It does, however, suggest that the law should, within certain limits, recognize individuals' authority to decide for themselves whether and when they may be open to certain

forms of touching in the absence of discretely contemporaneous subjective consent. We might say that the law should recognize a second-order
level of control: control over control. The doctrine of implied consent, in
the context of ordinary assault, gives effect to this intuition.

Once we take that view, though, it ceases to make sense to focus on
each moment in time as the site for a discrete exercise of control or autonomy. Instead, we must examine the individual's plans across a given
period of time. In doing so, we shift the focus away from autonomy,
narrowly construed, and toward agency. To the extent we are still concerned with autonomy, it is with relational autonomy – a model that emphasizes the influence of attachments and social norms on how we make
our choices and plans, and how we exercise control.

On "Implied Consent"

I argue that there is a place for the actus reus doctrine of implied consent
in sexual assault law. There is, however, a great deal of confusion about
what implied consent actually *means*. The term implied consent itself
might suggest that it is nothing more than an evidentiary doctrine – that
it amounts to the proposition that the trier of fact may infer subjective consent from the complainant's behaviour at the time of the alleged
touching. And as I argue in chapter 3, counsel in *Ewanchuk* seems to have
understood the doctrine to mean that a complainant shall be deemed
to have consented if, at the time of the alleged sexual touching, she appeared to subjectively consent (even if she did not in fact).

As I explain in chapter 3, implied consent in the context of ordinary
assault stands for neither of these propositions. It is not an evidentiary or
adjectival rule, but a substantive one. Nor does it apply merely because
the complainant appeared to subjectively consent to the specific touching in question at the time it occurred. Such a rule would be absurd in
any context, sexual or otherwise. Rather, if the doctrine applies at all, it
applies where there was no consent at all in the ordinary (*Ewanchuk*)
sense of the word. Any consent – insofar as we want to use that language – would be to the set of norms governing the practice in which
the defendant and complainant were engaged, and not to the particular
touching that occurred within that practice.

The confusion surrounding implied consent is understandable. Before *Ewanchuk*, neither courts nor legal scholars satisfactorily explained what implied consent means in the context of assault simpliciter, or why the law ought to recognize it. With one or two possible exceptions, that state of affairs has not substantially changed.[74] The question, then, is: why use the term here? Why not pick a different term that lends itself to greater clarity?

Indeed, the question can be stated more forcefully. In chapter 4, I argue that the doctrine of implied consent, insofar as it is extended to the sexual assault context, should be narrowed so that it (a) reflects important differences between, say, hockey and intimate relationships; and (b) takes into account valid concerns about objectifying gender stereotypes in Canadian culture. So the doctrine of implied consent I defend in this book is twice removed from the doctrine as it is commonly understood. Again, why use the language of implied consent at all?

These are not unfair criticisms. My decision to use the term is driven by two simple concerns. First, I want to highlight the fact that implied consent (in my sense of the term) is not pure invention, but finds some – albeit imperfect – grounding in Canadian law as it is. Second, I want to acknowledge the fact that my argument runs against the grain of *Ewanchuk* and subsequent authorities. No matter what label I applied to the doctrine I defend in this book, I would need to confront *Ewanchuk*. Better, I have decided, to be upfront about it.

Implied Consent and Advance Consent

In this book, I make a case for implied consent, not advance consent. I take the latter to refer to a subjective state of agreement, on the part of an individual, to permit a discrete instance of touching by another at some fixed point in the future. We would typically expect someone to claim advance consent where (as in *J.A.*) the complainant expected to be unconscious or asleep, and so unable to give consent at the time the touching was expected to take place, but perhaps also where she expected to be unwilling to give consent at the time of the touching. Implied consent, by contrast, refers to a subjective state in which the individual accepts a set of norms, applying to her at the relevant time, by which the sexual touching in question is legitimate.

The two concepts – implied consent and advance consent – have many superficial similarities but are distinguishable in a number of ways. First, advance consent, like ordinary consent, is determined by looking to the complainant's state of mind at a discrete point in time. The difference between them is that, whereas a complainant gives *Ewanchuk* consent at the time of the sexual touching in question, she gives advance consent at some earlier point in time. By contrast, implied consent refers to the complainant's ongoing attitude, stretching across a period of time.

Second, advance consent, again like *Ewanchuk* consent, is given to a specific course of action. An individual who gives advance consent agrees to be touched in a certain way at a certain time by a certain person. Implied consent, by contrast, involves acceptance of a set of norms according to which certain broad kinds of touching are permissible and legitimate. Thus, one could impliedly consent to touching even if the precise form of that touching was not anticipated. Indeed, as I will show, the very point in having a doctrine of implied consent is to allow people to inhabit spaces in which spontaneous and unexpected modes of physical interaction are legally possible. Just as the game of hockey would be impossible if *Ewanchuk* consent was required for every body check, so it would be impossible if advance consent was needed.

These first two differences entail a third. The case for implied consent, as I have suggested, rests on the importance of sexual agency. This is not simply to say that a choice made at one point in time (x_1) should bind the complainant at some subsequent point (x_2). It rests, instead, on the idea that certain ways of living reflect the complainant's deep normative commitments, and that we should respect those commitments. The case for advance consent, by contrast, takes its force (if it has any) from the idea that, having agreed to permit a kind of touching at x_1, the complainant is effectively bound at x_2. It is a case grounded, we might say, in quasi-contract. The trouble is that, in the absence of some claim that the complainant's state of mind at x_1 reflects anything special about her plans, long-term priorities, or values, we have no reason to believe that the complainant's agreement at x_1 should prevail over her lack of agreement at x_2. Since, on the liberal model of autonomy, we only ever look at control in the here and now, there is little reason to hold the complainant to a prior agreement. If, on the other hand, we say that the complainant's agreement at X1 does reflect some deep fact about her agency, then it is her agency and not her prior agreement that appears to be doing all of the normative work – in which case we seem to be appealing to implied consent and not advance consent.

One could object, of course, that the distinction I have drawn between advance consent and implied consent is stipulative. That's fine. Obviously, if one redraws the lines between advance consent and implied consent such that they overlap to a greater extent, one is liable to conclude that my argument has implications for the former. I am happy, at least for now, to let others decide what this book means for advance consent, and confine my argument to implied consent alone.

Heteronormativity

Throughout this book, I focus on male-female intimate relationships. That may strike some readers as objectionable. Same-sex relationships are, after all, just as important as those between men and women. It is worth taking a moment, then, to briefly explain why I don't say more about them.

Sexual assault is a gendered offence. Its victims are overwhelmingly female and its perpetrators overwhelmingly male. The central reforms to sexual assault law, over the past thirty years, have been made with this in mind. They reflect a well-founded preoccupation with gender norms and roles in Canadian society, and with the need to change (or at least unsettle) them. In particular, reforms and educational initiatives have been undertaken in the knowledge that, in our culture, there is a social expectation that men will be sexually aggressive and that women will be sexually passive and submissive. The doctrine of implied consent is regarded as problematic in large part because it could be seen as legitimizing or reifying men's sexual domination of women.

Sexual domination can be present in same-sex relationships, too. There is, however, less reason to think that gender norms play anything like the same role in those relationships.[75] For that reason, the doctrine of implied consent would be, if anything, less problematic in the same-sex context.[76] If the doctrine can work in the context of male-female intimate relationships, in other words, it should work at least as well in others.

The Road Map

In chapters 1 to 3 of this book, I set out some of the basic building blocks for the argument that follows. In chapter 1, I defend the claim that the problem I have described above is indeed a problem. Critics will contend that, since no one (or virtually no one) is being prosecuted for kissing and hugging their intimate partners, there is no *real* problem to be solved – that this work is academic in the pejorative sense of the word. In anticipation of that objection, I point out some of the difficulties with it, drawing upon the expressive function of the criminal law and the related principle of fair labelling.

In chapter 2, I consider the nature of the wrong targeted by the offence of sexual assault. I argue the offence is primarily directed at the wrong of sexual objectification, in the narrow sense of instrumentalization: one person's use of another as a mere tool for sexual gratification. In making the case that the offence of sexual assault is not directed simply at violence, but at a particular kind of violence that locates it among other crimes of sexual objectification, I consider its genesis. Activists and members of Parliament were committed to the idea that non-consensual sexual touching of any sort is an act of violence comparable to other acts of assault, and that the special language of "rape" should therefore be abandoned, along with substantive and procedural rules that reinforce a widespread view of women's sexuality as a commodity. At the same time, there was no clear rejection of the idea that sexual assault is different from other forms of assault – particularly when it involves penetration. This reflects a strong sense that, although sexuality is socially constructed, the subjective experiences of men and women are nonetheless real and deserving of respect. Furthermore, although it is often suggested that the wrong of sexual assault lies in the violation of another's sexual integrity, the law does not fetishize control. Rather, in determining whether a violation of sexual integrity has taken place, we must ask whether a person has been wrongfully used as a sexual object.

In chapter 3, I set out the essential case for a doctrine of implied consent in sexual assault law. I argue that the Supreme Court ruling in *Ewanchuk*, which rejected the doctrine in the sexual sphere, proceeded on the basis of a flawed grasp of it, and that properly speaking implied consent was not even on the table given the facts of that case. More importantly, the doctrine of implied consent – like ordinary consent – serves a valuable social function, allowing people to collaborate and challenge themselves and others in ways that would otherwise be impossible. This is no less true in the sexual sphere than in others, where the idea of implied consent is well accepted.

But what about section 273.1 of the Criminal Code? That provision defines sexual consent as "the voluntary agreement of the complainant to engage in the sexual activity in question." Commentators and courts have proceeded on the basis that it requires sexual consent to be purely contemporaneous. That is not obvious. The purpose of section 273.1 was to guarantee sexual autonomy – in particular, that of women. And it is often the case that we serve autonomy by holding individuals to their own normative commitments. As Nedelsky observes, a right to sexual autonomy encompasses more than a right not to be touched in certain ways – it includes the right to explore sexual possibilities, even in ways that leave us vulnerable to others. With that in mind, taking sexual autonomy seriously arguably requires the law to allow men and women to craft standing arrangements in which they may be sexually touched in the absence of contemporaneous consent. I raise these points in chapter 4.

Chapters 5 to 8 form the nucleus of this book. In the absence of a discrete decision to permit sexual touching at the time it takes place, there may yet be a norm, subjectively accepted as binding by both parties, legitimating the touching in question. Where that is the case, we may conclude that there is no sexual instrumentalization. To reach that conclusion, we first need to determine whether the ostensibly legitimating norms were formed and sustained under conditions of mutuality. That, in turn, requires a searching inquiry into the level of influence (or voice) each party had in shaping those norms, and the harmfulness of the touching putatively treated as legitimate. Where conditions of mutuality are satisfied, and an act of touching is justified or warranted with reference to a legitimating norm, we should conclude that the act is, for legal purposes, consensual. This reflects the importance in morality and law not only of sexual autonomy (in the narrow, classical liberal sense), but of sexual agency. It also underscores the fact that concerns about stereotyping and wishful thinking do not straightforwardly arise where sexual touching is based, not on assumptions about men and women generally, but on arrangements reached between individuals regarding one another as individuals with their own unique subjective values and priorities.

In chapter 5, I draw on Nussbaum's analysis of sexual objectification, and argue that certain kinds of sexual touching – particularly in the context of intimate relationships – may be non-instrumentalizing even where unaccompanied by discretely contemporaneous consent. This is because conditions of mutuality may exist. In chapter 6, I tie the preceding discussion of mutuality to wider questions of what autonomy is. Looking to Chambers's recent work, we can distinguish between two different kinds of autonomy: the first-order autonomy to decide, moment by moment, how to act and interact with others; and the second-order autonomy to engage in a way of life, in which one's future options may be constrained in certain respects. Chambers suggests that, even if we are uncomfortable with certain kinds of self-imposed constraints on first-order autonomy, we can still recognize a role for implied consent. In particular, the circumstances in which we will be most inclined to recognize mutuality in the absence of discrete and contemporaneous consent will be those in which there are relatively few concerns about influence and disadvantage.

In chapter 7, I argue that, although the offence of sexual assault is deeply concerned with gender stereotypes, these concerns are not centrally engaged where sexual touching is undertaken on the basis of norms constructed in the context of a particular intimate relationship (again, assuming that conditions of mutuality are satisfied). In making this point, I examine what makes stereotyping wrongful, how it contributes to gender inequality, and why mere conformity with a stereotype is not the same as stereotyping.

In chapter 8, I address the concern that transplanting the doctrine of implied consent into the sexual assault context would effectively restore the justly reviled marital rape exemption abolished in the 1983 legislative reforms. That could not have been Parliament's intention when it enacted section 273.1 during the 1992 reforms. It is, then, a serious challenge. Properly understood, though, the doctrine of implied consent bears no resemblance to the marital rape exemption. The fact that two people are in a spousal relationship does not, by itself, mean they are in a sexually intimate one. Nor does it tell us, if they are, what norms govern their sexual lives, or if the relationship is characterized by mutuality. The doctrine of implied consent, properly construed so that it advances sexual autonomy rather than destroys it, is available only after a deeply context-sensitive inquiry. The importance of context can be seen when we examine some of the few sexual assault cases involving long-term partners. Furthermore, the legislative debates on section 273.1 do not show an intention to impose a single set of sexual norms on those in intimate relationships. If anything, they show a preoccupation with women's freedom to explore sexual options.

This answer will be dissatisfying for many critics. Given social norms that treat spousal and other relationships as inherently sexually intimate, and that treat penetrative sexual intercourse as the paradigmatic form of intimacy, we may anticipate that the doctrine of implied consent – however well intentioned – would put women at risk. With that in mind, one might argue, the offence of sexual assault must be overbroad, in its moral if not its constitutional sense, if it is to protect sexual autonomy at all. It must assure women, and particularly women in intimate relationships, that they will not be subject to non-consensual sexual touching. In chapter 9, I note that this kind of justification finds a great deal of theoretical support. In chapter 10, the other shoe drops: though overbreadth may sometimes be justifiable, there are often means of giving assurance that do not involve defining the targeted wrong in an overbroad way. In particular, I argue that the difficulties with an overly contextualized analysis may be resolved by employing a legal presumption.

Naturally enough, I hope that readers find the argument on the whole compelling – at least sufficiently compelling that it cannot be rejected out of hand. But there is room to reject certain aspects or premises and still (I hope) find something of value. Not everything in this book, in other words, stands or falls together. For example, one could deny that the criminal law's function is primarily expressive or educative, yet accept that the offence of sexual assault essentially targets sexually instrumentalizing conduct. One could reject the latter claim, yet think there is merit in establishing or exploring the boundaries of instrumentalization – perhaps by way of determining what moral obligations we owe to each other. One could accept the suggestion that conduct is instrumentalizing only when it fails the condition of mutuality, and yet conclude that mutuality does not answer concerns about stereotyping. And one could accept the entirety of my argument about the ideal boundaries of sexual assault law, yet find that overbreadth is an acceptable option given the world we live in.

In this book, in short, I attempt to make a single overarching argument, but in doing so get involved in a series of wider debates about, among other things, the point of the criminal law; the nature of the wrong targeted by the offence of sexual assault; what makes consent morally and legally significant; the importance of mutuality in how we make sense of that wrong; the circumstances under which we can say that a person has been stereotyped; what it means to have sexual autonomy and agency; the value of assurance; and the need for overbreadth in criminal legislation. Though my argument takes its point of departure from Canadian legislation and case law, I hope it will be of interest to lawyers and legal academics in other jurisdictions.

CHAPTER 1

The Criminal Law's Expressive Function

Introduction

In the introduction to this book, I referred to a class of cases in which there is no discretely contemporaneous (or *Ewanchuk*-type) consent to sexual touching, and yet where intuition suggests that there is no criminal wrong – or at the very least, that the wrong is not properly described as sexual assault. These cases, I suggested, are most likely to arise in the context of intimate relationships, and involve relatively trivial acts of sexual touching – paradigmatically, kissing and hugging.

Right away, one could ask, "So what?" There has not been, since *Ewanchuk*, a great influx of prosecutions of men who give their intimate partners unexpected kisses and hugs. Who cares if the law technically catches that sort of conduct? What should trouble us, some will say, are actual threats to the liberty of criminal defendants, not the merely theoretical possibility of prosecutions and convictions.

In this chapter, I take issue with that view. I argue that the role of the criminal law is, first and foremost, not to punish but to teach. Its primary responsibility is to authoritatively articulate, for the public, the boundaries of permissible conduct.[1] If the law falsely suggests that certain innocent forms of conduct are criminally wrongful, it fails to discharge this educative function – indeed, it loses some of its credibility and authority as a moral guide. This idea finds (albeit imperfect) expression in Canadian constitutional case law. I also address the closely related objection that the de minimis doctrine resolves this problem. That doctrine has a questionable place in the law of assault and sexual assault. To the extent it has any role to play at all, moreover, it begs the very questions that my account of implied consent attempts to answer.

So What?

In an article written shortly after the Supreme Court's ruling in *Ewanchuk*, Don Stuart expresses fears that the decision would effectively criminalize the "art of seduction" – that is, the use of touching to "test" and build another's interest in engaging in more (or more intimate) sexual contact.[2] He rests this criticism on a fairly straightforward premise: interactions in which sexual touching takes place between relative strangers – say, in the context of a first date – are often characterized by ambiguity. It will not always be obvious to one party how he should read the other's body language or signals. If the defence of honest but mistaken belief in consent is available only when the defendant acts on the basis of a clear "yes," Stuart argues, we have effectively criminalized sexual touching that many will regard as unremarkable and blameless. A number of conservative commentators in the popular press echoed this concern.[3]

Craig presents two responses to Stuart's critique. First, she argues that, in cases of ambiguous signals, courts applying *Ewanchuk* have tended to find that there is sufficient basis for leaving the defence of honest but mistaken belief with the trier of fact.[4] They have done so in spite of language in the Criminal Code, and in *Ewanchuk*, indicating that it is an error of law to proceed with sexual touching on the basis that "silence, passivity *or ambiguity*" amounts to consent.[5] Stuart's problem, she suggests, is more hypothetical than real.

Her second response is, for my purposes, more interesting. Craig notes that the scenario Stuart describes does not represent the kind of case typically prosecuted.[6] We are, she observes, more likely to encounter cases in which the complainant and defendant were both heavily intoxicated, and in which the defendant touched the complainant while she was passed out or so stupefied that she was unable to either consent or signal consent.[7] Since prosecutors have not, by and large, applied the law to the cases Stuart has in mind, Craig wonders whether there is any basis for criticizing *Ewanchuk*. We could similarly reason that, even if the law clearly precludes us from saying that those involved in intimate

IMPLIED CONSENT AND SEXUAL ASSAULT

relationships ever impliedly consent to sexual touching by their partners, it is a non-issue so long as the Crown chooses not to prosecute.

This would be an unsatisfactory way to proceed.[8] As McLachlin C.J. observed in *J.A.*, it is not for the courts to decide when and whether to give effect to Parliament's social policy determinations in the absence of some serious question of constitutional compatibility.[9] We should be at least as uncomfortable with suggestions that the Crown is entitled effectively to nullify the law. That is true as a general proposition, but it is especially true when the very point of the criminal offence in question is to change social attitudes – attitudes shared by police, prosecutors, and trial judges. As I discuss in chapter 2, the 1983 legislative reforms to rape and sexual assault law were driven by concerns that legal officials, and the public at large, were inclined to dismiss many instances of non-consensual sexual touching as morally unproblematic. Advocates for women's rights have long – and rightly – argued that the low conviction rate for rape and sexual assault is partly a function of blinkered police and prosecutorial policies, and have for that reason sought to change those policies to reflect a broader understanding of sexual assault.[10]

If the conduct I described in the introduction amounts to sexual assault, we should want the Crown to prosecute those who engage in it. The lack of prosecutions ought to be a source of complaint rather than comfort, for it suggests that the Crown has failed to vindicate the physical and sexual autonomy of women who have been wronged by their partners on the basis of law enforcement stereotypes about what a sexual assault (and what a victim) must look like.

In the scenarios I have described – in which men caress and kiss their sleeping partners, or give unexpected squeezes – there would rarely be a police investigation, never mind a prosecution. We would not expect the victims in these cases to report having been assaulted. Even if they knew that sexual touching took place, they may not perceive themselves as wronged. If they do, they may see no realistic prospect of prosecution. Again, though, if we proceed on the basis that these are cases of sexual assault, this lack of reporting is surely a problem to be solved, not a state of affairs to blithely accept. Certainly, the lack of reporting in other sexual assault contexts has rightly been treated as an urgent issue.[11] The women involved should be encouraged to think of themselves as wronged, to bring their grievances forward, and not simply accept their fate.

We should not interpret an absence of criticism of investigative and prosecution policies as an endorsement.[12] It may be only a strategic decision not to invite controversy by suggesting too forcefully that a commitment to sexual autonomy requires us to abandon longstanding ideas about how men and women in intimate relationships can interact with each other. One may hesitate to push the reasoning of *Ewanchuk* to its logical conclusion for fear that doing so will invite a wholesale re-appraisal of the ruling. But this line of thinking is itself telling, since it hints at some awareness that the public is not ready to see the kinds of sexual touching I have described as criminal assaults – that a suggestion to that effect runs headlong into common moral intuitions. The question is *why*. So far, there is no satisfactory answer.

Finally, it is neither here nor there that the paradigm cases of seductive touching, or of playful sexual touching in the context of long-term partnerships, are not typically brought before the courts. The point of the criminal law is, first and foremost, to guide citizens away from wrongful courses of action.[13] In a healthy legal order, it should perform that function whether or not there is any meaningful threat of prosecution or conviction.[14] Indeed, we might say that, however important it is generally to separate the guidance function of the criminal law from the threat of sanctions, it is especially important in the context of sexual assault, an offence which is under-reported, poses unique problems of proof, and continues to be difficult to prosecute. If we are to say that the offence of sexual assault provides guidance at all, its effectiveness cannot be attributed to any credible threat of punishment. But if we say that the offence of sexual assault guides (some) citizens with or without such a threat, then it should concern us if they are guided away from courses of action that are not, strictly speaking, wrongful, or that are not the kinds of wrongs that Parliament intended to discourage.[15]

The Criminal Law's Expressive Function[16]

In *The Concept of Law*, H.L.A. Hart purports to show that laws are not merely "orders backed by threats" akin to the demands of an armed bandit.[17] We may obey the bandit only insofar as she has the power to oblige us to do so – that is, to the extent she makes sufficiently terrible threats and convinces us she is willing and able to enforce them.[18] By contrast, Hart argues, at least some people obey the substantive criminal law because they regard themselves as obligated to do so – i.e., because they believe they ought to follow its substantive rules – whether or not a threat of punishment is attached to a criminal prohibition, and whether or not there is any realistic prospect that violations of the prohibition will be investigated, prosecuted, or punished. For these people, represented in *The Concept of Law* by the figure of the puzzled man, the very fact that the state has declared a course of conduct criminal provides a reason to regard it as wrongful, and therefore as a course of action to be avoided. The criminal law's normative significance distinguishes it from the orders of the bandit.[19]

Once we look at the criminal law through the eyes of the puzzled man, Hart claims, we are better able to understand how it is distinct from other legal rules. The law is shot through with provisions setting out the circumstances under which a member of the public may be subjected to one sort of deprivation or another. Income tax legislation sets out the conditions under which a person may be moved into a higher tax bracket. Civil forfeiture laws articulate some of the conditions under which a person may be deprived of property. Civil commitment legislation sets out some of the circumstances under which the mentally ill may be forcibly detained. Each of these statutory provisions aims to distribute benefits and burdens. At first glance, we might regard the substantive criminal law in the same way as we regard these other provisions – as statements of the conditions under which a person will undergo a deprivation (either in the form of a fine or a term of imprisonment). To the puzzled man, though, they are not the same. Income tax legislation is not intended to discourage people from earning more. Property may be seized as proceeds of crime whether or not it was obtained in a blameworthy fashion. If the mentally ill are forcibly committed, it is for the sake of their own well-being or others' protection and not necessarily because they have done anything to warrant disapproval. Criminal punishment, on the other hand, necessarily is administered to censure the offender for engaging in wrongdoing – for breaching an obligation. In this sense, a fine is materially different from a tax; a prison sentence is different from state-imposed quarantine.

To say that criminal sanctions are supposed to censure wrongdoing, rather than distribute benefits and burdens, is to make a common-sense (but, before Hart, surprisingly elusive) observation: the primary purpose of the substantive criminal law is not to tell police officers when they can arrest citizens,[20] prosecutors when (and what) they can charge, triers of fact when they can convict, and judges what kinds of sentences they can deliver. Rather, it is to guide citizens away from the kinds of wrongful conduct that, if proven, warrant criminal deprivations in the first place. If the criminal law truly functioned as it should – if it successfully and authoritatively conveyed the wrongfulness of all the courses of action it seeks to condemn – there would be no crimes to prosecute or punish.[21]

In creating a criminal offence, Parliament purports to settle disagreements about what courses of action are wrongful – so wrongful that one must answer for them in a public hearing and, if found guilty, endure grave deprivations of liberty and security by way of forced attrition.[22] The latter point is important. We do not tend to think that one is answerable in a criminal court for every wrong under the sun: lies, insults, acts of ingratitude, miserliness, or unsociability. We may be criticized for these things, but we typically blanch at the idea that Parliament should make them criminal. Thus, the Supreme Court in R. v. Mabior was able to say that mere lies are not sufficient to constitute "fraud" vitiating consent, without suggesting that lies are anything other than wrongful.[23]

Perhaps more importantly, we need to remember that particular offences target particular wrongs. In fulfilling its expressive function, the criminal law must, as far as possible, attempt to fairly capture differences in wrongdoing.[24] Andrew Ashworth, discussing the principle of fair labelling, states: "Its concern is to see that widely felt distinctions between kinds of offences and degrees of wrongdoing are respected and signaled by the law, and that offences are subdivided and labelled so as to represent fairly the nature and magnitude of the law-breaking."[25] To a degree, this ensures that offenders receive proportionate sentences that reflect the respective wrongs in which they engaged. But fair labelling does more than guarantee fair sentencing.[26] As Doug Husak observes: "Labeling is crucial for determining what punishment is just, for evaluating the relevance of prior convictions, and, perhaps most importantly, for sending appropriate expressive signals to the public. The crimes for which persons are convicted should provide an accurate and authoritative description of what defendants have done."[27] Stuart Green, in his work on theft, likewise emphasizes the need to distinguish between different kinds of wrongful takings, for example, embezzlement, loot-ing, fraud, and armed robbery.[28] The authority of the criminal law, he observes, is based in large part upon the public's sense that it tracks and reflects morally salient distinctions between wrongs. He states:

> It is not merely the case that social norms play a role in shaping the criminal law. The criminal law also plays an important role in informing, shaping, and reinforcing social norms. Children and adults learn what is wrong in part from what the law says is wrong. When the law deviates too far from existing norms, its instructive function is impaired as well. Maintaining consistency between the law and social norms is important not only in connection with de-ciding which conduct should or should not be criminalized; such consistency is also vital in deciding how much to punish. If the legal system imposes more, or less, punishment on some crimes than citizens believe is deserved, the system seems unfair; it loses its credibility and, eventually, its effectiveness.[29]

This statement contains an obvious tension. The criminal law, as Green notes, should track existing social norms – but it should also, to some extent, change them. The mere fact that a course of action is not cur-rently regarded by large swaths of the population as wrongful – whether it be impaired driving in the 1970s or online file-sharing in the 2000s – may be more, not less, reason to criminalize it. In a sense, though, this is precisely why the legislature must be attentive to questions of fair label-ling: if it creates the impression that courses of action are criminalized or lumped together willy-nilly, the public will have more difficulty taking its pronouncements seriously.[30] The legislature, and the criminal law, will lose their moral authority. Paul Robinson and John Darley state: "The criminal justice system's power to stigmatize depends on the legal codes having moral credibility in the community. The law needs to have earned a reputation for accurately representing what violations do and do not deserve moral condemnation from the community's point of view. This reputation will be undercut if liability and punishment rules deviate from a community's shared intuitions of justice."[31] In much of this book, I proceed on the basis that the boundaries of criminal offences – most notably, for my purposes, sexual assault – should reflect the specific wrongs they are intended to target. The remainder of this chapter merely underscores that the principle of fair labelling finds some expression in Canadian criminal and constitutional law.

Child Pornography and Fair Labelling: One Illustration

To illustrate the significance of fair labelling, consider a recent case in which a seventeen-year-old woman was convicted of distributing child pornography after spitefully texting a photo of her boyfriend's ex-girlfriend.[32] There is no doubt that she engaged in a wrongful course of action that the criminal law may appropriately target.[33] Nonetheless, it will strike most of us as intuitively obvious that the child pornography provisions target a very different kind of wrong, and that prosecuting her under section 163.1 of the Criminal Code seriously misrepresents the nature of her wrongdoing. This is true whether or not the sentence she ultimately receives is roughly proportionate to the gravity of her wrongdoing.

In explaining this intuition, we might start with the nature of the wrong targeted by the child pornography provisions. In *R. v. Sharpe*,[34] the Supreme Court of Canada held that the purpose of the child pornography provisions is "to prevent harm to children by banning the production, distribution and possession of child pornography, and by sending a message to Canadians 'that children need to be protected from the harmful effects of child sexual abuse and exploitation and are not appropriate sexual partners.'"[35] It seems inapt to characterize the seventeen-year-old's behaviour as exploitive. We do not have, here, the sort of inherent power imbalance found between adults and children. No one alleges that, by prosecuting this case, we are sending a message about child sexual abuse, or that the victim in this case is, by virtue of her age, an "[in]appropriate sexual partner" (at least, for individuals in her immediate peer group). The problem with the defendant's conduct simply has nothing to do with the complainant's age. It has everything to do with the fact that the defendant violated the complainant's privacy interest in images given (however unadvisedly) to her boyfriend, and in doing so exposed her to a campaign of slut shaming.

Many lawyers would suggest that the distinction makes no practical difference. As long as serious wrongs are prosecuted, many will say, it doesn't matter how we label them.[36] But that's a short-sighted view.

Prosecuting conduct as though it amounts to one kind of wrong, when it amounts to another, obscures the message that Parliament intended to send. It also makes the criminal law look like an absurd game of gotcha instead of a deadly serious enterprise whereby citizens are held accountable for clear and articulable wrongs.

In its 2013 report, the CCSO Cybercrime Working Group proposed a new offence of non-consensual distribution of intimate images.[37] It nonetheless expressed concern that prosecutors would use the new offence in cases where child pornography charges were more appropriate. The result, the working group feared, would be a watering-down of the child pornography prohibitions.[38] It was concerned, in other words, with overlap – with the expansion of prosecutorial discretion that results when there is more than one way to prosecute a given course of action.[39] The very fact it was concerned, though, shows the force that the principle of fair labelling has. After all, if we ignore the fact that different offences target different wrongs, then this added discretion is unproblematic. Each offence, in that case, is basically equivalent. A conviction is a conviction is a conviction. It is only when we see each offence as an attempt by Parliament to address a unique kind of wrong that it starts to look important that prosecutors not use their discretion in certain ways – specifically, by using a criminal offence, designed to target one kind of wrong, to convict people for a different wrong. The upshot is this: although the elements of the proposed offence overlap with those of distributing child pornography (and other prohibitions), prosecutors do not have a license to choose between them on a whim.[40]

In the end, the working group "recommend[ed] that the proposed new offence should take into account how to provide prosecutors with appropriate flexibility while maintaining the integrity of related offences."[41] But the mere fact it perceived an issue in the first place underscores my point: to know how Crown discretion should be exercised, we must be more careful in articulating the precise nature of the wrong that Parliament means to address.

Fair Labelling in Canadian Law

The Supreme Court has not expressly said that Parliament is constitutionally required to adhere to the principle of fair labelling, but it has drawn upon at least a watered-down version of it on a number of occasions. In *R. v. Vaillancourt*,[42] a majority of the court held that section 213(d) (now section 230(d)) of the Criminal Code violated sections 7 and 11(d) of the Charter. It found that the provision allowed a defendant to be convicted of murder in the absence of evidence that death was an objectively foreseeable outcome of her conduct. This was unconstitutionally unacceptable in light of the punishment and stigma attached to the offence of murder. Lamer J. (as he then was) observed:

> [T]here are, though very few in number, certain crimes where, because of the special nature of the stigma attached to a conviction therefor or the available penalties, the principles of fundamental justice require a *mens rea* reflecting the particular nature of that crime. Such is theft, where, in my view, a conviction requires proof of some dishonesty. Murder is another such offence. The punishment for murder is the most severe in our society and the stigma that attaches to a conviction for murder is similarly extreme. In addition, murder is distinguished from manslaughter only by the mental element with respect to the death. It is thus clear that there must be some special mental element with respect to the death before a culpable homicide can be treated as a murder. That special mental element gives rise to the moral blameworthiness which justifies the stigma and sentence attached to a murder conviction.[43]

Importantly, the majority did not rely simply on the fact that a conviction for murder carries a particularly harsh punishment. It drew upon the stigma attached to the offence – to the fact that those convicted of it face especially grave social opprobrium. This is particularly apparent from the fact that theft – an offence that does not carry a minimum sentence anywhere near as great as that of murder – also requires proof of a subjective state of mind. The label of theft connotes dishonesty. Parliament is not, Lamer J. suggested, free to misleadingly label honest conduct "theft" and thereby distort the message that a theft conviction sends about the nature of the offender's wrongdoing. Without suggesting that this would be a constitutional problem, it might also be jarring if Parliament declared that theft amounted to a "dishonest taking," since this would unacceptably blur the lines between true theft, fraud, and armed robbery.[44]

MacIntyre J., writing in dissent, observed that the majority had not found that section 7 precludes Parliament from creating a new offence – one that targeted the sort of behaviour in which the defendant had engaged, and punished it with a severity perhaps equal to that of section 213(d). The majority had only articulated a restriction on what such a new offence could be *called*. He thought this was absurd:

> The principal complaint in this case is not that the accused should not have been convicted of a serious crime deserving of severe punishment, but simply that Parliament should not have chosen to call that crime "murder." No objection could be taken if Parliament classified the offence as manslaughter or a killing during the commission of an offence, or in some other manner. As I have observed before … while it may be illogical to characterize an unintentional killing as murder, no principle of fundamental justice is offended only because serious criminal conduct, involving the commission of a crime of violence resulting in the killing of a human being, is classified as murder and not in some other manner.[45]

We should not be too quick to accept MacIntyre J.'s objection.[46] Perhaps it rests on the premise that criminal prohibitions address themselves primarily or exclusively to legal decision-makers rather than to members of the public, and that they can set out what the Crown needs to prove in order to win a conviction no matter what the offence in question is named. But, for the reasons I discussed above, that is a peculiar starting-point to adopt. In any case, the Supreme Court has plainly rejected MacIntyre J.'s position. In *Martineau*, a majority of the court voted to strike down section 213(a) (now section 230(a)) of the Criminal Code. Sections 7 and 11(d) of the Charter, the majority held, preclude a conviction for murder in the absence of proof of subjective foresight of death.[47] In reaching that conclusion, the majority again looked to the degree of stigma and punishment attached to the offence. Lamer C.J., writing for the majority, remarked: "A conviction for murder carries with it the most severe stigma and punishment of any crime in our society. The principles of fundamental justice require, because of the special nature of the stigma attached to a conviction for murder, and the available penalties, a *mens rea* reflecting the particular nature of that crime."[48] He continued:

The rationale underlying the principle that subjective foresight of death is required *before a person is labelled and punished as a murderer* is linked to the more general principle that criminal liability for a particular result is not justified except where the actor possesses a culpable mental state in respect of that result ... Murder has long been recognized as the "worst" and most heinous of peace time crimes. It is, therefore, essential that to satisfy the principles of fundamental justice, the stigma and punishment attaching to a murder conviction must be reserved for those who either intend to cause death or who intend to cause bodily harm that they know will likely cause death.[49]

Notably, Lamer C.J. explicitly drew support from four foundational texts on fair labelling.[50]

Though there have been some high-profile constitutional rulings implicating the principle of fair labelling, it is important to see them for what they are: a nod in the direction of a central idea in criminal law theory, not a body of law purporting to define it. In particular, I would make three observations about the limits of the Supreme Court case law. First, it is important not to confuse the fact that fair labelling has been invoked chiefly to impose mens rea standards with the claim that it has nothing to say about actions. Rather, state of mind matters, at least in part, because it helps to indicate the kind of action targeted by the offence.[51] An inadvertent killing is not a lesser kind of murder – it is not a murder at all.[52] If I take your cellphone in the mistaken belief it is mine, I cannot be said to have engaged in "honest theft" – I have not engaged in theft in the first place.[53] The language of "attempts" generally implies an intention to carry out an act – it would make no sense to say that a person who recklessly runs along a subway platform and, as a result, slips and falls onto the tracks has attempted suicide.[54]

Second, simply focusing on the severity of the stigma attached to a given offence ordinarily tells us little about the kind of label that should be applied to a given course of action.[55] Some allusion to this point was made in *R. v. Darrach*.[56] There, the Ontario Court of Appeal observed that the stigma criterion is an "unstable" basis "for making important constitutional decisions."[57] But the problem is not just that it is difficult to measure precisely how stigmatizing an offence is.[58] It is that, if we are worried about fair labelling, we should also want to know what kind of stigma the offence label is intended to convey. Murder, terrorism, and treason all carry considerable stigma, yet no one would argue that the labels applied to them are interchangeable.[59] That point is quite obscured by the emphasis on severity in the case law.

Where the label applied to a course of action is unconventional because it is meant to capture a new kind of wrong – or a type of conduct not traditionally regarded as wrongful – considerations of fair labelling may be especially tricky.[60] But even in that case, we are not left completely unmoored. We can use ordinary principles of statutory interpretation to determine what the legislature broadly intended to target with the offence in question. And it is certainly fair to proceed on the basis that the language that was used – however unconventionally – was deployed for a reason. A legislature might conceivably engage in Orwellian doublespeak to conceal what it is actually targeting with an offence – it could choose, that is, to label unfairly.[61] Rarely, however, would it use a label designed to utterly defeat any attempt at interpretation by the public; for example, by naming an offence "Brenda."[62]

Third, dangers arise when we rely too heavily on Supreme Court jurisprudence in making sense of the principle of fair labelling. Because these cases tend to emphasize the need for fairness vis-à-vis the defendant, they tend not to dwell on the significance of fair labelling for the victims of crimes.[63] Yet that is, for criminal law theorists, at least as important as the fairness of the label to the defendant. It would be deeply problematic to label an offence that targeted wrongful killing in a way that entirely elided the victim's death – for instance, by describing it as a mere species of assault. To return to my earlier example, it is wrong to conflate distribution of child pornography with the distribution of revenge porn at least in part because doing so elides the nature of the wrong done to the victim – the betrayal of having intimate photographs, given to a partner in a spirit of openness, trust, and affection, passed along to others for no other reason than to shame.[64] It obscures the kind of domestic violence done to her.[65] It also explains the discomfort that many have when sexual consent is fraudulently obtained through the non-disclosure of one's HIV-positive status, and the defendant is subsequently charged with aggravated assault rather than sexual assault. The sexual nature of the touching, it is widely thought, should be acknowledged in the charge.[66]

Many of these observations about fair labelling take on particular significance when we consider "sexual assault," a label that, until 1983, did not exist. It was created for the express purpose of dislodging a certain set of assumptions about what does and does not constitute violence against women. The language of assault was intended to alert the public to the fact that non-consensual sexual touching is every bit as much an act of violence as a bar fight. Underpinning the creation of the offence, though, is a presupposition that sexual assault is not the same as other acts of violence inasmuch as it reflects and perpetuates a culture in which the sexual objectification of women is rife. By rebranding non-consensual sexual touching as assault, moreover, it was hoped that the offence would better reflect the experience of its victims.

De Minimis Non Curat Lex?

There is an alternative formulation of the "so what?" problem. In the introduction, I largely (though not exclusively) drew upon examples in which long-term intimate partners engage in relatively tame or non-intrusive sexual touching. But if the modified doctrine of implied consent would chiefly apply to "harmless" or "trivial" sexual touching anyway, why not simply rely on the old doctrine of *de minimis non curat lex*?[67] That would weed out many or most of the sexual assault cases I have identified as inappropriate for the courts, without resuscitating the implied consent doctrine.

There are several problems with relying upon the de minimis doctrine in this way. First, it is far from clear that it applies to assault or sexual assault at all. Members of the Supreme Court have occasionally suggested that certain instances of assault or sexual assault may be de minimis. In *Canadian Foundation for Children, Youth, and the Law v. Canada*, Arbour J. argued in dissent that certain uses of corrective force by parents would be too trivial to properly attract criminal sanctions.[68] In *R. v. Hinchey*,[69] L'Heureux-Dubé J. expressly noted that the doctrine might still exist.[70] Later, in *R. v. Cuerrier*, she suggested in her concurring opinion that an expansive understanding of fraud vitiating consent could be addressed by recognizing that some assaults and sexual assaults are de minimis.[71] But these represent the strongest expressions of support for the de minimis doctrine in the assault context – Canadian appellate courts have generally shied away from giving it the judicial stamp of approval.[72] Indeed, in *Ewanchuk*, the court strongly intimated that no intentional application of force without consent could be too trivial to be regarded as a criminal wrong. Major J. remarked:

> The rationale underlying the criminalization of assault explains this. Society is committed to protecting the personal integrity, both physical and psychological, of every individual. Having control over who touches one's body, and how, lies at the core of human dignity and autonomy. The inclusion of assault and sexual assault in the *Code* aspect expresses society's determination to protect the security of the person from any non-consensual contact or threats of force. The common law has recognized for centuries that the individual's right to physical integrity is a fundamental principle, "every man's person being sacred, and no other having a right to meddle with it, in any the slightest manner" ... It follows that any intentional but unwanted touching is criminal.[73]

In *J.A.*, the court was expressly invited to import the de minimis doctrine into the assault context. McLachlin C.J. did not treat the suggestion as abhorrent, but responded with skepticism:

> The Crown suggested that this Court could allow for mild sexual touching that occurs while a person is unconscious by relying on the *de minimis* doctrine, based on the Latin phrase *de minimis non curat lex*, or the "law does not care for small or trifling matters" ... Without suggesting that the *de minimis* principle has no place in the law of sexual assault, it should be noted that even mild non-consensual touching of a sexual nature can have profound implications for the complainant.[74]

So I am not altogether convinced that using the de minimis doctrine in the sexual assault context would be less controversial than bringing back some limited form of implied consent. But there is a second issue.

Assuming the doctrine does apply, we need some basis for distinguishing "trivial" cases of sexual assault from "serious" ones. My point, in discussing the expressive function of the criminal law, is in part that the ·Crown ought to have good reasons for prosecuting one person but not another, and one offence rather than another. If we simply declare that the Crown is free to ignore de minimis crimes, without setting out a principled test for determining what those are, we effectively grant prosecutors carte blanche.

What would a principled test for the de minimis doctrine look like? It is woefully under-theorized. There is, however, often an implicit understanding that triviality must refer to the degree of harm sustained by the victim.[75] Look back to McLachlin C.J.'s passage from *J.A.* On one reading, her rejection of the doctrine was based on the presupposition that sexual assault victims typically sustain significant physical or psychological harm. On such a reading, the case says nothing at all about cases in which no such harm results. And where is the harm in someone caressing his sleeping intimate partner or embracing her at an unguarded moment?

The trouble with this kind of reasoning is that it proves (or comes dangerously close to proving) too much. Consider the "pure case of rape" imagined by John Gardner and Stephen Shute.[76] In it, a woman is raped while in a state of deep sleep or unconsciousness. No physical injuries are inflicted, and there are no physical signs of penetration. The perpetrator leaves before the victim regains consciousness and never sees her again. The victim wakes up and lives the rest of her life wholly unaware that she had been used in any way. There is, therefore, neither physical nor psychological harm. If that is enough to trigger the de minimis doctrine, we seem committed to saying that the conduct in the pure case is not properly the subject of criminal sanctions. That, however, seems a shocking conclusion. Even those who would argue that this is an example of a lesser rape would surely agree that it is not trivial.[77] And the Supreme Court has made a number of remarks suggesting that the wrongness of sexual assault cannot be reduced to the physical and psychological harms it causes victims. In *R. v. McDonnell*, a majority of the court indicated that it is at least logically possible for the trier of fact to find a criminal defendant guilty of sexual assault without finding that the victim suffered any physical or psychological harm.[78]

The above passage from *Ewanchuk* proceeds on the basis that assault and sexual assault are inherently wrongful, because they entail interference with another's physical or sexual integrity and autonomy, and not only wrong if and when they cause physical or psychological harm to others.[79] More recently, in *R. v. Mabior*, the court observed: "In keeping with the Charter values of equality and autonomy, we now see sexual assault not only as a crime associated with emotional and physical harm to the victim, but as the wrongful exploitation of another human being. To engage in sexual acts without the consent of another person is to treat him or her as an object and negate his or her human dignity."[80] All things considered, the court has indicated that sexual touching in the absence of *Ewanchuk* consent is wrongful whether or not physical or psychological harm results. Is the test, then, one of social harm? The Supreme Court has sometimes suggested that the state's interest in combatting social harms – particularly those associated with the sexual objectification of women – amounts to a "pressing and substantial objective." Its reasoning in *R. v. Butler* and *R. v. Labaye*, for example, emphasized the social harm to women produced by depictions of exploitation and degradation. In explaining the wrongfulness of distributing violent pornography or engaging in acts of public indecency, the court was less focused on physical and psychological harm.[81]

Once we consider social harms, though, it is far from obvious that the de minimis doctrine could apply to *any* instances of sexual touching without *Ewanchuk* consent. In the few cases where the de minimis doctrine has been successfully invoked in the context of assault, the non-consensual touching has tended to involve minor pushing or shoving of grown men.[82] It is difficult to say that a kiss or hug (in most cases) could be trivial in anything like the same way, given our concerns with sexual objectification. If some cases of sexual touching without *Ewanchuk* consent should be prosecuted and punished, but others should not, there must be a way to distinguish between forms of objectification that are worthy of criminal sanctions and those that are not. It is difficult to imagine how we could do so without tacitly appealing, in some way, to the idea of implied consent – to the idea that people can exercise a form of sexual autonomy by licensing their intimate partners to engage in sexual touching in the absence of contemporaneous consent.[83] The de minimis argument, in other words, collapses into the very argument I am making.

There is, potentially,[84] a more fundamental objection. Where one invokes the de minimis doctrine, one effectively concedes that a wrongful act was committed, but claims that the wrong was trifling, and so not properly addressed in a criminal court.[85] Many, however, intuit that the sort of conduct I described in the introduction is not wrong at all – that one can be justified in physically demonstrating affection for a partner even in the absence of express contemporaneous consent. To say, then, that the touching is wrongful, even if only triflingly so, is arguably to miss the point: the law should tolerate this type of behaviour not in a spirit of contemptuous forbearance, but as one mode of living well.

This point has been seized upon by Hamish Stewart, albeit in a different context.[86] He observes that the de minimis doctrine may be an inappropriate means of smuggling a defence of corrective force into the law of assault. Stewart remarks: "[E]ven if the [corrective force] could somehow be characterized as trifling, excusing it through the defence of *de miminis* would send the wrong message: it would say that the parent or other caregiver had done something wrong, not that he or she had used force that was permissible and proportionate."[87] Indeed, something like this reasoning may have been used *sub silentio* by the majority in *Canadian Foundation*. Arbour J., in her dissent, argued that the de minimis doctrine might allow parents to use corrective force. The majority objected, in part on the basis that the doctrine is intolerably vague.[88] Surely, though, that vagueness would not be so problematic if we wanted only to discourage parents and teachers from physically disciplining their children – without knowing in advance whether their use of corrective force would trigger criminal sanctions, parents and teachers could be expected to read the offence of assault in the broadest reasonable terms. The vagueness of the defence is only problematic if we think that parents and teachers should (or at least can justifiably) use corrective force on occasion, but that they will be frightened away from doing so in the absence of clear legal authority. Applying this reasoning to the context of sexual touching, we may be concerned about relying upon de minimis to cure overbreadth concerns with sexual assault if we do not want to discourage the conduct in question.

All in all, then, the de minimis doctrine does not resolve the problems I raised in the introduction to this chapter – it simply repackages them. Taking the criminal law's expressive function seriously, we cannot avoid wrestling with difficult problems of statutory interpretation and moral and political philosophy. That enterprise begins in chapter 2.

CHAPTER 2

The Wrong of Sexual Assault

Introduction

In 1983, the offence of rape was abolished and replaced with the offence of sexual assault. This legislative change, according to the orthodox understanding, was intended to convey the fact that sexual assault is a crime of violence, not of sex.[1] As Wilson J. said in *R. v. Bernard*:

> Sexual assault is a crime of violence. There is no requirement of an intent or purpose beyond the intentional application of force. It is first and foremost an assault. It is sexual in nature only because, objectively viewed, it is related to sex either on account of the area of the body to which the violence is applied or on account of words accompanying the violence. Indeed, the whole purpose, as I understand it, of the replacement of the offence of rape by the offence of sexual assault was to emphasize the aspect of violence and put paid to the benign concept that rape was simply the act of a man who was "carried away" by his emotions.[2]

With that as a starting point, it seems relatively easy to conclude that sexual assault is intended to promote only sexual integrity in the narrow sense of the term, meaning women's ability to restrict others' access to their bodies, and not their ability to express themselves sexually however they choose. To say that the offence of sexual assault is purely about protecting women from violence – that it addresses their negative liberty – is to say that it is not (quite) about empowerment in a richer, more positive sense.[3]

In this chapter, I want to problematize the orthodox reading. The offence of sexual assault is indeed about protecting women from violence. It also protects them from a certain kind of violence – the kind that reflects, and is part of, a wider culture of sexual objectification. Throughout the debate on rape reform, there was an appreciation of the fact that rape and sexual assault are made possible by a pernicious set of gender and sexual norms. The 1983 amendments were, in large part, an attempt to address not just rape, but rape culture. Some writers emphasize remarks by the Supreme Court in *R. v. Chase* and elsewhere that the offence of sexual assault targets violations of sexual integrity. But those comments do not necessarily stand for the proposition that, as a matter of law, women cannot relinquish control over who can sexually touch them, and we should hesitate to read them in that way.

The 1983 Rape Reforms

In 1978, the Law Reform Commission of Canada proposed the abolition of the offence of rape.[4] Concerns of fair labelling animated the suggestion from the outset. The commission, in its working paper, observed: "The term 'rape' is said to stigmatize. This stigma attaches to both victims and offenders. The offender becomes labelled a 'rapist' and the victim sometimes becomes somehow morally suspect even if her complaint is amply proved and vindicated in law. These hard to describe but nonetheless real attitudes constitute that which is said to be the folklore relating to rape. What is prohibited is, of course, not sexual intercourse *per se* but its attainment through an assault."[5] In its final report, the commission reiterated the concern that "use of the word 'rape' attaches a profound moral stigma to the victims and expresses an essentially irrational folklore about them."[6] The perceived problems with the label of rape were, from the outset, closely bound up with the fact that it is sexually evocative. The commission noted that rape and assault are distinguishable only insofar as the former requires sexual intercourse:

> An assault is essentially an intentional application of force on another, or an attempt or threat to apply force without that person's consent. Rape is the intentional application of force in order to accomplish sexual intercourse without the victim's consent. On this basis, it can be seen that all of the legally defined elements

of rape are contained in the concept of assault, with sexual intercourse being a specific ingredient in addition to the force applied or threatened by the accused. The concept of sexual assault, therefore, more appropriately characterizes the actual nature of the offence of rape because the primary focus is on the assault or on the violation of the integrity of the person rather than the sexual intercourse. In addition, *it has been suggested that change in the focus of the offence from sexual intercourse to assault could in some measure help to lessen the unnecessary and embarrassing stigma which still adheres to rape victims by virtue of folklore about rape.*[7]

Shifting the emphasis away from the sexual aspect of rape, and toward its inherent connection to other forms of assault, would make it less likely that victims would be unfairly labelled.

Throughout the debate on Bill C-53, this need to recast rape as a crime of violence rather than sex was heavily stressed.[8] This would be done, in part, by simply doing away with the term "rape" and replacing it with "sexual assault." But it would also be accomplished by moving its replacement offences to a different part of the Criminal Code. Before Bill C-53 became law,[9] the crime of rape was situated under "Sexual Offences, Public Morals and Disorderly Conduct" – suggesting, it was said, that rape was only a crime of sexual morality.[10] Ultimately, it was moved alongside other offences in the assault family.

There was a further, pivotal step. The commission did not only say that the offence of rape should be called something different – it proposed that the elements of the offence should be changed so that proof of sexual penetration would no longer be required. Instead, all forms of non-consensual sexual contact would be lumped together under "sexual interference." Where force or threats of violence were used, the defendant could be convicted of "sexual aggression."[11] Bill C-53 did not use this language, preferring instead "sexual assault" and "aggravated sexual assault." But it did pick up the idea that nothing should turn on the question of penetration until the sentencing stage of criminal proceedings. The law of rape's focus on penetration was problematic, of course, because it privileged a distinctly male idea of which kinds of sexual touching matter and which do not.[12] Ron Irwin, moving the bill for second reading, remarked: "It would no longer be necessary to prove penetration. That requirement in section 143 of the Criminal Code has caused much embarrassment to complainants. It has done little, if anything, to protect these victims. Also it has created an anomaly in the law. Some brutal and injurious sexual attacks not involving penetration have been charged, out of necessity, as the lesser offence of indecent assault."[13] He then quoted the commission: "To retain penetration as a distinct element of one of the offences would be to emphasize the sexual character of the proscribed behaviour rather than to stress the aspect of violence or threatened violence."[14] Renaming the offence of rape without changing its underlying elements would be purely cosmetic. As the commission observed: "To conserve [the requirement of proof of penetration] would increase the risk of having the concept of 'rape' reappear, albeit under a different name, and of accomplishing therefore no more than a nominal reform."[15] In the absence of legislative definition of the term "sexual," the courts would read the new offences narrowly and would effectively make them pointless.

One further significant aspect of the 1983 amendments was the abolition of the marital rape exception. On the terms of the Criminal Code, it was impossible for a man to rape his wife. This, it was reasonably thought, sent the message that marriage conferred upon men a right of sexual access.[16] It also reinforced a view of women, and their sexuality, as a kind of property to be owned and controlled by men. As I discuss in the next section, this vision of what women are in our culture was believed to underpin the view that sexual coercion (commonly described as seduction) is, within narrow limits, socially acceptable. By abolishing the exception, it was implicitly hoped that Parliament would buttress its broader message that *all* forms of non-consensual touching amount to violence.

Because an entire spectrum of male-female sexual relations was to be problematized under the new legislation, it was ultimately decided that the offence of sexual assault simpliciter should cover the entire range of non-consensual sexual touching. At the same time, it would be a hybrid offence with a minimum punishment of only ninety days' imprisonment. It was understood that not all forms of non-consensual sexual touching could deserve punishment for an indictable offence. To use one example cited commonly during the Parliamentary debates, non-consensual "bum pinching" could not deserve a minimum of one-year imprisonment.[17] Yet there was resistance to the suggestion that this sort of touching should be punished as something other than sexual assault. There was plainly a concern that the sexual aspect of non-consensual touching is an important part of what makes such conduct uniquely wrongful, and that the legislation should acknowledge that fact even at the less serious end of the spectrum. Forms of sexual touching that legislators perceived as more serious, like those involving penetration, would meet with more severe sanctions – but, again, would not be treated as fundamentally different in kind from bum-pinching incidents.

Because sexual assault covers the complete spectrum of sexual touching, there has been persistent controversy over whether the new offence effectively diminishes the seriousness of rape.[18] The pre-1983 law expressly set rape apart from other offences, highlighting its special wrongness.[19] After the legislative changes, rape became a crime that was different only in degree from forms of sexual touching that, rightly or wrongly, were and are commonly accepted in our culture. As I show in the next section, the 1983 amendments were driven at least in part by the conviction that rape is not unique – that it is a natural outgrowth of widespread social attitudes and patterns of behaviour in society. This idea, however, is deeply controversial.[20]

Rape and Sexual Assault as Crimes of Objectification

It would be foolish to suggest that there was a single feminist position on rape in the 1970s and 1980s. It is, however, useful to look to Clark and Lewis's 1977 *Rape: The Price of Coercive Sexuality*,[21] since it represents a sustained and particularly influential treatment of the subject in Canada and has been described as a "major impetus behind reform."[22] In our culture, women's sexuality is treated as a commodity – indeed, since women were traditionally valued primarily for their ability to reproduce and provide sexual gratification for men, as their only marketable asset. That being the case, they have no choice but to bargain with it. Like other commodities, however, sexuality is valued according to its scarcity. Women are expected to withhold sexual gratification from anyone to whom they are not committed in a lifelong romantic partnership. Clark and Lewis wrote:

[I]t is an indisputable fact that women do become socialized to accept the view that they cannot make free use of their sexuality or their reproductive ability. Women almost always feel guilty

IMPLIED CONSENT AND SEXUAL ASSAULT

about having sexual relations with anyone other than their actual husbands, the men to whom they are engaged, or, at least, the men with whom they are "in love" or having a "serious" relationship. And the only explanation for this guilt is their acceptance, however unconscious, of the belief that their sexuality is something they hold in trust for the mythical Mr. Right.[23]

There is, then, an irresolvable tension in how women are expected to interact with men: they must hold themselves out as sexually available when in fact they are not. They are "placed in the contradictory position of having to use the reward of sexual contact or the threat of sexual deprivation in order to get what they want, and of being regarded as under a special obligation to devote themselves to the minimization of threats to their sexual purity."[24] Men, meanwhile, are expected to use bargaining, coercion, and fraud to obtain sexual gratification from women.[25] Clark and Lewis continued: "Women are seen as the hoarders and miserly dispensers of a much desired commodity, and men must constantly wheedle, bargain, and pay a price for what they want. And if anything lies at the root of misogyny, this does. Men naturally come to resent and dislike women because they see them as having something which they want and have a perfect right to, but which women are unwilling to give them freely. The right to female sexuality must be purchased."[26] Coercion is unavoidable in this kind of social environment. At the most benign level, the lack of socio-economic opportunities for women makes it impossible for them to avoid bargaining with men over the sexual use of their bodies. But men who lack the social, economic, or sexual capital to negotiate with women may think themselves entitled to resort to varying degrees of harassment, extortion, or force. This is the natural extension of a logic that treats women and their sexuality as things to be bought and sold, possessed and used.[27] The important observation made by Clark and Lewis is that, in our culture, coercion is not the exception in male-female sexual relations, but the rule. The line between rape and seduction is not a line between coercion and no coercion – it simply marks the point at which a socially unacceptable amount or kind of coercion has been used.[28]

The shame that rape victims experience, Clark and Lewis argued, is directly tied to the sexual nature of the offence. Since rape was not fundamentally different in kind from other forms of sexual coercion, its victims could be blamed for failing to take adequate steps to protect their "property" (even if they did not consent), and could be dismissed as lacking "credibility" when they did not fit the profile of the stereotypical victim whose sexuality was perceived as having market value.[29] They remarked:

> It is men, and not women, who have defined rape as the worst thing that can happen to a woman. For a man to have his exclusive sexual property defiled by an intruder is one of the worst things that can happen to him, but it most assuredly is not the worst thing that can happen to a woman, even though it frequently verges on this because of its accompanying risk. What woman would not rather have a penis inserted in her vagina, even against her will, than suffer death or mutilation? Women accept the judgment that rape is a disgrace because they, too, have been brainwashed into placing pre-eminent value on their sexuality, and because they know from experience that rape will, in fact, lead to their social and personal devaluation.[30]

Clark and Lewis proceeded to argue that rape is nothing other than a kind of assault. The fact that the assault is upon one body part rather than another is neither here nor there. The victim experiences rape as an assault, and it is arbitrary for the law to treat it as something sui generis.[31] With this in mind, Clark and Lewis recommended the redefinition of rape as a crime of violence, rather than as a sexual offence.[32]

Underpinning the rape-as-violence-not-sex argument, then, is much more than the claim that rape shares certain features with assault. The argument is premised on an understanding of "ordinary" sexual relations between men and women as socially constructed – as grounded in a set of norms that define what it means to engage in permissible rather than impermissible coercion. On this understanding, men are expected to be aggressive and domineering in their treatment of women, whereas women are expected to be passive, and to withhold their sexual services in the absence of a compelling offer of security, protection, and affection.[33] Furthermore, this analysis presupposes that women are systematically treated as objects of male sexual gratification, and that their bodies and sexuality are regarded (if unconsciously) as commodities or property. These themes likewise run through Susan Brownmiller's work.[34]

Taking these observations on board, we can begin to see that the 1983 rape amendments were not intended, at least by their principal proponents, merely to relabel rape. They were intended to rebrand ordinary sexual transactions as a kind of violence, and to alert the public to wider equality issues facing women. Because men are expected to take on a dominant role in sexual scripts, whereas women are expected to take on a passive role, the violence inherent in rape is obscured: how are we to readily distinguish the domination by a man over a woman in the context of rape from that which occurs in ordinary sexual intercourse?[35] As Kinnon remarked: "The similarities of [convicted sex offenders and a control group of men in the community] implies that motivations, values, etc., of men in general do not vary greatly from men who are convicted of sexual assault, except in the degree of aggression."[36] By desexualizing the offence of rape, the legislation arguably purported to draw a bright line between violence and a model of sexual relations that respects the equality of women. In doing so, it would transform not just the way we think about rape, but how we think about norms that govern sexual relations generally. By highlighting that rape, under existing norms, lies along a continuum that includes popularly acceptable forms of sexual conduct, one might hope to rebrand the continuum as a whole as one of violence.

And yet there is something deeply jarring about the idea that rape is purely an act of violence – that it bears no relation to sex. Women are treated as sexual objects, and are shamed for having been touched in ways that have been culturally coded as sexual. To act as though rape is nothing more than assault is to pretend that those norms do not exist, and that rape victims' experience of having been sexually violated can be explained only by appealing to their own pathology, and not to anything "real" in the world. Łoś writes:

> The focus on the legal relabeling ... may create a fiction that somehow the sexual degradation of women, integral to the traditional notion of rape, has been reduced, or is going to be reduced, by the changed label. On the one hand, it is true that the new label more easily locates the offender within the broader culture that promotes and perpetuates patterns of male domination over women and increasingly associates sex with violence. On the other hand, however, through this concept, women's experience of rape as a *sexual* violation is deliberately minimized.[37]

This is, of course, partly the point. The way in which men and women think about rape was and is informed largely by how we think about sex. Those who have internalized existing gender and sexual norms will not perceive ordinary sexual relationships as defined by violence. For them, the offence of rape is horrifying because it transforms an unproblematic exchange, defined by love (or at least affection) and intimacy, into something altogether different.[38] As Cohen and Backhouse remarked: "Rape transforms what is for many women an intimate act into a completely impersonal one, used for the expression of hate, conquest or contempt."[39] It represents a radical corruption of a fundamentally positive act – not the logical extension of the domination and objectification that was always present in the sexual sphere. From that point of view, it is nonsensical to distance the act of rape from its sexual aspects: part of what makes rape so humiliating and psychologically harmful to its victims is the sense that they have been forced to engage in the simulacrum of an act signifying love.[40] To deny that rape has a sexual dimension radically fails to reflect the lived reality of its victims, and might so seem to invalidate their experiences as "distorted" or as "false consciousness," which in itself amounts to a kind of violence, however well motivated.

On this basis, Cohen and Backhouse took issue with the idea that rape could or should be desexualized. Doing so, they argued, would fail to do justice to an essential aspect of victims' experience: "Rape victims perceive rape as an act which is qualitatively different from other forms of physical assault. The fear that it engenders can best be likened to the male fear of castration. As one rape victim said, 'For me, the trauma was the total humiliation of not being treated as a person. There's something worse about being raped than just being beaten.'"[41] Rape, Cohen and Backhouse argued, is only possible in a culture in which women are treated as sexual objects: "Sexual penetration would [in a non-sexist culture] be inconceivable as a means of expressing hostility."[42] The attempt to desexualize rape is, in part, driven by the desire to transform sexist ways of thinking about women – to undercut the perception that "the most important thing about a woman is that she's a sexual receptacle."[43] But to men and women who have internalized existing gender norms, it may be impossible to avoid this way of thinking. For them, it is absurd to try to separate the offence of rape from its sexualized character. In trying to desexualize the offence of rape, one again risks invalidating the experience of its victims – those, at any rate, who are insufficiently "enlightened" to appreciate that their experience of the attack as sexual has been socially constructed. As Łoś remarks: "[T]he elitist tendency to impose the concepts worked out by a few feminists upon all women remains questionable and may add to the oppression and devaluation of some women."[44]

Likewise, MacKinnon argued that it is a mistake for feminists to link rape too closely or exclusively to violence. Taking that approach, she claimed, sends the message that rape is something altogether different from sex:

> While intending the opposite, some feminists have encouraged and participated in this type of analysis by conceiving rape as violence, not sex. While this approach gave needed emphasis to rape's previously effaced elements of power and dominance, it obscured its elements of sex. Aside from failing to answer the rather obvious question, if it is violence not sex, why didn't he just hit her? this approach made it impossible to see that violence is sex when it is practiced as sex. This is obvious once what sexuality is, is understood as a matter of what it means and how it is interpreted. To say rape is violence not sex preserves the "sex is good" norm by simply distinguishing forced sex as "not sex," whether it means sex to the perpetrator or even, later, to the victim, who has difficulty experiencing sex without re-experiencing the rape. Whatever is sex cannot be violent; whatever is violent cannot be sex. This analytic wish-fulfillment makes it possible for rape to be opposed by those who would save sexuality from the rapists while leaving the sexual fundamentals of male dominance intact.[45]

On one central point, there is no serious disagreement between Clark and Lewis and Cohen and Backhouse (or between Brownmiller and MacKinnon): the problem of rape emerged from a social environment in which women were and are systemically treated as nothing more than sexual objects. All agreed that anti-rape legislation, to succeed in its aims, would need to tackle pervasive social norms about what men and women are, and how they should interact. They simply disagreed about whether it would do more harm than good to emphasize the message that rape is violence, not sex. Fundamentally, they agreed that what makes sexual assault uniquely wrongful as a form of violence is its intersection with sexual objectification.

This last point finds expression in *A Feminist Review of Criminal Law*, where the authors begin the chapter on "Offences against Women" with these remarks:

> Obviously women can be the victims of all criminal offences, but one common distinguishing thread runs through [sexual assault, prostitution, and distribution of pornography] i.e., they are offences against women as women, rather than against people who simply happen to be women. They reveal in the deepest sense just what women are, are for, in our society. Thus the commission of all these offences plays a major role in the subordination of women; they are in the forefront of the means of oppression.[46]

The authors continue: "Thus these offences are about the humiliation and degradation of women, the expression of hatred against them, and their use for sexual purposes either through economic or coercive means. They are also about the sexual exploitation and objectification of women, and symbolize the fact that a major aspect of being a woman is belonging to the sex to whom these things can happen. Whether on the mind or the spirit or the body, these offences fall into a general class of gender assault."[47] The point is clear: though sexual assault belongs to a family of offences against the person, it also belongs to a family of offences against sexual objectification.[48]

It is interesting to consider this suggestion in light of John Gardner and Stephen Shute's analysis of the English offence of rape. Like others, they argue that the offence primarily targets the wrong of objectification.[49] Understood in this way, Gardner and Shute reason, rape would be criminally wrongful even in circumstances where it is arguably "harmless" – that is, in circumstances where the victim had no knowledge of the violation and suffered no physical injuries.[50] Rape is wrongful not because its victims perceive themselves as having been wronged, but because they have been used as sexual objects. As they put it: "That a rapist objectifies his victim by treating her as a mere repository of use-value is, in our view, what is basically wrong with rape."[51]

On Sexual Integrity

There is sometimes a suggestion that the offense of sexual assault targets not wrongful objectification, but violations of sexual integrity. The Supreme Court has said so on a number of occasions, starting with its decision in *Chase*.[52] By using the language of "sexual integrity," the court might seem to have invoked rough comparisons to "territorial integrity" or "bodily integrity," suggesting that the offence of sexual assault is directed at certain kinds of boundary crossings. It is meant to confer control upon the intended object of the touching. On this view, it does not matter whether touching is wrongfully objectifying or not.

That, it seems to me, is an unnecessarily narrow understanding of sexual integrity. Yes, having control over others' sexual access to one's body is important. But it is part of a larger concern for sexual autonomy. Elaine Craig remarks:

> Bodily integrity constitutes one aspect of sexual integrity, but sexual integrity should mean something much more than simply "freedom from" bodily violations. It should also include, along with "freedom from," the "conditions for" sexual fulfillment, sexual diversity, the safety necessary for sexual exploration, and sexual benefit. To suggest that sexual integrity extends beyond the notion of bodily invasion invokes the notion of protecting sexuality itself ... To suggest that sexual integrity is about one's sexuality and not simply "freedom from" bodily invasion is to suggest that the promotion of sexual integrity also requires promoting certain "conditions for" – for example, the conditions necessary to create the capacity for developing a sense of sexual self, sexual self-esteem, the opportunity for sexual exploration, and beneficial sexual interactions.[53]

Craig, following Jennifer Nedelsky,[54] suggests that sexual autonomy is a relational good: it is made possible only if we live in a community in which we have the assurance that we can express our sexuality safely and free of shame or ridicule.[55] In her view, sexual integrity should be interpreted in this richer sense, as encompassing not only bodily integrity but also sexual autonomy. Moreover, Craig argues that the Supreme Court, in *Chase* (which I discuss in a moment), used "sexual integrity" in something like this sense:

> [T]he manner in which the Court [in *Chase*] employed [the term sexual integrity] signaled a shift that has had significant impact. It is a shift towards a substantive meaning of criminally prohibited sexual violence that, at the definitional stage, flipped the analytical perspective from that of the accused or the community to that of the complainant ... Determining whether the complainant's sexual integrity was violated will of necessity require consideration of the complainant's perspective and experience. This makes it different than the analysis for the former offence of indecent assault. Indecent assault based its objective determination on the sexual propriety, morality, and standards of the community, not on the integrity of the complainant.[56]

As I noted earlier, when Parliament replaced the offence of rape with sexual assault, it also moved it out of the part of the Criminal Code addressing morals offences. In doing so, it effectively backed away from the (implicit) idea that the offence of sexual assault is designed to police women's sexual choices. Its purpose is not to regulate access to women's bodies at the expense of their sexual autonomy. This, according to Craig, is the message conveyed by the Supreme Court's invocation of sexual integrity.

On Craig's reading, we can lack sexual integrity even when our physical boundaries have not been transgressed, insofar as the law has failed to create the conditions under which we can explore sexual possibilities. A person whose consent is not legally recognized, and who is therefore unable to engage in sexual intimacy without being labelled (or having her partner labelled) a criminal, has had her sexual integrity and autonomy violated in an important sense.[57] This is significant because one way in which men and women express their sexual autonomy is by relinquishing control. In the ordinary assault context, the law makes it possible for people to engage physically with one another, stripped of control, by recognizing the idea of implied consent. We understand this not as a violation of their physical integrity or autonomy, but as a means of legally extending it. By not recognizing implied consent in the sexual sphere, the criminal law arguably undermines sexual integrity or autonomy.

Leaving aside implied consent for a moment, Craig's discussion of sexual integrity shows the extent to which the question of what counts as a violation of sexual integrity turns on whether we regard a certain kind of sexual touching as impermissibly *objectifying*. As I observe in chapter 5, there is a sense in which one objectifies another by treating him or her as someone who lacks self-control. As Martha Nussbaum shows, however, the mere fact that someone surrenders control is not morally significant in itself. To decide whether and when a loss of control is wrongful, we need to ask deeper questions.

Chase and the Definition of "Sexual"

Equipped with the idea that the ability to relinquish control is an important part of integrity – physical or sexual – we can begin to see the significance of a line of authority, starting with *Chase*, that the complainant's subjective experience of the touching in question is not dispositive when determining whether it is sexual or not.[58] In *Chase*, McIntyre J. stated:

> The test to be applied in determining whether the impugned conduct has the requisite sexual nature is an objective one: "Viewed in the light of all the circumstances, is the sexual or carnal context of the assault visible to a reasonable observer" ... The part of the body touched, the nature of the contact, the situation in which it occurred, the words and gestures accompanying the act, and all other circumstances surrounding the conduct, including threats which may or may not be accompanied by force, will be relevant.[59]

The complainant's experience is certainly relevant. Such evidence can give us insight into how a reasonable third-party observer would have understood the touching under the circumstances. But the complainant's testimony is only circumstantial – not direct – evidence of the sexual nature of the touching. It may help the trier of fact draw inferences about how a reasonable third party would have perceived matters. The trier of fact may believe the complainant experienced the touching as sexual, yet find the touching non-sexual.

Consider, too, the Supreme Court's single-paragraph judgment in *R. v. Robicheau*.[60] The defendant was acquitted of sexual assault. In giving reasons for judgment, the trial judge stated: "There's no doubt that what [the complainant] experienced was a violation of her sexual integrity."[61] The judge nonetheless had a reasonable doubt about the sexual nature of the assault. A majority of the Nova Scotia Court of Appeal held that the ruling was internally inconsistent, and ordered a new trial.[62] Roscoe J.A., dissenting, found that the trial judge, in making the above remark, was merely describing the complainant's state of mind. It was possible, he argued, for the trial judge to believe that the complainant subjectively experienced a violation of her sexual integrity, and still conclude that the touching was not sexual. There was therefore no inconsistency.[63]

The Supreme Court allowed the appeal, endorsing Roscoe J.A.'s reasoning. To say the least, the complainant's experience of the touching was not treated as "determinative."[64] Though the trial judge appears to have believed the complainant's testimony that she regarded the touching as sexual, there was no finding that a reasonable third-party observer would have regarded it in the same way. On this basis, the court restored the acquittal.

The Supreme Court's ruling in *R. v. Litchfield* is also instructive.[65] There, the defendant was a male physician accused of sexually assaulting his patients on fourteen separate occasions. A central issue in each of the counts was whether the touching was of a sexual nature. The counts were severed. The defendant was ultimately acquitted. The Crown appealed on the basis that, by severing the counts, the trier of fact was unable to consider all of the circumstances relevant in determining whether the *Chase* test was satisfied. The Supreme Court agreed. Iacobucci J., writing for the majority, stated: "[T]his Court emphasized in *Chase* that the court must look to all the circumstances surrounding the conduct in determining the nature and quality of the act. For example, if the respondent acted improperly toward a complainant during one part of a physical examination, evidence of that improper conduct would be relevant to assessing the respondent's conduct at other times during the examination."[66] He continued:

The [severance] order denies the reality of how the complainants
experienced the conduct which they have alleged constituted
sexual assaults. Each aspect of one complainant's contact with the

respondent interlocks with all the other aspects to form the larger context within which that complainant felt that the respondent's actions were inappropriate. Further, the message that a division and severance order in a sexual assault case based on the complainant's body parts sends to women is that the complainant's physical attributes are more important than her experience as a whole person.[67]

One could seize upon this passage, arguing that it places the complainant's experience at the centre of the *Chase* inquiry.[68] It should, though, be taken with a grain of salt. The passage emphasizes that if we are to understand the nature of the touching in a given case, we must look at it in context. It is no good parsing each instance of touching that takes place in a single examination, since any particular instance may appear medical. That is how the defendant was alleged to have perpetrated the assaults – i.e., by giving them a veneer of legitimacy. The trier of fact was being called upon to decide whether the defendant's touching was indeed pursuant to a bona fide medical examination, as opposed to a mere simulacrum. To make that determination – to properly interpret the context within which the touching occurred – we need to look at all of the allegations together.

As this quick analysis of the ruling makes clear, the central issue was not whether each complainant subjectively regarded the touching as sexual, but whether the defendant engaged in it in his professional capacity. That question cannot be answered by looking to the defendant's motives – a person may act unprofessionally whether or not he believes he is – but neither can it be resolved by asking what the complainants felt about the touching.

That the issue was not really the complainants' subjective experience of the touching can be seen in the fact that the court also found that the evidence of one complainant could be relevant when assessing the nature of the touching of other complainants. Iacobucci J. stated: "[T]he evidence provided information highly relevant to understanding the context in which the alleged offences occurred and shed light on the nature of the respondent's relationship with his patients, particularly the standard of medical treatment he provided."[69] Again, none of this is to say that a complainant's experience of the touching in question is irrelevant. But it is relevant only insofar as it sheds light on what a reasonable third party observer would think was going on.

It is worth discussing another case: *R. v. Larue*.[70] There, the defendant was charged with aggravated sexual assault. He pleaded guilty to the included offence of aggravated assault. The only issue to be decided was whether the *Chase* test was satisfied. It was common ground that the defendant had attacked the complainant with a knife, and had climbed on top of her while she was unconscious and naked from the waist down. The trial judge acquitted. Unable to say who had removed the complainant's clothing – the defendant or the complainant – the judge had a reasonable doubt as to the sexual nature of the touching.[71] The Supreme Court found that, in light of the complainant's state of undress at the time of the assault, its sexual character was apparent irrespective of how she came to be undressed.[72]

Again, *Larue* might seem to illustrate a more complainant-centred focus in sexual assault law.[73] It would certainly have been more open to the trial judge to have a reasonable doubt about the sexual nature of the touching had the inquiry turned entirely on whether the defendant had a sexual motive.[74] But nothing in the decision suggests that the complainant's experience of the touching has special significance in the analysis. We are concerned with whether her sexual integrity was actually violated, not simply with whether she believed it was.

Finally, consider the Supreme Court's approach to the sexual fraud provisions in the Code, starting with *Cuerrier*.[75] There, the court was called upon to decide whether and when deception as to HIV status would constitute fraud vitiating consent to touching.[76] Cory J., writing for the majority, held that where the deception caused a deprivation or risk of deprivation involving a serious risk of bodily harm, consent would be vitiated.[77] In her analysis of the case, Craig observes: "Rather than focusing solely on the specific sexual act [by dwelling on whether the fraud went to its 'nature and quality'], Justice Cory adopted an interpretation that takes into consideration the entire sexual interaction as well as the complainant's perspective not just regarding the specific physical act ... but also regarding the context of the interaction as a whole."[78] Again, the complainant's perspective is not dispositive. After all, the court in *Cuerrier* did not say that, in determining which risks are serious, we should ask what the complainant herself regards as serious. We are concerned with what is actually a serious risk. Thus, in *Mabior*, the Supreme Court held that, where the risk of HIV transmission is sufficiently low, it will not be regarded as serious enough to satisfy the *Cuerrier* threshold.[79] The fact that the person who ostensibly consented would not have done so had she known that there was any risk at all of contracting HIV was treated as neither here nor there: the deception would not be regarded as the sort that Parliament intended to criminalize.[80]

This stance on sexual fraud is made all the more apparent from the decision in *R. v. Hutchinson*.[81] The defendant had assured the complainant that he would wear a condom to avoid impregnating her, but poked holes in it. The question was whether the complainant's consent had been vitiated, or indeed whether she had consented at all to the sexual touching that took place. Though the Supreme Court unanimously found that a sexual assault had taken place, it was split on the reasoning. Three members of the panel, concurring in the result, found that there was no consent to anything. The complainant, they held, had consented to "sex with a condom." Since there was, in effect, no condom, they found that the complainant had never consented to the encounter.[82] A thin majority disagreed. It found that the complainant consented to "intercourse" – i.e., with or without a condom. That being the case, there was consent to the sexual act. But, it found, the complainant's consent was vitiated by fraud: the defendant's behaviour entailed both dishonesty and a significant risk of serious bodily harm inasmuch as pregnancy entails significant biological changes and hardships.[83]

In preferring to resolve the case as one of fraud rather than no consent, the majority took the road that gives the complainant less control. On the approach taken by the concurring judges, a sexual assault can occur whether or not the defendant has acted dishonestly, and whether or not the complainant has been subjected to any risk. The majority balked at this approach, and preferred to construe in a relatively narrow way the circumstances under which sexual touching would be treated as criminal – even though this necessarily strips a degree of control from the complainant.[84]

Ewanchuk on Control and Integrity

With the above in mind, what are we to make of the Supreme Court's decision in *Ewanchuk*? There, the majority emphasized "control" and "physical integrity" as common concerns animating sexual assault and other forms of assault.[85] Major J. remarked:

> Society is committed to protecting the personal integrity, both physical and psychological, of every individual. Having control over who touches one's body, and how, lies at the core of human dignity and autonomy. The inclusion of assault and sexual assault in the Code expresses society's determination to protect the security of the person from any non-consensual contact or threats of force. The common law has recognized for centuries that the individual's right to personal integrity is a fundamental principle ... It follows that any intentional but unwanted touching is criminal.[86]

Major J. purported to explain why consent in sexual assault cases must be understood as the complainant's purely subjective experience in sexual assault cases; and, further, why the doctrine of implied consent should be rejected. There is, however, a gap in Major J.'s reasoning. If a concern for personal integrity led inexorably to the conclusion that consent must refer exclusively to a discretely contemporaneous subjective experience, we would expect the court to reject the doctrine of implied consent not just in the sexual assault context, but in all assault contexts. It has not done so. On the contrary, a majority of the court in *J.A.* expressly reaffirmed that the doctrine applies in many assault contexts.[87] That is a good thing. As I discuss in chapter 3, the doctrine of implied consent in an important sense enhances autonomy – it makes it possible for people to engage in practices in which some relinquishing of control is both valuable and necessary. But this begs the question: if a concern for integrity and autonomy permits or even demands a place for implied consent in the context of ordinary assault, why believe there is no place for it in the context of sexual assault?

The tentative answer, of course, is that sexual assault is a gendered offence. The debate over the 1983 reforms was grounded in the understanding that women are the victims of a pervasive rape culture in which they are treated as mere instruments of sexual gratification for men. The relative uniqueness of sexual assault – the fact that it does not target precisely the same wrongs as other assault offences – has been remarked upon by the Supreme Court on several occasions. In *R. v. Osolin*, Cory

J. acknowledged the offence's unique nature, noting that it both assaults human dignity as well as denies gender equality.[88] In *R. v. Seaboyer*, the court unanimously held that many of the evidentiary reforms to the law of sexual assault were designed to address myths and stereotypes about sexual assault victims.[89]

Returning to *Ewanchuk*, the court recognized that the defence of honest but mistaken belief in consent is not available where the belief rested on the complainant's silence or passivity.[90] As three members of the court observed, this approach was necessitated by pervasive myths and stereotypes about women – particularly, that they are "passive, disposed submissively to surrender to the sexual advances of active men."[91] In other words, it implicitly recognized the wrongfulness of "honestly believing" that another human being is little or no more than a sexual object ready and willing at all times to satisfy one's own sexual desires. This theme was developed in *J.A.* Holding that consent does not persist once a person loses consciousness, the majority noted that the consent provisions in section 273 exist in part to prevent sexual exploitation, and that consent must be voluntary and revocable at all times during the sexual activity in question.[92]

These are all good reasons to be suspicious of any doctrine that threatens to undermine women's ability to control others' sexual access to them. At bottom, though, the concern is not about lack of control per se, but wrongful sexual objectification. We are concerned about exploitation, with men using women as instruments of gratification, as consumable and disposable things. And, as I noted earlier, the fact that one person touches another under conditions where the latter lacks control does not mean that the physical touching is problematically objectifying – i.e., it need not amount to a "violation of sexual integrity." It may, indeed, reflect and honour the latter's autonomy. That being the case, it is worth asking whether it is possible to recognize a limited doctrine of implied consent without licensing the wrongful objectification of others.

Conclusion

In this chapter, I have argued that the offence of sexual assault targets acts of wrongful sexual objectification. Though the language of sexual integrity abounds in the case law, there is a credible argument that it does not refer merely to sexual boundaries but to sexual capacities – including the capacity to relinquish control over others' physical and sexual access. In determining whether a given loss of control amounts to a violation of sexual integrity, we must ultimately look to what makes objectification wrongful.

CHAPTER 3

Implied Consent and *Ewanchuk*

Introduction

Any discussion of implied consent must begin with the Supreme Court of Canada's 1999 ruling in *Ewanchuk*. There, the court categorically rejected implied consent in the sexual assault context. It has never looked back.[1]

But it is worth asking whether the reasoning used in *Ewanchuk* can truly support the conclusion that implied consent could have *no* place in the sexual sphere. Writing for the majority, Major J. seemed to proceed on the basis that the doctrine of implied consent treats the complainant's subjective state of mind as irrelevant. That is simply not true. The doctrine applies where the complainant subjectively accepted a set of norms under which the touching in question is legitimate. The complainant need not subjectively want or accept the specific act of touching as it occurs, and in that respect there is not consent in the usual sense of the word. We are, however, no less concerned with the complainant's subjective state of mind.

The doctrine of implied consent applies only where the complainant and defendant were engaged in a practice governed by norms capable of legitimating the touching in question. Understood in this way, it is clear that the defence could not conceivably have arisen given the facts in *Ewanchuk*, where the sexual touching occurred in the context of a job interview. The defendant's sexual touching was driven by stereotypes about women, and not by any reasonable interpretation of the norms governing the relationship between an interviewer and interviewee. On any plausible interpretation of the law and facts, implied consent was not an issue that should have been before the court.

Had the court more fully considered the question, it may have found good reasons for acknowledging a limited role for implied consent in sexual assault law. The doctrine exists in recognition of the fact that certain plans and goals can only be realized if we are able to cede control over how and when others engage physically with us. Like ordinary consent, implied consent is a way to expand and enhance the autonomy of the recipient of the touching. We may not, for reasons that will receive greater attention later, be able to simply transplant the doctrine of implied consent into the sexual sphere. It would require modification. But the essential reasons for having a doctrine of implied consent in the law of assault apply as surely when we turn to the offence of sexual assault.

Implied Consent in *Ewanchuk*

The court in *Ewanchuk* discussed and rejected the defence of implied consent in a single paragraph. Major J. stated:

> Counsel for the respondent submitted that the trier of fact may believe the complainant when she says she did not consent, but still acquit the accused on the basis that her conduct raised a reasonable doubt. Both he and the trial judge refer to this as "implied consent." It follows from the foregoing, however, that the trier of fact may only come to one of two conclusions: the complainant either consented or not. There is no third option. If the trier of fact accepts the complainant's testimony that she did not consent, no matter how strongly her conduct may contradict that claim, the absence of consent is established and the third component of the *actus reus* of sexual assault is proven. The doctrine of implied consent has been recognized in our common law jurisprudence in a variety of contexts but sexual assault is not one of them. There is no defence of implied consent to sexual assault in Canadian law.[2]

The passage reflects some confusion at the trial level (and among counsel) about what implied consent means. If counsel was arguing only that evidence of a complainant's conduct is logically capable of casting doubt on her claim that she did not subjectively consent, the argument was and is uncontroversial. Major J., only a few paragraphs before, indicated as much: "While the complainant's testimony is the only source of direct evidence as to her state of mind, credibility must still be assessed by the trial judge, or jury, in light of all the evidence. It is open to the accused to claim that the complainant's words *and actions, before and during the incident*, raise a reasonable doubt against her assertion that she, in her mind, did not want the sexual touching to take place."[3] In rejecting the doctrine of implied consent in the sexual assault context, the court did not take issue with the proposition that the trier of fact is entitled (though not required) to draw inferences about a person's state of mind from evidence that he or she behaved in a certain way.[4] The court was making the far less radical claim that, having found beyond a reasonable doubt that the complainant did not subjectively consent to sexual touching, it would not be open to the trier of fact to constructively impute consent to the complainant on the basis that her conduct at the relevant time would, to a reasonable third-party observer, have appeared consistent with subjective consent. The appearance of consent has no freestanding significance. In asking whether the complainant subjectively consented, or whether the defendant had an honest but mistaken belief in consent, the trier of fact may well find evidence of the complainant's behaviour and demeanour helpful. If the trier of fact answers both of those questions in the negative, however, evidence of the complainant's conduct ceases to be relevant.

To a degree, the court's reasoning is unobjectionable. It is far from obvious why we would want to say that the mere surface appearance of consent should have the same moral effect as actual consent. The trouble is that the doctrine of implied consent, in the context of *ordinary* assault, does not stand for the proposition that the simulacrum of subjective consent is substantively significant. Nor does it suppose that the complainant's subjective state of mind is irrelevant. The doctrine is both more modest and more radical than either proposition would indicate. It suggests that we may sometimes find something morally equivalent to consent (or comparably powerful), but not by looking to the complainant's subjective attitude to the particular act of touching in question at the precise time of that touching. Instead, we may find it by examining the complainant's normative commitments – the norms that constitute the social practice in which the complainant was engaged, and that she subjectively regarded as binding upon her. Implied consent, then, does not abandon the idea of subjectivity. Quite the contrary, it deepens the subjective inquiry.

What Is Implied Consent?

Consider the use of the doctrine in the context in which we have been most comfortable asserting it – that of contact sports.[5] Let us imagine an adult who agrees to participate in a hockey game and, in the course of play, receives a devastating (but, within the rules of the game, "legal") check. It is unlikely that the complainant subjectively consented to the application of force. As Stewart notes: "Quite the contrary, [the hockey player] subjectively does not want to be checked, hooked, or tripped precisely because these actions impede his or her effectiveness as a member of the team."[6] We can go further: often a player is unaware that she is about to be checked, and therefore has no opportunity to decide whether she consents to the particular application of force. Yet the courts have held that a kind of consent may be imputed to the complainant. In *R. v. Cey*, the Saskatchewan Court of Appeal stated: "It is clear that in agreeing to play the game a hockey player consents to some forms of intentional bodily contact and to the risk of injury therefrom. Those forms sanctioned by the rules are the clearest example. Other forms, denounced by the rules but falling within the accepted standards by which the game is played, may also come within the scope of the consent."[7] Nothing in *Cey* suggests that we are imputing consent to our hypothetical complainant on the basis that she behaved like someone appearing to consent to physical contact. First, it is not obvious that hockey players do appear to consent, even in the sense of acquiescence – they are, after all, actively trying *not* to be hit. But let us also consider a hypothetical scenario. Imagine that the defendant and the recipient of the hit had been engaged not in an actual hockey game, but in an elaborate pantomime which, to a third-party observer, would have appeared all but indistinguishable from the real thing. (Perhaps something like the fake contests played by the Harlem Globetrotters.) No one (surely) would argue that, on the reasoning in *Cey*, we should impute consent to the complainant merely because she looked like a hockey player. For the reasoning in *Cey* to directly apply, the complainant must be a *real* hockey player playing a *real* game. If we were only concerned with the appearance of consent, the authenticity of the game would be neither here nor there.

When we look to implied consent outside the sporting context, we get an even clearer picture that the appearance of consent is not the touchstone. The Ontario Court of Appeal, in *R. v. E. (A.)*, observed that children are deemed to consent to applications of force by parents or guardians insofar as they are consistent with the "customary norms of parenting" or "in the best interests of the child."[8] In *R. v. Palombi*,[9] the court of appeal explained:

> Infants ... require care that will call for the intentional, although usually minor, application of force. In addition, parents have a statutory and common law duty to provide the necessaries of life to children under their care ... [T]he performance of this type of duty will require the use of force. It is awkward to attempt to excuse the use of force through the application of the rigorous standards of the necessity defence. The courts have instead developed the concept of deemed consent.[10]

More recently, in *R. v. D.J.W.*, the British Columbia Court of Appeal accepted that children are deemed to consent to parental force to the extent it is reasonable.[11] In each of these cases, the force in question was held not to have been administered in the child's best interests, and so the defence of implied consent did not apply. These remarks could, therefore, be read as *obiter*. On appeal in *D.J.W.*, however, the Supreme Court endorsed the court of appeal's reasoning and expressly reserved for another time the question of whether the conduct in issue, had the defendant exercised greater care, could have been regarded as in the child's best interest.[12] That suggests willingness on the part of the court to recognize the defence in the context of the parent-child relationship. Indeed, Gonthier J. indicated in *R. v. Jobidon* that something like a defence of implied consent would need to be recognized in that context:

> Assault has been given a very encompassing definition in s. 265.
> It arises whenever a person intentionally applies force to a person "directly or indirectly," without the other's consent. The definition

says nothing about the degree of harm which must be sustained. Nor does it refer to the motives for the touching. If taken at face value, this formulation would mean that the most trivial intended touching would constitute assault. As just one of many possible examples, *a father would assault his daughter if he attempted to place a scarf around her neck to protect her from the cold but she did not consent to that touching, thinking the scarf ugly or undesirable.*[13]

Let us take as given, then, that implied consent has been recognized in the parenting context, though with the understanding that there tend not to be prosecutions in cases where the parental application of force might reasonably be regarded as appropriate to the parent-child relationship.[14] For now, the significant point to observe is that the defence is not thought to apply only where the recipient of the touching appears to consent to it. To borrow Gonthier J.'s example, we are hardly surprised when a child actively resists or protests her parents' attempts to place a scarf around her neck. A child who does not want to go to bed may holler at the top of his lungs – even struggle – when physically compelled to do so. Such reactions are not a reason not to impute consent. If anything, the apparent *absence* of subjective consent makes it important for the courts to constructively impute consent to the child in the first place.

It is easy to see why one might think that the doctrine of implied consent appeals in some way to the appearance of consent. Implied consent is most well established in the sporting context. In that context, the complainant has voluntarily engaged in conduct that might superficially be construed as an invitation to opposing players to apply physical force. She wears the sort of uniform frequently worn by people who receive checks. She is present on a playing surface in which people frequently receive forceful blows, and where those pursuing or carrying a puck frequently get checked. With that, and only that, in mind, we might be tempted to conclude that the hockey player must have invited the touching.

But this interpretive approach would be deeply flawed: it focuses on the incidence of hits given and received by people who wear hockey uniforms, and neglects the meaning of those hits for players. This approach would be fine if we simply wanted to predict whether someone is *likely* to be struck by a heavily padded person with blades attached to her feet – e.g., if we wanted to calculate insurance premiums.[15] The point here, though, is not just to predict the incidence of hits, but to determine whether those hits are wrongful. That is not a question we can answer without examining the normative framework within which those checks take place. It is for precisely this reason that we do not ask whether a person has an obligation not to assault or mug people in a particular part of town by asking whether that sort of conduct is common in the area: the mere fact that a person strolling in a given neighbourhood at night might attract certain kinds of violence does not change the normative framework within which those acts occur – that is, it does not affect their criminal wrongfulness.[16]

Distinguishing Implied Consent and Ordinary Consent

To make sense of implied consent, then, we cannot look only to the surface appearance of the complainant's behaviour – we must consider what the complainant thinks she (and others) are doing. We must examine her subjective state of mind. But that does not mean we are engaging in the same sort of analysis that we would use for ordinary consent.

When we consider the significance of checks to the players themselves, two points become reasonably clear. First, it is impossible to see those hits as invited in any meaningful sense.[17] So far as the players are concerned, getting hit represents a failure of sorts – an inability to evade a check and, as a result, put one's team in a better position to score and win. Indeed, it is difficult to imagine how many of the defining features of a game of hockey – stick-handling, puck-passing, goal-scoring – could occur if players were standing around inviting their opponents to hit them. One could go further and say that, if the point of hockey is to be hit, it cannot make sense to speak of opposing players. The fact that we do suggests that there is something fundamentally misleading about speaking of checks as invited.

The second point is that, although checks cannot be construed as invited, the participants in hockey do not regard them as inherently wrongful. Quite the contrary, the players in a pick-up game of hockey might well complain if they came to realize that the opposing team was so disengaged or lazy (or otherwise unmotivated) that its players were not even *trying* to physically strip them of (or prevent them from reaching) the puck. The game would become too easy – no longer any fun. The participants in the hypothetical pantomime I described earlier could rightly complain if someone began to hit them as though they were real hockey players. By the same token, the players in a real game could rightly complain if their opponents so failed even to attempt to physically challenge them that they were no longer playing hockey at all – that they were engaging in a mere pantomime.[18] We might say that, although checks are uninvited and unwanted, there is also a norm that opposing players will genuinely attempt them and an expectation (in the sense of a prediction) that some of those attempts will succeed. Participants do not tend to think that they have a good reason to censure other players for such attempts.

One might argue that all I have said here is that hockey players consent in one sense but not in another – that they do not consent to being checked in the sense of wanting to be hit by opposing players, but that they acquiesce to it. They are, according to this imaginary interlocutor, ready to be hit, resigned to their likely fate, but not enthusiastic about it. But speaking of consent in this way again misconstrues what is going on. A person who walks through a dangerous neighbourhood may be resigned to the prospect of being accosted by hooligans, but we would never equate this attitude with consent. And if, by "acquiescence" we mean something more than mere resignation, perhaps something like being okay with being struck, then it now seems that the hockey player could not consent in that sense: she may be positively resentful and angry about any checks she receives, and regretful that she could not avoid them, even while she accepts that she was not wronged.

This last suggestion – i.e., that the hockey player accepts that the hit upon her was legitimate – may be taken to suggest that there must be some sort of consent. But even if we want to call this consent, it is reasonably clear that this is different from what we usually mean by the term. I can accept that another is within her rights to impose a burden without consenting to it being imposed upon me. I can, for example, accept that a police officer with a search warrant is entitled to enter my home, and yet withhold my consent. It would, indeed, be strange to suggest that everyone who yields to an officer brandishing a warrant necessarily consents to the search. My acquiescence may not be to the entry of my home specifically, so much as to the legal regime within which

IMPLIED CONSENT AND SEXUAL ASSAULT

police officers can acquire the authority to enter someone's home.[19] In broadly the same way, a hockey player may object to being checked and yet accept that, within the rules of the game, players are entitled to deliver hits upon each other.

From the above, we can draw two further, closely related conclusions. First, the doctrine of implied consent operates in spite of the absence of what we normally mean by consent, insofar as we ordinarily think that one must subjectively deliberate on the specific touching in question and not merely on and within the normative regime within which it occurs. The Saskatchewan Court of Appeal, in *Cey*, attempted to articulate something very like this point: "Ordinarily consent, being a state of mind, is a wholly subjective matter to be determined accordingly, but when it comes to implied consent in the context of a team sport such as hockey, there cannot be as many different consents as there are players on the ice, and so the scope of implied consent, having to be uniform, must be determined by reference to objective criteria."[20] To say that there is no subjective state of mind in play, here, is again wrong: what makes the sporting context significant is the fact that the complainant is one of the players – that she voluntarily submitted to the normative regime governing her at the time.[21] There is a sense in which the inquiry is objective. The norms of a hockey game, after all, are not simply whatever the individual players think they are. But those norms matter because the players are, on some level, subjectively invested in them.[22]

In *Ewanchuk*, the defendant apparently took the latter half of the above passage from *Cey* to mean that, rather than look to the complainant's subjective state of mind, he could establish implied consent by considering whether there was an appearance of consent uninfluenced by fear. But that is not at all what the court meant by "objective criteria." Rather, it was alluding to the point I have made, that we must look to the rules and aims of the game in order to see what sorts of touching the participants would regard as legitimate. These are objective criteria insofar as no individual player sets the rules – at least, not while the game is being played.

To see what courses of action are legitimate in a social practice like hockey, we must examine not only the rules of play, but also the point of having such a practice at all. Thus, it would not make sense, in determining whether checks in hockey are legitimate, to ask simply whether they are against the rules – the rules might say nothing about checks for no other reason than that it has never occurred to anyone to deliver one. (Imagine someone bothering to articulate a rule prohibiting body checks in a game of chess or badminton.)[23] It is necessary, too, to consider the special kind of challenges hockey is meant to pose for its participants and what it means to excel in meeting them.[24] To the extent that hockey, unlike other games, challenges not only players' athleticism, speed, and dexterity, but also their physical fortitude,[25] we will be inclined to think it legitimate that opposing players test each other by using certain kinds of physical force.[26]

I have so far focused on implied consent in the context of contact sports because that is its least controversial milieu, and because it is most tempting in that context to say that something like consent in the traditional sense exists. But there is a risk of distortion here. The doctrine of implied consent does not apply only to competitive activities. Consider the context of parenting. No one would seriously argue that a parent is in competition with his or her child, or that insofar as uses of force are legitimate they are permissible because the object of parenting is to test a child's physical fortitude or endurance. That does not preclude us from applying the doctrine to the parenting context. It simply means that the doctrine extends to non-competitive social practices. Just as the legitimacy of physical contact within the hockey context can be assessed only by looking to the rules and aspirations of that practice, so the same can be said of physical contact in the parenting context. The rules and aspirations of those two practices, however, are obviously quite different. Whereas hockey challenges players to overcome (through speed, stamina, endurance) the physical obstacles opposing players throw up, parenting challenges those raising children to nurture them.[27] To the extent that physical force must be used to protect children from themselves, as by a father wrapping a scarf around his daughter's neck,[28] we can (and regularly do) say that the exercise of force is legitimate in light of the norms and aspirations that constitute the practice of parenting.

Admittedly, discussions of implied consent in the parenting context can be distorting in their own way. In my earlier discussion of hockey, I observed that players who receive checks typically experience them as legitimate, if unwelcome, which is helpful in understanding why one might see a kind of quasi-consent to those hits. It is senseless to ask, though, whether a child who is forcibly restrained while being bundled into snow pants perceives the restraint as legitimate or not, or whether the child opted into a set of norms – indeed, for much the same reason it would be senseless to ask whether the child consents. One of the challenges a parent must face as a parent is in teaching his or her child to appreciate authority and social obligations.[29] The practice of parenting would not survive if children themselves helped to define the norms that constitute it. It would, in fact, be strange to suggest that children are "participants" in the practice of parenting in the first place, rather than beneficiaries. The relationship between parents and children more closely resembles that of fiduciary-beneficiary than of two people involved in a shared cooperative activity.[30] This does not prevent us from appealing to the legitimacy of certain forms of physical contact. It merely underscores that, at least in the parenting context, we should not look to the perception of those who are parented when determining what courses of action are legitimate. In other contexts, where the participants in a non-competitive social practice are predominantly adults, we can more reliably look to participants' experiences in identifying the rules and aspirations that constitute a practice and, therefore, what forms of touching are and are not legitimate.

There is a further risk in drawing upon the sporting context. As Cheryl Hanna argues, it is far from clear that the considerations that make the doctrine of implied consent appropriate in sporting apply to the sexual sphere. In chapter 4, I discuss the problems with transplanting the doctrine, in an unmodified form, to the sexual assault law context. As I show, substantial changes are necessary. For now, and moving forward in this chapter, I want only to explain what the doctrine is, and why it is worth having at all.

Why Have Implied Consent?

To see why we might want to recognize an alternative form of sexual consent under some circumstances, it is worth considering why we commonly think that consent should have moral and legal significance at all. John Gardner argues that consent can matter in one of two ways. Sometimes, it transforms an otherwise wrongful act into a permissible one. When you take something of mine without my consent, for example, it is theft. When you engage in the same act with my consent, it typically becomes a morally and legally valid transfer – i.e., a gift or a sale. When I step upon your property without your consent, it is trespass. With your consent, it is not. In this sense, consent works a kind of "moral magic."[31] It may have significance, however, even when it does not transform the moral quality of the act. Sometimes, we may want to give people the power to licence others to wrong them. To take an example by Gardner and Shute, we may want to say that it is wrongfully objectifying to hire a prostitute, and yet at the same time say that the prostitute should be entitled to decide whether the client should be able to wrong her in that way.[32] As this language suggests, we can both condemn the client's conduct and say it should not be criminalized.

For my immediate purposes, I want to set aside the second understanding of the significance of consent. (I return to this point in chapter 4.) Even focusing on the narrower justification of consent, it is reasonably plain why we think that consent makes a difference to the wrongfulness of certain courses of action. To use my body or my property without regard to my feelings on the matter is to treat me as an object – a means to your ends, rather than an end in myself. To act as though my non-consent matters is to treat me as someone with ends of my own that deserve respect in their own right. But we can go further. We fail to treat someone as an autonomous being with ends that deserve respect when we deny that the presence of his or her consent makes a difference to how another is entitled to behave. Many of our most important projects and plans would be impossible if we were unable to deploy others' bodies and possessions for our own ends, and our own bodies for the ends of others. As Arthur Ripstein observes, consent "serves to make cooperative activities among responsible agents possible."[33] The doctrine of consent permits us to make use of each other[34] in ways that are mutually beneficial and that effectively expand our autonomy.

It should be equally clear, though, that many complex social practices would be impossible if discretely contemporaneous consent was required on an ongoing basis. Hockey again provides a good example. One of the things that makes hockey interesting to its participants is the way it challenges them to overcome physical obstacles at high speed. That challenge would be diminished – indeed would disappear altogether – if players had to alert each other in advance to oncoming hits by way of securing consent. We would make it impossible for players to demonstrate their on-ice awareness, their speed and agility, or their physical stamina and endurance. The very idea of what it means to achieve excellence in hockey would be narrowed or eviscerated. To put it another way, the game would cease to be fun.

It is precisely because hockey is defined and justified in part with reference to the speed with which it is to be played that we say that the doctrine of implied consent applies not only to checks that are permitted by the rules, but to at least some checks that occur outside the rules. The rules do not permit certain kinds of physical interference with opposing players – tripping and hooking, for instance, are prohibited, punishable with two- or five-minute penalties. But even these kinds of behaviour cannot be regarded as assaults. The speed with which the game is played makes it inevitable that players will occasionally stray outside the confines of permissible interference and that they will react to opposing players on an instinctual level. A requirement that players maintain at all times an awareness of just how far they can go to interfere with their opponents, on pain of being charged with assault, would effectively preclude them from losing themselves in the game. If the practice of hockey is to be sustained, we cannot regard every check, trip, and hook as an assault. We must recognize people's ability to give a kind of quasi-consent to these applications of physical force, without requiring discrete exercises of consent on each and every occasion they are inflicted, if we are to make it possible for people to be hockey players.

We can make much the same point about many other social practices. If we are to make it possible to use crowded buses and subways,[35] dance in nightclubs, or shop in busy malls during the Christmas season, we cannot say that an assault has taken place each time a person pushes through a crowd. Many conventional displays of friendship or appreciation – for example, handshakes and backslaps – would become less conventional and less warm if, but for the presence of contemporaneous consent, we had to treat them as assaults.[36]

The doctrine of implied consent, in other words, is liberty expanding – both for the person who engages in the touching and for the person who receives it. It allows people to engage in worthwhile practices that require a measure of social coordination. In this respect, it reflects the reasons we have for recognizing subjective consent as a defence: if we did not allow people to consent to certain kinds of intrusions, it would be impossible for us to work together in any number of socially and personally valuable projects.[37] The doctrine of implied consent pushes that reasoning further by recognizing that some practices would be unsustainable if discretely contemporaneous consent was needed on an ongoing basis.

A modified form of this line of reasoning applies just as well as to the parenting context. As the passage from *Palombi* indicates,[38] the defence of implied consent is recognized in the parent-child context because, quite simply, parenting would be impossible otherwise. The practice of parenting is important precisely because infants and children need someone to make decisions for them, to teach them habits they may not in their immaturity want to inculcate, to protect them from themselves (and others), and ultimately to help them become autonomous agents.[39] To require subjective, contemporaneous consent would be disadvantageous not only to the parents involved, but also to the children who would be forced to live with the consequences of decisions they are not yet ready to make.[40]

What makes parenting a valuable social practice, in other words, is inextricably tied to the undesirability or impossibility of requiring subjective, contemporaneous consent every time parents handle their children. We could put the burden on children to exercise consent, and force them to live with their mistakes, but doing so would undermine the benefits that children enjoy (if only when they have grown up) from being parented. At the same time, parenting would be a very different, and manifestly less significant, practice if we required subjective, contemporaneous consent from children.

The example of parenting poses special problems because the children who are subject to physical force may not subjectively recognize the legitimacy of its use. Furthermore, children obviously do not voluntarily submit to being parented. In many other contexts, though, those subject to applications of force in the course of a social practice will have become participants by virtue of a volitional act,[41] will accept the practice's rules and aims as their own, and will regard the kinds of touching as legitimate – even if they do not necessarily want it to occur at a specific time and place. Acceptance of the rules and standards of excellence that constitute a practice is not, I have argued, identical to an attitude of consent (as we traditionally understand it). Nonetheless, we should not ignore the fact that adult participants themselves regard the animating aims of the practice as sufficiently compelling that, in their view, acts of touching occurring within it are legitimate. This, again, follows from the idea that the law should respect the autonomy of persons, and allow them to pursue their own ends to the extent that doing so does not interfere with the autonomy of others.

The mere fact that a social practice exists is not reason enough for the law to permit it to continue. The criminal law should not only reflect existing social values, but also shape them to some extent. A practice like hockey might be defended on the basis of its value as a recreational activity, as a means of promoting physical health, as a way for people to engage socially, and perhaps (at least for Canadians) as a means of connecting with a common cultural heritage. The value of a practice like parenting is self-evident. But other social practices may also be regarded as sufficiently important to ground the doctrine of implied consent. Looking ahead, I want to suggest that people may engage in just such a practice, albeit one vastly more complex than hockey, when they are involved in certain intimate relationships.

Before we turn to that stage in the argument one further point is worth raising. Many social practices may be deeply problematic as they are constituted in the here and now. They may, for example, involve an unacceptable degree of violence or risk to public health. Such concerns have arisen in the context of both hockey[42] and American football,[43] as well as in the context of the parental use of corrective force.[44] These problems may be so ingrained in the practice as to create an all-or-nothing choice between preserving it, risks and all, or denying that the doctrine of implied consent can be used to sustain it – effectively condemning it. But often the difficulties can be cured by tweaking the constitutive rules of the practice – by confining how and when checks can be delivered, requiring helmets, barring parents from using weapons to chastise children, or prohibiting the use of corrective force on children of a certain age.[45] In those instances, the practice can be sustained, but with the law taking a leadership role in refining its aims and recalibrating the rules that set out how its defining challenges can be met.

Ewanchuk Redux

With the above in mind, I now return to the Supreme Court's brief discussion of implied consent in *Ewanchuk*.[46] To the extent the court suggests that the doctrine applies where there is an appearance of consent, it is simply wrongheaded – in the ordinary assault context, the question is not whether there is an appearance of consent. Rather, the question is whether the touching occurred within a social practice that, given its defining rules and aims, legitimates it. In denying that the doctrine is ever available as a defence to sexual assault, the court effectively refused to recognize that there is any social practice worthy of protection by the criminal law that could have rules and aims which legitimate sexual touching in the absence of subjective consent to the particular touching in issue – a debatable conclusion. As I suggested earlier, the spontaneous physical expression of affection, tenderness, and warmth strikes many individuals as not only acceptable for partners in long-term committed relationships, but as praiseworthy – as an example of what it means for people to achieve a kind of excellence as partners.

But let us leave that point aside for now. What should be transparent from even a cursory examination of the facts in *Ewanchuk* is that the defendant and complainant were engaged in no social practice capable of legitimating the sexual touching that took place. Recall, the defendant invited the complainant into his trailer, ostensibly as part of a job interview.[47] They met only a short time before the touching occurred. Under those circumstances of anonymity, in which the complainant and defendant were supposed to be determining whether they would have a professional relationship, and in which the complainant displayed little or no interest in any other kind of relationship, the defendant assumed that she consented to sexual touching. Whatever social rules we imagine might be built into a job interview, it is difficult to conceive of any sort of touching (beyond a handshake) as integral to the sort of challenge undertaken by the complainant.

Indeed, we are better able to see just why the defendant's behaviour was so objectionable when we assess his conduct in light of the norms of the practice in which the complainant was engaged. The defendant, on the interpretation of his actions most favourable to him,[48] presupposed that whatever norms might typically govern job interviews did not apply in this instance with this complainant. He effectively assumed that the complainant was not taking the interview seriously as an interview – i.e., as an exercise whereby she would demonstrate her professional skills for employment – and that she would be prepared to abandon it as soon as she received a signal of sexual interest. For the defendant in *Ewanchuk*, the complainant was interested in only one social practice: dating. Anything she did between dates was, in his apparent view, a pretence or killing time until the next expression of sexual interest from an eligible partner. The defendant, in short, was indulging in the objectifying fantasy that women are always sexually available to men – that they exist, first and foremost, to fulfill the sexual needs of men. L'Heureux-Dubé J. was right to point out that *Ewanchuk* was "not about consent," but about "myths and stereotypes."[49]

The conclusion reached in *Ewanchuk* was correct, then, but the court did not need to reject the doctrine of implied consent in order to reach it. (Indeed, as L'Heureux-Dubé J. observed, it is far from clear how implied consent could have arisen on the facts even if the doctrine was triggered by the mere appearance of consent, since the complainant said "no" three times.)[50] Given the facts of *Ewanchuk*, the Supreme Court's sweeping language is quite understandable. The case graphically illustrated why it is wrong as a matter of principle to permit defendants in sexual assault cases to argue honest but mistaken belief in consent on the basis of deeply misogynistic understandings of women's sexual availability. One would need to be utterly oblivious to the significance of gender equality in our legal culture to believe, as Ewanchuk seems to have, that he was entitled to treat all interactions with women as dates – an error which, as Vandervort and McInnes and and Boyle respectively argue, is one of law rather than fact.[51]

Fraser C.J.A., writing a dissenting opinion for the Alberta Court of Appeal in *Ewanchuk*, attempted to explain why the doctrine of implied consent could not apply to the sexual sphere. Her reasoning, though, is question begging. She remarked:

[The] approach to implied consent in sports cases has no application to cases of sexual assault. The differences between the two situations are self-evident and hardly need explanation. A woman does not consent to sexual activity in a vacuum. Nor is she in a state of constant consent and subject to sexual contact unless and until she says "No." She consents to sexual activity with a specific person in specific circumstances at a specific time ... What this means in the context of this case is that the complainant's right to sexual autonomy which the Code protects is her individual right and she did not relinquish it when she went to the job interview and stepped into Ewanchuk's trailer.[52]

In its submissions to the Supreme Court in *Ewanchuk*, Fraser C.J.A.'s analysis was picked up by the Women's Legal Education and Action Fund: "The development of the concept of 'implied consent' in the sports cases is inapplicable in sexual assault law. In sport, those who decide to play a *particular* game consent to some bodily contact necessarily incidental to the game. In those cases, the issue is the scope of the consent, not whether 'implied consent' exists. In their interactions with men, women are not engaged in an unrelenting and continuous sexual game in which consent to sexual touching is implied."[53] Fraser C.J.A. alludes to an important objection to the transplantation of implied consent from the sporting context to the sexual sphere. Whereas sporting contests have clear spatial and temporal limits, the sexual sphere is potentially boundless. In chapter 4, I discuss this objection, which is echoed in the work of Cheryl Hanna.[54] For now, though, I want to make an observation. Fraser C.J.A. acknowledges that the doctrine of implied consent is context sensitive: it applies only where the kind of touching in issue is legitimated by the rules and aims of the social practice in which it occurs. The question, then, is whether a similar sort of context-sensitive analysis is appropriate when the touching is sexual.[55] In subsequent chapters, I present the case that it is – or, at least, might be.

Conclusion

Though *Ewanchuk* was not a Charter case, it was a defining moment in achieving greater equality rights and sexual autonomy for women. In this chapter I have not taken issue with its importance, the correctness of the outcome it reaches, or with the broad values that run through the judgment as a whole. But the decision has come to seem almost untouchable, as if one cannot challenge aspects of the reasoning employed in *Ewanchuk* without tearing down the entire edifice.[56] The treatment of implied consent in *Ewanchuk* may have been unnecessary, was certainly too fleeting, and should be revisited.

CHAPTER 4

Autonomy and Section 273.1(1)

Introduction: Section 273.1(1) before *Ewanchuk*

In chapter 3, I argued that the Supreme Court of Canada may have been too quick to dismiss the idea of implied consent in the sexual assault context. Perhaps, though, I have missed the point. *Ewanchuk* was written in the shadow of section 273.1 of the Criminal Code. That provision sets out what it means to consent to sexual touching. If it requires sexual consent to be discretely contemporaneous, allowing no other form of consent under any circumstances, then of course the Supreme Court rejected the doctrine of implied consent. What else could it do?

There is little doubt that the court in *Ewanchuk* proceeded on the basis that section 273.1 did indeed rule out non-contemporaneous sexual consent. But it did not ground that conclusion in a careful reading of Bill C-49. Arguably, section 273.1 was not subjected to sustained interpretation until the court's 2014 ruling in *Hutchinson*.[1] (I say more about the critical interpretive passage in that case in chapter 7.) Rather, the *Ewanchuk* court implicitly took the view that the question of when sexual consent must be given had already been settled. Major J. simply observed: "The absence of consent ... is subjective and determined by reference to the complainant's subjective internal state of mind towards the touching, at the time it occurred."[2]

For that proposition, the majority cited three authorities: a passage from Don Stuart's treatise on the criminal law,[3] a decision by the Ontario Court of Appeal,[4] and L'Heureux-Dubé J.'s opinion in *R. v. Park*.[5] The relevant passage from Stuart is as follows:

As was made clear in *Donovan*, where consent is raised as a
defence the issue is the actual state of mind of the alleged victim.
This is a rare example of the state of mind of a third party determining the accused's culpability. The approach is subjective. The
proper question is: what did the alleged victim believe? On analogy
with an inquiry into subjective *mens rea* of an accused whether
the alleged victim's belief was reasonable is only relevant on the
evidentiary issue of whether the victim is to be believed.[6]

The passage is inelegant, but the thrust is clear enough: in determining
whether consent exists, we should look at the complainant's subjective
state of mind. The excerpt was subsequently cited by a majority of the
Ontario Court of Appeal in *R. v. Jensen*, in support of the proposition that
"[w]here consent is in issue the actual state of mind of the complainant is
determinative. The approach is subjective."[7] The court was wrestling with
a case in which the Crown argued the complainant was either too intoxicated to have capacity to consent, or did not consent despite having the
capacity to do so. Rosenberg J.A., writing for the majority, found there
was no evidence of lack of capacity. The complainant herself testified that
she was "alert" at the time of the alleged assault. To buttress its capacity
argument, the Crown referred to the defendant's statement to the police
that the complainant had been "too drunk" and that "he didn't finish."[8]
It was in this context that the majority observed that the test for consent, as an element of the actus reus, is subjective. Rosenberg J.A. stated:
"Even if the [defendant's] statement could be read as an assertion that
the complainant lacked the requisite capacity, it was at best an assertion
of a 'belief' in lack of capacity to consent. Consent, and capacity to consent, are mental states experienced only by the complainant and against
the [defendant's] equivocal statement stood the complainant's uncontra-
dicted evidence as to her own state of mind."[9] The majority, then, did not
refer to the above passage from Stuart in order to counter suggestions
that the complainant had consented – whether impliedly or otherwise.
Rosenberg J.A. used the passage to parry claims by the Crown that it
could prove a lack of capacity to consent without adducing supporting
evidence by either the complainant or a qualified expert. Furthermore,
the Supreme Court did not affirm the result in *Jensen* on the basis that

the majority had correctly articulated the law of consent. It affirmed, rather, because the Crown's appeal did not raise a question of law alone.[10]

Rosenberg J.A.'s ruling in *Jensen* also referred to L'Heureux-Dubé J.'s opinion in *Park* – the third source relied upon in *Ewanchuk*. The core question in *Park* was whether the trial judge should have instructed the jury to consider the defence of honest but mistaken belief in consent. The defendant at trial denied that the sexual touching in question occurred at all. In the alternative, he claimed he had an honest but mistaken belief in consent. The trial judge refused to leave the second defence with the jury, finding that it lacked an air of reality. The court held that the trial judge did not err. In reaching that conclusion, L'Heureux-Dubé J. observed that, to claim honest but mistaken belief in consent, it is not necessary for the defendant to concede the actus reus issue of consent. Since consent is subjective, she noted, the defendant can only ever provide evidence of his belief in it: "Given that consent is, itself, a mental state experienced only by the complainant, an accused's assertion that the complainant consented must mean that he in fact believed she was consenting ... The distinction between asserting a belief in consent and asserting consent, itself, is therefore both artificial and potentially misleading."[11] Again, the point that consent is subjective is relied on not to defeat defence claims that the complainant gave implied (or advance) consent, but to explain the circumstances under which it is inappropriate to deny the defence of honest but mistaken belief.

The fact that these cases are not about implied consent affects what we can read into them. In both *Jensen* and *Park* – as well as in the passages by Stuart – the claim is that in assessing whether there was consent, we should look to the subjective state of mind of the complainant. That point will be dispositive in many sexual assault cases. But none of the above passages propose that the relevant subjective state of mind can only be found at the time of the sexual touching, or that it must be directed at the instance of touching in issue. They certainly do not provide clear authority for the idea that what I will call the complainant's future-directed intentions are necessarily irrelevant to the consent inquiry.

Stuart, of course, does consider implied consent – indeed, immediately after his discussion of consent as subjectively determined.[12] In that discussion, he objects to the Saskatchewan Court of Appeal's suggestion in

Cey that implied consent must be determined on the basis of an objective standard. He remarks: "This resort to the objective standard appears far too pragmatic and unprincipled. In all other contexts, including sexual assault, courts have not invoked an objective standard simply because different alleged victims consent differently. Consent must involve what the alleged victim actually had in mind. It is confusing to make the inquiry into implied consent something different."[13] Implied consent, then, is acceptable for Stuart – but only because it must be determined subjectively. That, however, begs the question. As I discussed in chapter 3, it is not tenable to suppose that the participants in a sport like hockey consent in any meaningful sense to the contact they receive when opposing players check them into the boards. Stuart's confusion is revealed in the fact that he thinks himself bound to reject any possible role for implied consent in the medical context where a patient is unconscious. He states: "It is sometimes said that implied consent occurs where a doctor treats or operates in a situation of emergency or where the patient is incapable of giving consent. This fiction of retrospective consent is unsatisfactory. There might well be situations in which the patient, had he been aware, would not have consented. It is vastly preferable to consider the justification for the treatment in such cases as being the defence of necessity."[14] Stuart wants to say that, insofar as implied consent cannot be equated with subjective consent, we should not recognize the former. That is a coherent position so far as it goes. But he is not prepared to follow that line of reasoning to its obvious conclusion – that a doctor is legally required to allow an unconscious patient to die. Instead, he suggests that the doctor who operates should be acquitted under the defence of necessity. The trouble with this proposed solution is that necessity operates as an excuse, meaning that we are committed to condemning the doctor's behaviour even while we deny that she should be found criminally liable[15] – a peculiar outcome. Yet it is unclear how we can avoid it unless we allow that something like a doctrine of implied consent can step into the breach and explain why the doctor's behaviour is not just noncriminal but permissible.

We can cut this knot by supposing that implied consent, like consent generally, must be subjective, but that the subjective states of mind with which we should sometimes concern ourselves include the complainant's background norms and beliefs about how it is legitimate to be treated under the circumstances. When it is appropriate for the law to give effect to these norms is the subject of chapters 5 and 6. For now, it is enough to observe that *Park* and *Jensen* do not rule out the possibility of taking individual plans and norms into account when assessing subjective consent.

So we should be skeptical of any claim that the possibility of noncontemporaneous sexual consent was genuinely precluded by the doctrine of *stare decisis*.[16] What about the language of section 273.1(1)?

On Voluntariness

Section 273.1(1) defines consent as "the voluntary agreement of the complainant to engage in the sexual activity in question." One could argue that the use of the word "voluntary" places a premium on the complainant's subjective state of mind at precisely the time of the sexual touching in question. After all, if we say that a person has "consented" to an activity even though, at the time it occurs, she does not want to engage in it, her participation in it is, in a sense, involuntary: she has been required to submit to physical touching on the basis of earlier decisions from which she might now prefer to depart. By treating the individual as bound by her earlier decisions, one might say, we deny her a meaningful choice in the here and now. This seems to be Sheila McIntyre's view in her discussion of the 1992 rape shield reforms. Recalling the consultation process that gave rise to Bill C-49, she states:

> The consent clauses did not go as far as urged by the coalition, but five of our proposals did appear in the tabled legislation. Section 273.1(1) positively defined consent to require "voluntary" (but not "unequivocal") agreement to engage in the sexual activity in question, thereby underlining that consent requires active, hence verifiable (not projected) conduct freely chosen (not coerced or presumed) and focusing law enforcement on the specific interaction in dispute, not on past history or self-serving myths. [17]

McIntyre acknowledges that the word "unequivocal" was specifically not included in section 273.1(1). The minister of justice pointedly denied that the legislation would radically transform sexual norms by requiring men and women to engage in formal negotiations. This is symptomatic of the fact that although parliamentarians expressed unqualified support for the legislation, their support was driven by a narrow set of concerns. Nonetheless, McIntyre proceeds on the basis that the term "voluntary" signals that we should look for an "active" and "verifiable" state of mind on the part of the complainant at the time of the sexual activity.

In *Ewanchuk*, Major J. appealed to the value of sexual autonomy in explaining why consent under section 273.1(1) should be understood as "subjective and determined by reference to the complainant's subjective internal state of mind towards the touching, at the time it occurred."[18] He stated:

> Society is committed to protecting the personal integrity, both physical and psychological, of every individual. Having control over who touches one's body, and how, lies at the core of human dignity and autonomy. The inclusion of assault and sexual assault in the Code expresses society's determination to protect the security of the person from any non-consensual contact or threats of force. The common law has recognized for centuries that the individual's right to personal integrity is a fundamental principle ... It follows that any intentional but unwanted touching is criminal.[19]

The concurring judges in *R. v. Hutchinson* later relied on this passage.[20] L'Heureux-Dubé J. in *Park* likewise emphasized the connection between sexual autonomy – again couched in the language of control – and the offence of sexual assault: "[T]he primary concern animating and underlying the present offence of sexual assault is the belief that women have an inherent right to exercise full control over their own bodies, and to engage only in sexual activity that they wish to engage in. If this is the case, then our approach to consent must evolve accordingly, for it may be out of phase with that conceptualization of the law."[21] This passage was cited with approval, again by L'Heureux-Dubé J., in *Ewanchuk*.[22] Indeed, few take serious issue with the idea that sexual integrity and autonomy underpins contemporary sexual assault law.[23] The question is whether we should or must understand sexual autonomy to mean only the power to decide in the here and now whether to permit others to engage in sexual touching. In fact, sexual autonomy can mean something more.

Voluntariness and Planning Agency

Above, I observed that there is a sense in which, when we bind others to their earlier decisions, we interfere with their autonomy. There is a sense in which they are made to participate in a course of action involuntarily. But that is not the only way to think about autonomy or voluntariness. In some cases, a person bound by her earlier choices can seem more autonomous.

Consider the person who decides that she wants to be a concert pianist, or a chess grandmaster, or a karate black belt. To realize any of these goals, she will need to practice every day. She knows, however, that on any given day she will be sorely tempted to neglect her training in favour of watching television or playing video games. With that in mind, she arranges to have someone supervise her at a set time each day, and to make her pay an exorbitant fine each time she misses her practice. When the time comes to practice, she predictably would rather not. The threat of the fine, though, effectively compels her to do it.[24]

Has she been deprived of her autonomy? Yes, but only if we look at the activity as nothing more than an isolated event. If we look at it as part of a broader plan that the individual has devised for herself, matters are not so clear. Faced with the prospect of yielding to temptation, and depriving herself of a life path she desires, she has chosen instead to deprive herself of certain options in the future. That strikes (most of) us as a perfectly intelligible and rational thing to do. If it is very important for her to realize her goal of becoming a concert pianist, we may think her approach quite sensible. It is intelligible as an example of what Michael Bratman calls "planning agency."[25]

A plan is a future-directed intention.[26] Though lawyers tend to focus on present intentions (i.e., intentions to do whatever it is one is already doing), future-directed intentions are what define us as human beings. Many of the things we want to do are complex: they require not a single discrete step, but a series of steps. Even simple plans have an element of complexity to them. If I want a casserole for dinner tonight, I must first buy the ingredients. That means I need to go to the supermarket. Getting to the supermarket may require me to fill the tank of my car, which may in turn require me to leave my office early. My simple goal requires me to coordinate my present and future activities. If we were to try to understand these steps without appealing to my plan to eat a casserole tonight, we would miss something important: that they are bound together. It does not just happen to be the case that I (a) left work early; (b) travelled to the gas station and filled the tank; (c) went to the supermarket; (d) bought groceries; and (e) went home, where I prepared a casserole. I behaved in that way because my plan gave me reasons for doing so.[27] To strip out the normative underpinnings of my course of action, treating each step as discrete and atomistic, is to short-change the act of agency running through it.

That, of course, is an example of a simple plan. Other plans – the ones around which we construct our individual identities, and which set out the terms of success or failure in our lives – are so core to who we are that we can see their pull in almost everything we do.[28] To become (and be) a lawyer, a skilled amateur tennis player, a physically fit or financially responsible or well-travelled person, a parent, someone who lives in Saskatoon, a good citizen, a connoisseur of fine wines or whiskeys, or anything else requires the inculcation of habits of mind and action. They require extensive coordination over long periods of time. Many of the actions we perform daily make sense only against the backdrop of one or more long-term plans which, to be executed, require sub-plans, sub-sub-plans, and so on.[29]

Plans often require not just the coordination of our own "present and future activities,"[30] but the coordination of our activities with those of others.[31] It is here that ideas of consent are most germane – as Ripstein observes, we care about consent in large part because it allows people to engage in cooperative activities with each other.[32] Our agency and autonomy would be badly – fatally – undermined if we could not do so. As I discussed in chapter 3, it is this insight about why consent matters that gives rise to the suspicion that something like implied consent also deserves recognition.

The person who decides to play a game of hockey governed by a particular set of rules likewise forms a plan of sorts. She agrees that, for the duration of the game – at least for so long as she participates in it – she may be compelled to receive certain forms of physical contact notwithstanding the fact that, at the time of the contact, she would choose differently. She commits herself because she wants to participate in a game in which she faces a particular kind of challenge, and it would be impossible

IMPLIED CONSENT AND SEXUAL ASSAULT

to embark upon that challenge if she was able to opt out of body checks whenever she chose. By binding her future self, a hockey player is able to exercise a deeper form of agency. It is this kind of agency that political liberals aim to protect.

The question is whether something like this kind of reasoning could apply when the touching is sexual. Could an individual effectively bind her future self by reaching an understanding with her intimate partner that certain forms of sexual touching are presumptively legitimate – even without providing an opportunity to deliberate on its acceptability at the time? There is no doubt that special concerns arise.

First, note that a hockey game is an activity with a defined start and finish. In agreeing to play hockey according to the standard rules, a player binds her future self, but only for the duration of the game – not while she is unprotected on the street. The fact that hockey games are local to a time and place means that, even in the absence of further negotiation before or during the game, the players have assurance that their physical integrity will not indefinitely be at risk. Once the game is over, it is understood that the ordinary rules of social life immediately apply again – rules in which any application of force is suspect. There is, we might say, a *default* rule. The fact that I have agreed to play hockey with you does not now mean that, if I want to be free from violence in the future, I must negotiate with you. Rather, once the game is over, and we have defaulted to the ordinary rules of civilized life, you must renegotiate with me for the right to apply any amount of physical force. The locality of the game gives me a meaningful *voice* in determining how secure I will be in the future.

Intimate relationships, however, are not necessarily local in that way. An intimate partnership need not have any geographical or temporal limits. (Though it could.) An agreement by an individual to allow her partner to touch her in certain ways potentially flips the default rule ("no touching in the absence of express, contemporaneous consent") for all time and in all places: suddenly, if she wants to restrict her partner's sexual access in some way, she must negotiate with him. Depending on the conditions under which she must negotiate, this may be more or less problematic – but it does affect the voice she has.

Second, the rules in a game of hockey tend to be well defined. Participants have a clear sense of the boundaries of permissible conduct, and are therefore able to push against the limits of acceptable touching. Insofar as the speed of the game makes it difficult to conform precisely to the rules, players nonetheless have a relatively good idea of what kinds of rule violations they can expect. But the rules surrounding sexual touching are often fuzzier, requiring the person who gives implied consent either to negotiate more frequently or to submit to unwanted physical contact.

Third, the fact that hockey games are refereed and played in public, whereas intimate relationships are typically not, makes an important difference. The existence of a third-party adjudicator can diminish the extent to which parties are dominated by illiberal values and norms. Again, this is inextricably tied to the voice we have in shaping the norms that govern our lives. As Cheryl Hanna notes, it matters that sexual practices tend to be treated as relatively private.[33] There is no referee or audience to ensure that touching occurs in accordance with the rules – nothing to sanction or restrain violence when it erupts.

Finally, the fact that objectifying gender norms are pervasive in our culture should trigger special concerns. Given that women are expected to be sexually passive and men to be sexually aggressive, we can anticipate that there will be pressure on women to "agree" to various forms of sexual touching. At least some of these, arguably, are physically harmful or psychologically damaging. The dominant social norms in play may discourage women from complaining about acts of sexual violence – and indeed feed into their sense that certain kinds of touching are not acts of violence at all, but acts of love.

So we have good reasons not to treat sexual touching exactly the same as non-sexual touching. That conclusion fits with the very existence of section 273.1(1). The section, after all, applies only to the sexual assault offences in the Criminal Code; it does not apply to the ordinary assault provisions. It is, then, plainly intended to signal that consent should mean something different in the sexual sphere. We have already seen, in the discussion of the 1983 reforms, why this is the case: rape and sexual assault are gendered offences, in that they are made possible by a set of objectifying and pervasive gender norms.[34] Indeed, we might say that rape and sexual assault are the logical extension of those norms – a point expressed by the term "rape culture." In creating a new offence of sexual assault in the first place, Parliament sought to address this problem of wrongful sexual objectification or instrumentalization.

The existence of rape culture makes it inappropriate simply to transplant the doctrine of implied consent into the sexual assault context. The doctrine would require serious modification. It is not enough to say that an individual had (in Bratman's terms) a plan to live her life according to these rules (or, looking ahead, that the individual engaged in an exercise of second-order autonomy).[35] We need to examine the context in which the norms governing an intimate relationship are formed and refined over time, and the extent to which those norms require an individual to sustain harms or disadvantages.

But if the inquiry is made more sophisticated, so it accounts for those factors, then it is not clear why we should not respect actors' planning agency. Indeed, some of the factors that should make us wary of introducing implied consent into the sexual assault context should also make us hesitate to not do so. In particular, the fact that intimate relationships cannot necessarily be compartmentalized in the way a hockey game can be – that it strikes at people's identities and lives in an especially profound way – suggests it is important that people be permitted to decide for themselves what norms should govern them in that context.[36] Some support for that view can be found in the work of Jennifer Nedelsky.

Nedelsky on Sexual Autonomy

In her important book, *Law's Relations*, Nedelsky discusses the "reasonable steps" requirement in section 273.2(b) as a positive move away from the criminal law's unrelenting focus on the defendant's motives and beliefs.[37] She stresses the fact that section 273.2(b) imposes at least something approaching an "objective" test of reasonableness.[38] Her relational theory provides the resources for explaining why the doctrine of implied consent is both problematic from the point of view of sexual integrity, and arguably necessary to give effect to women's sexual autonomy.

Nedelsky's relational theory emphasizes the extent to which autonomy is possible only in an atmosphere of "assurance."[39] It is not just that the law should more effectively protect "negative liberty"[40] – it should, as far as possible, create the conditions under which people can confidently use their autonomy to pursue their own aims and life plans. Gender norms of male dominance and female passivity undermine women's autonomy by forcing them to either retreat from the social world – that is, to "choose" not to use their sexual autonomy – or else take the chance that they will become objects of sexual violence.[41]

Following MacKinnon, Nedelsky observes that gender norms eroticizing female passivity and male domination can and should be stripped away so that women have greater assurance that they will not be subject to unwelcome sexual touching by men.[42] A progressive law of rape and sexual assault, Nedelsky argues, must impose on men an obligation to "make a respectful effort to determine whether and what kind of touch (or contact) is desired." She continues: "In addition, [men] need to maintain a continued alertness to this desire rather than treat the relation as an on/off one in which once permission (which actually implies acquiescence rather than desire) is acquired no further attention to desire is necessary. Of course, calling for respectful attention to desire is addressing the vastly more common form of sexual assault, that among people who know each other, rather than stranger rape."[43] The reasonable steps requirement in section 273.2 of the Criminal Code, in Nedelsky's view, serves just this function.[44] It assures women that they can be sexually touched only after they confirm that they desire or consent to the touching. Stated this baldly, Nedelsky's reasoning would seem to rule out something like a doctrine of implied consent in the sexual assault context. It appears to suggest that one's understanding of reasonableness cannot and should not be informed by the norms of a social practice insofar as they permit sexual touching in the absence of active, subjective consent. But that conclusion would be too hasty. If we consider some of the nuances in Nedelsky's theory, particularly in light of my qualifications in chapter 3 as to what implied consent could mean in the sexual context, the matter ceases to look so straightforward.

A prominent theme running through Nedelsky's work is the idea that autonomy does not boil down to control. The mere fact that we lack control over some aspect of our lives, or lack as much control as we would like, does not mean that we cease to be autonomous beings. Autonomy is a spectrum, not an all-or-nothing proposition. This point is often raised by way of arguing that even those who have been figuratively or literally beaten down by social and legal norms that place human beings in a position of subservience nonetheless deserve our respect as autonomous beings.[45] It blocks the tendency we sometimes have of thinking that if a person has been subject to degrading treatment, he or she is degraded and so unworthy of respect. But Nedelsky also wants us to appreciate that, by reconfiguring social and legal norms so that some need to give up their power over others, or by predicating autonomy on forces beyond our direct control in the first place, we are not thereby taking autonomy away from anyone or giving up on the idea of autonomy altogether. We are simply reconceiving what it means to be autonomous.

Recent work by Deborah Tuerkheimer is instructive.[46] Though she uses the language of agency rather than relational autonomy, she also challenges the classical liberal model of autonomy which puts a premium on the individual's self-containment – on the idea that our "tastes, opinions, ideals, goals, values and preferences are all authentically [our own]."[47] Tuerkheimer places considerably greater emphasis on the extent to which we are shaped by social norms that reflect entrenched power relations.[48] The fact that our desires are socially constructed – that they are, in a sense, porous – does not diminish our agency as sexual beings, nor deny it.[49] Our subjective experience of the world is important. This matters, Tuerkheimer says, because from a subjective point of view, sexuality – though it is "constructed in a world of rampant gendered violence" – is still experienced as both pleasurable and a way to assert power.[50]

From the point of view of sexual agency, there is nothing special about consent being given under less-than-perfect conditions. That is the typical state of affairs. Robin West remarks:

> Heterosexual women and girls, married or not, consent to a good
> bit of unwanted sex with men that they patently don't desire,
> from hook-ups to dates to boyfriends to cohabitators, to avoid
> a hassle or a bad mood the endurance of which wouldn't be
> worth the effort, to ensure their own or their children's financial
> security, to lessen the risk of future physical attacks, to garner
> their peers' approval, to win the approval of a high-status man
> or boy, to earn a paycheck or a promotion or an undeserved A
> on a college paper, to feed a drug habit, to survive, or to smooth
> troubled domestic waters. Women and girls do so from motives of

self-aggrandizement, from an instinct for survival, out of concern for their children, from simple altruism, from friendship or love, or because they have been taught to do so. But whatever the reason, some women and girls have a good bit of sex a good bit of the time that they patently do not desire.[51]

The passage is compelling because it makes clear that, although some of the reasons for engaging in sexual activity can be boiled down to co-ercion, others may be attributed to a sense of obligation – whether to a partner or to someone else. Understanding this point allows us to strip away some of the romanticism that tends to inform thinking about sex. Individuals may consent to sexual acts, like other acts, for a range of rea-sons – many of which are consistent with personal agency. "[C]onsent and wanting," Tuerkheimer observes, "can diverge."[52] "When they do," she continues, "women engage in sex that is neither rape nor apparent cause for celebration."[53] She observes: "[Consent] cannot be discounted solely by virtue of its imperfection. Otherwise, in a world where sexual agency is constrained in all sorts of ways, there could be no valid consent."[54]

Nedelsky, then, is not the only thinker to argue that it is a mistake to fetishize control, as if we only deserve respect as persons if we are in-sulated from others, utterly self-sufficient, and unaffected by the social forces swirling around us. Nussbaum also makes this point in *Upheav-als of Thought*.[55] She rejects the Stoic view that we should emotionally distance ourselves from the things important to us, and argues that we should instead accept that our well-being depends to an important degree on fortune, both good and bad. Like Nedelsky,[56] Nussbaum emphasizes the embodied nature of persons; the fact that we are subject to emotions, physical urges, and desires that are not in conflict with our rationality, but expressions of it. They reflect things that matter to us as individuals, and so deserve respect, even – perhaps especially – when they make it impossible for us to exercise complete control over ourselves.[57] Though Nedelsky takes issue with Nussbaum in certain respects, on this broad point they are not obviously at cross-purposes.

Nedelsky states, "[t]he essence of rape is coercive, unwanted inter-course or attempted intercourse."[58] She makes this point in the course of arguing that rape is not wrongful simply because it involves the crossing of physical boundaries or the use of force, but because it is unwanted.

She does not suggest that the law of sexual assault precludes men and women from playing roles that at least outwardly might appear to conform with traditional gender norms. She accepts that women can consent to sexual acts that involve physical violence[59] or a "show of force."[60] Indeed, Nedelsky points out that the criminal law would interfere with the autonomy of women if it imposed blanket prohibitions on certain kinds of sexual touching, or if it took certain contextual factors as conclusive evidence that consent was coerced:

> Since what is required to end violence against women is, ultimately, a transformation of the relations between men and women, we need language that directs our attention to these relations and laws that shift them. Few of the basic protections adult women need can be captured adequately by simple prohibitions. Most of the words and touching that can be threatening, frightening, demeaning, and assaultive in one context can be welcome in another. That is the inherent problem in rape as well as sexual harassment. Simple prohibitions are a problem because coercion is often not simple.[61]

Nedelsky rejects the idea that men are entitled to presume that coercion is a turn-on for women.[62] But she does not want to resort to the criminal law to impose limits on what women can consensually do. "Assurance," as Nedelsky notes on several occasions, does not just refer to the assurance that physical boundaries will not be crossed.[63] It refers to the assurance that women will be able to use their autonomy – sexual and otherwise – in ways they find rewarding and satisfying. Even if we believe that it would be better if men and women chose not to adopt norms that arguably reinforce pernicious gender stereotypes, it is important that they *choose* not to adopt those norms. Why? Because individuals' ability to apply their own practical reason to the question of how they ought to live is a core dimension of human well-being.[64] We can (and should) use the law to encourage men and women to rethink their traditional assumptions about gender roles and norms – to think critically about what they find erotically pleasing.[65] It is another matter altogether to say that we can or should use the criminal law to bludgeon couples into behaving (or pretending to behave) like enlightened people. Joseph Raz – whose project is similar in some ways to that of Nedelsky[66] – argues that the law should promote "morally valuable activities" and "eliminate repugnant ones." Nonetheless, he resists the conclusion that the criminal law should necessarily be used to achieve these purposes.[67] He observes that the criminal law "expresses a relation of domination and an attitude of disrespect for the coerced individual."[68] Raz has in mind the individual whose conduct is specifically targeted by the offence in question – in this instance, the man who is told that he "takes his chances" if he engages in sexual touching without express consent, whether or not he and his partner have adopted norms that allow for such conduct – but there is no less domination over the partner whose own ideas of how her relationship should proceed are effectively trampled upon.

For Nedelsky, too, the domination of women by the law is just as problematic as their domination by private actors.[69] It is for this reason that, as the above passage suggests, she is suspicious of "simple prohibitions."[70] For the law to tell women that they categorically cannot be touched or spoken to in certain ways is not to advance their autonomy, or to give them assurances, but to limit their options. Better to impose a duty on men to take reasonable steps in determining whether consent and desire are present, she argues, than to impose bright-line rules on which kinds of touching or words can be used, and which cannot.[71] But if, in determining whether reasonable steps have been taken, we cannot consider the background norms settled upon by the parties to the relationship, we come perilously close to the very kind of simple prohibition Nedelsky rejects, for we are then using the criminal law to tell women how they can and cannot choose to run their own lives.

Autonomy and the Role of Consent

In this chapter, I have tried to show that section 273.1(1), insofar as its central aim was to advance women's sexual autonomy in a culture of sexual objectification, need not rule out the possibility of implied consent. A concern for women's autonomy, as the work of Bratman, Tuerkheimer, and Nedelsky shows, can be understood as a concern for women's planning agency. We must be alert to the special problems that arise when we attempt to transplant the doctrine of implied consent from the sporting realm to the sexual sphere. But that alone does not mean we should ignore implied consent altogether. To do so is to give a kind of autonomy – one that is deeply important to many people – short shrift.

In interpreting section 273.1(1), we should keep in mind that the criminal law does not only permit people to consent to activities of which it approves. Consent, as I noted in chapter 3, does two things. Sometimes, it makes otherwise wrongful conduct morally permissible – it works a kind of "moral magic."[72] At other times, it merely licenses others to engage in wrongful conduct.[73] In determining how consent is operating, and what its limits should be, it is important to reflect on what role it is playing at a given time. If you and I both treat me as nothing more than an instrument for your ends, we are surely not engaging in a morally justifiable line of conduct. We have made the same moral mistake in regarding me as something less than an end in myself – but it is no less a mistake. Does that automatically mean the law should prevent me from giving legally effective consent to the course of action? Not at all. It may be that, for the law to treat me as an autonomous moral agent, it must give me a fair bit of leeway to exercise my autonomy in experimental and arguably problematic ways.[74] It should defer to at least some of my judgments about how it is appropriate for you to interact with me. At the same time, it is not at all clear that the law must give me limitless scope to injure and degrade myself.

As a general proposition, the law should be readier to allow the licensing of wrongs when consent is discretely contemporaneous rather than implied. Contemporaneous, *Ewanchuk*-style consent – precisely because it is given to a discrete, reasonably well-defined instance of touching, taking place in a context relatively apparent to the consenting party – offers some assurance that she appreciated the risks and dangers associated with it. Even if, on close examination, it turns out that the course of action so compromised her well-being that she should not have exercised her autonomy in this way, there is a compelling reason for the law to defer to her judgment on the matter. Implied consent, by contrast, is open-ended and often somewhat hazy in its implications. We have a tendency to underestimate risks and harms that lie in the future – though also to overestimate them.[75] Perhaps more to the point, we may be concerned that individuals' willingness to abandon their fate to others itself suggests the undue influence of social norms and pressures, inadequate attention to their own well-being, or both.

All other things being equal, then, the law should have a heightened degree of suspicion when autonomy is asserted through implied consent rather than contemporaneous consent. And, given the pervasiveness of gender norms, it should be all the more skeptical of implied consent in the sexual sphere. Earlier in this chapter, I observed that the sexual context is quite different from the sporting context, in which claims of implied consent have been most confidently asserted. They are different in part because contact sports feature safeguards that are lacking in the sexual context – e.g., they take place in public and referees are present. But it is also a function of the norms that govern gender relations in our culture, and that pose special dangers. As I discussed in chapter 2, concerns about a culture of sexual objectification animated the 1983 rape law reforms that culminated in the Supreme Court's ruling in *Ewanchuk*.

But it is one thing to adopt a healthy skepticism with respect to implied consent in the sexual sphere, and quite another to deny it altogether. There are two reasons for this. The first is tied to the role of consent as a means of making it possible for people to cooperatively engage in morally permissible acts. If we can engage in sexual touching, in the absence of contemporaneous consent, without engaging in wrongful objectification, then that should be reflected in the law of consent. The second reason is tied to the role of consent as a means of licensing wrongs. Even if a course of action is wrongful – say, because it does amount to wrongful objectification – it may still be appropriate for the law to defer to the consenting party's decision on the matter in the name of respecting her as an autonomous individual. It would be strange for the law to take sexual autonomy less seriously than other kinds of autonomy. After all, as I discussed in chapter 2, it was a concern for women's sexual autonomy that largely drove the reforms to rape and sexual assault law in the first place.

The next two chapters build on these points. In chapter 5, I draw upon the work of Nussbaum and her analysis of sexual objectification. She implicitly takes the view that sexual touching, under certain narrow circumstances, can be morally permissible even in the absence of contemporaneous consent. In chapter 6, I ask a somewhat different question: under what circumstances is it appropriate for the criminal law to defer to normative arrangements that regard sexual touching as legitimate even in the absence of contemporaneous consent? To a degree, in chapter 6 I set aside the question of permissibility and instead consider the factors that warrant consideration as we decide whether and when certain kinds of wrongs can be licensed.

Put in those terms, it might seem like there is a neat line to be drawn between chapters 5 and 6. Not so. One reason to emphasize consent's dual-purpose nature, after all, is to avoid having to reach hard-and-fast conclusions about the moral permissibility of a course of action by way of deciding whether the law should allow individuals to consent to it. With that in mind, it matters if there is even a plausible case that certain forms of sexual touching are morally acceptable even in the absence of con-temporaneous consent. At the very least, the fact that such a case can be made suggests that those who form normative arrangements, in which contemporaneous consent is not required, are not necessarily acting ir-rationally or unreflectively, and that the claim that they are exercising their autonomy should not be dismissed out of hand. Furthermore, the various forms of mutuality that inform Nussbaum's analysis, and that ostensibly make certain instances of sexual touching non-instrumental-izing, also have implications for the proper scope of legal deference. As I show, the fact that two people share a similar socio-economic back-ground, or share a commitment to one another, makes a difference when we consider questions of voice and influence in chapter 6. Finally, and more generally, I want to use chapter 5 to make the obvious yet crucial point that, as Nussbaum puts it, "context matters." This is no less true when we consider the scope of legal deference.

CHAPTER 5

Mutuality and Sexual Instrumentalization

Introduction

In chapter 2, I suggested that the wrong of sexual assault is, first and foremost, the wrong of sexual objectification. In chapter 5, I use the work of Martha Nussbaum to explore the circumstances under which sexually objectifying treatment is morally wrongful such that it is arguably eligible for criminalization. As I show, the central question is whether a particular instance of objectifying treatment is instrumentalizing – that is, whether it involves the mere use of another as a sexual object. In this chapter, I discuss how the presence or absence of mutuality makes a critical difference to whether sexual touching is instrumentalizing in Nussbaum's sense of the word.

Mutuality is significant in three broad ways. First, the fact that two parties share a fascination with each other suggests that they are not merely using each other's bodies as instruments or to subvert one another's autonomy, but rather are responding to each other as embodied persons. Second, the fact that the parties share a broad socio-economic status gives us some reason to believe the relationship is something other than exploitive. Finally, whether or not the parties share a life plan, a history, and a future with each other – whether, we might say, they are loyal to one another – makes an important difference when morally assessing sexual touching. Indeed, the presence of loyalty can make such a moral difference that Nussbaum suggests it can make sexual touching non-instrumentalizing even in the absence of contemporaneous consent.

Before going further, it is worth drawing attention to the approach I have undertaken in interpreting Nussbaum's work on objectification. Her analysis is largely undertaken through a close reading of literary passages and texts, and not through a study of sexual desire and touching in the abstract. This makes perfect sense in light of her contention that context is all-important. It does, however, make it rather difficult to extrapolate a list of general propositions about how and when sexual touching is instrumentalizing. To fill out her analysis of how and why sexual desire is not generally instrumentalizing, I draw heavily on the work of Roger Scruton, the conservative philosopher. Some readers may find that curious. For anyone who is interested, I explain this approach in the appendix.

Nussbaum on Objectification

Nussbaum observes that one may objectify another in one of several ways.[1] First, one may treat a person as an instrument, i.e., as "a tool of his or her purposes." Second, one may treat her "as lacking in autonomy and self-determination." Third, one may treat her as inert, in the sense that she "lack[s] ... agency, and perhaps also ... activity." Fourth, one may treat her as fungible, that is, as interchangeable with other people or even with non-persons. Fifth, one may treat her as violable, in the sense that she lacks "boundary-integrity," and may be "br[oken] up, smash[ed], br[oken] into." Sixth, one may treat her as "something that is owned by another [or] can be bought or sold." Last, one may deny her subjectivity by treating her "as something whose experience and feelings (if any) need not be taken into account."[2]

These different forms of objectification are by no means mutually exclusive. Objectifying a person in one sense frequently entails objectifying her in one or more other senses – sometimes in every sense. To deny that a person has a subjective life often implies that she cannot exercise autonomy; that she has no distinct personality of her own, and is interchangeable with others; and that she has an inert quality. We may treat a person as non-autonomous in the course of using her as an instrument for our own ends. In treating her as violable, we frequently act as though she is an inert object, and often as someone whose subjective feelings, because they can be manipulated, need not be respected.

At the same time, Nussbaum shows that one form of objectification need not be accompanied by others. I may treat a child as non-autonomous without thinking her fungible, and certainly without thinking of her as an instrument to be used for my own purposes.[3] I may treat a person as fungible without regarding her as non-autonomous – at least, as Nussbaum suggests, "in the limited sense of [being] fungible with other autonomous agents."[4] A slave may be regarded by her "owner" as neither inert nor fungible.[5]

More to the point, not all forms of objectification are invariably objectionable on moral grounds. We do not engage in moral wrongdoing merely because we treat children as lacking autonomy. In the employment context, we regularly treat individuals engaged in non-specialized tasks (like assembly line or fast-food workers) as interchangeable with others, and all but ignore their subjective experience of their work environments. To be sure, it is possible to criticize this practice on moral grounds – and many have[6] – but the fact that it is so well established might lead us to wonder how seriously such criticisms are taken. A person may be committed to certain points of view, be content with the life those values and beliefs make possible, and find challenges to them discomfiting, but we do not necessarily think it morally objectionable to pose such challenges. This is the case even though, in doing so, we ignore her preference not to engage in public debate, and to some extent treat her mental landscape as something we are entitled to "invade" with ideas and arguments.

Whether or not a given kind of objectification is morally problematic largely depends on context.[7] When I tell my seven-year-old child to do something, I treat her as non-autonomous whether or not my instruction is for her own good. Morally speaking, though, it makes an important difference whether I am telling her to wash behind her ears, do her homework, or donate blood to her ill sibling. Whenever I set out to change another's mind, I in a sense treat the boundaries that separate us as porous and violable. It makes a moral difference, though, whether I do so through reasoned debate, coercion, or brainwashing; whether she is a willing participant in the debate or someone I effectively bludgeon with argument; and whether my reasons for wanting to change her mind are disinterested or self-interested. Whether we find objectification in the employment context problematic will in large part depend on how much mobility we think workers have, and whether they are treated as equal contracting parties or as mere property.

Among the various forms of objectification, Nussbaum regards instrumentalization – which she understands narrowly as the *mere* use of another person[8] – as the most inherently troubling.[9] At the bottom of what makes the other forms of objectification morally problematic, when and if they are, is the intuition that they involve the treatment of another as a mere instrument for one's own use. The treatment of a person (such as a child) as non-autonomous is troubling to the extent it involves treating her as a means to another's ends, but less so insofar as it comes with treating her as an end in herself. If we think the treatment of workers as fungible is problematic, it is because and to the extent that such treatment involves the suppression of creativity and individual personalities, which suggests that the lives of workers are dominated not by their own ends, but by those of their employer. (This concern abates insofar as we envision workers as freely contracting parties whose working life is informed by their own priorities and commitments.)

For our purposes, it is significant that Nussbaum does not regard the kinds of objectification that occur in the sexual context as necessarily instrumentalizing nor, therefore, as morally problematic. Indeed, she is prepared to conclude that objectification "might be a wonderful part of sexual life."[10]

Isn't Sexual Desire Inherently Instrumentalizing?

Not infrequently, sexual pleasure and sexual desire are treated as if they were purely physical (or "animal")[11] in nature; that is, as if sexual desire was simply the desire for a warm body that will bring the desirer to orgasm, and sexual pleasure was reducible to a collection of intense physical sensations. The thinker most associated with this view is Kant. He argues that sexual desire floods the individual with sensations, rendering him or her unable to spare any thought for the dignity or humanity of the other.[12] Until that desire is sated, he claims, the other will be regarded as nothing more than "a set of bodily parts that are useful tools for one's pleasure."[13]

If Kant's understanding of sexual pleasure and desire were accurate, it would be inherently objectifying in many of the senses Nussbaum discusses. To the extent that sexual desire entails treating a human being as a set of body parts, it means treating her as an inert thing and denies that she has any subjective life worth considering. Insofar as the body parts matter, rather than the person to which they are incidentally attached, it suggests that human beings are interchangeable and fungible – not just with other human beings, but with rubber dolls, animals, sex toys, and anything else capable of penetrating or being penetrated. There is, moreover, a hint of the attitude that one may violate the other at will. Finally, there is an instrumentalizing attitude built into this conception of sexual desire – an attitude that one human being can use the body of another simply for the sake of a pleasurable sensation culminating in orgasm.

Plainly, some forms of sexual desire are objectifying in the problematic sense Kant describes. To suggest, though, that sexual pleasure and desire are inherently objectifying in that way is flatly wrong. It suggests that sexual pleasure is nothing more than a "pleasure of sensation experienced in the sexual parts" – a sensation that might be had as a result of a willing partner's cooperation, but might just as (or more) easily be had with an unwilling partner, one's own hand, or a sex toy alone.[14] This impoverished conception of sexual pleasure neglects the fact that, even when we masturbate, we tend to picture ourselves with other human beings, imagining their faces, their exclamations, and their reactions to our touch.[15] This imagining is not simply a quirk that people happen to share. Much of sexual pleasure is, as Scruton would say, "intentional" – it is the pleasure we have at pursuing a meaningful activity with someone who will recognize its significance.[16] When we are aroused by the thought of being sexually involved with another, we do not typically imagine a "partner" with no awareness of our touch, or with no appreciation of the connection between the physical sensations we create and the fact that our touch creates them. We imagine a partner attuned not only to physical sensations, but also to the intentional content of the acts that produce them; a partner who recognizes our intentions toward her, and who has intentions toward us.

It is because sexual pleasure cannot be reduced to physical sensations that we can experience it not only during intercourse, but also in giving a kiss or caress.[17] When we take such sexual pleasure, it is not only because of any physical sensation in our lips or fingertips, but also in part because we see, in the other's response, a recognition of what that kiss or caress means.[18] Indeed, we can go further. Much of the pleasure of a kiss or caress is often drawn not only from the other's recognition of our intentions, but from her recognition of our intention that she recognize those intentions; that is, from the fact that she knows not just that we are sexually interested in her, but also that we regard her knowledge as an indispensable part of what we desire.

To see why, we need only briefly consider another intentional pleasure – that of chess. Suppose I sit across a chessboard from someone with whom I hope to play a game of chess. There would be no pleasure in moving a pawn forward two squares on a chessboard, even if the person across the board recognized its significance as a move in chess, if she did not also realize that I intended her to play with me. She would not, in that case, be engaged in a cooperative activity with me, but merely think herself a spectator or perhaps an intruder. I, in turn, would be engaged in an activity fundamentally different from that which I intended; I would be shifting pieces around a board, but I would not be playing chess. In much the same way, if the person I erotically kiss does not appreciate that I intend her to recognize my sexual interest, she will think herself only a spectator to expressions of interest playing out on her lips and body – not someone expected to have any sort of attitude toward them. Once more, I will be engaged in an activity qualitatively different from that which I intended.

My point, here, is not that we treat people in morally acceptable ways merely because we wrap our intentions up with their own. I may intend someone to recognize the fullness of my intentions without treating her as a true participant in a cooperative endeavour. I may, for example, want another to know that I know she appreciates the significance of moving chess pieces around a board because I dislike her and, out of spite, wish to pointedly convey that I do not want to play chess with her. Likewise, I may want the object of my sexual interest to know that I intend her to recognize that interest not because I hope she will consent, but because I hope she will not consent and I sadistically take pleasure in *that*. As Nussbaum observes, it is possible to instrumentalize a person while caring about her subjective thoughts and feelings.[19]

Nonetheless, then, sexual pleasure and desire, at least as we frequently experience, cannot be objectifying in the particular sense Kant suggests. No plausible account of sexual pleasure can neglect the fact that its delights are largely those "of the mind."[20] Simon Blackburn describes the "Hobbesian unity" we can experience in the sexual act: "I desire you, and desire your desire for me. I hope that you desire my desire for your desire, and if things are going well, you do. There are no cross-purposes, hidden agendas, mistakes, or deceptions. Lust here is like making music together, a joint symphony of pleasure and response."[21] The sort of mind-set Blackburn discusses – in which our thoughts are not only about the physical sensations we are experiencing, but also about the physical and mental experience of our partner – is radically different from that supposed by Kant. Far from ignoring or denying the subjective life of the object of desire, sexual pleasure often presupposes it: we anticipate a partner capable of interpreting our kisses or caresses, of recognizing in them an expression of sexual interest, and of perceiving that our intentions are bound up with her own. This understanding of sexual pleasure, in turn, is to a degree incompatible with attributing inertness to the object of desire; there is, we might say, too much psychic "movement" and adjustment involved.

At the same time, we have no reason (at least, yet) to suppose that sexual pleasure must involve treating people as autonomous entities – we can acknowledge that people have a subjective life without believing that their preferences and choices ought to affect the way we behave toward them. Moreover, that we acknowledge another person's inner life does not necessarily mean that we will treat her non-instrumentally. It may affect only how we use her; what kind of tool we perceive her to be. Finally, there is a sense in which we can recognize another's subjective life without recognizing her as unique or special: we may think it important that the object of our desire has intentions and desires, and yet think it unimportant what they are, or deny they distinguish her in any meaningful way from others. There is surely some moral difference between treating a person as interchangeable with a piece of plastic and treating her as interchangeable with other human beings. Nonetheless, we may still find this attitude of fungibility intuitively troubling. Indeed, I argue that concerns about this kind of fungibility are closely tied to questions of instrumentalization.

Desiring the Embodied Person: Mutuality as Shared Openness

Our relationship to our bodies is not simply that of an owner to property, though it is tempting to think otherwise.[22] We often act as though our bodies are separate from our core selves – things that are ours to use but not reducible to us. Furthermore, as Gardner and Shute note, we tend to treat our homes and belongings as if they define our identity, and to compare experiences of burglary to that of rape.[23] Reasoning from both directions, it would not be unusual to conclude that our bodies are just another kind of property – less alienable and more personal than our other possessions, but not fundamentally different. But that view is deeply troubling. It suggests that someone who was not "using" her body, because she was asleep or unconscious, is not wronged in more than a technical sense if a rapist decides to use it for his own ends.[24] No victim of rape, moreover, would compare her experience to that of a victim of burglary or theft, and for good reason.[25] Her body is not just a tool or piece of property that she uses; it is a part of who she is.[26] Rape is so deeply offensive to the dignity of a human being because it is not just her body that is used – it is *her*. As Scruton argues, it is impossible to "perceive the true horribleness of murder, torture, and rape" without appreciating that the human body is not just an instrument, but also an embodiment of a moral agent.[27]

The fact of embodiment is not only central to understanding the wrongness of rape; it is also key to understanding sexual pleasure and desire. The pleasure we take in our partners as we kiss and caress them, as I have shown, is in part the pleasure of imagining their subjective experiences, and therefore draws upon an appreciation of them as agents.

This point, however, should not be confused with the suggestion that sexual pleasure is based upon an appreciation of partners' voluntary responses. Quite the contrary, many of the responses we most crave are involuntary.[28] Blackburn notes: "[A] partner who can decide at will whether to feel desire is not quite the real thing. We don't want control. We want to feel swept away ourselves and especially we want each other to be swept away, just as we require blushes to be involuntary, and it is no sign of shame that they are."[29] What makes these responses involuntary is that they are bodily – that a smile emerges out of a joy that is felt and not willed; that a blush is a physiological response to a feeling of embarrassment or exposure; that a need to return our kiss is, above all else, experienced as a physical compulsion. How we understand these responses' moral significance depends, in part, on how we understand the relationship between a person and her body. If we take the view that the body is simply a kind of property – that it is a tool used by the self – then we will be more inclined to think of these responses as a subversion or overcoming of the person's agency by the passions and sensations of the flesh. The person who delights in the ability to manipulate those sensations, in turn, begins to appear to be indulging in the pleasures of power. We will be inclined, that is, to understand a seductive caress or kiss as a kind of instrumentalization of another's body, a way to overcome another's resistance for our own ends. It seems, as well, to reduce the other to bodily parts and sensations. There may be appreciation (as I have shown) that the other has a subjective life and is capable of forming intentions and beliefs, but there is also a suggestion that these intentions are unimportant; that, ultimately, the other's decisions will be directed by uncontrollable physical sensations. This suggests an attitude that the other, in the end, is really just an inert thing (to be, in that telling phrase, turned on). The other is also treated as something violable, as someone whose desires may be adjusted at the whim of another. Finally, there is a clear sense in which the other's autonomy seems not to be taken seriously. We would, in short, be inclined to see this sort of revelling in the involuntary responses of another as objectifying in several morally problematic ways.

Our perspective changes if we understand the body as not only the property or instrument of the self, but as partially constitutive of it. On this view, the smiles and blushes we provoke are not simply animalistic responses independent of the other's attitudes, beliefs, and values. They are not, that is, signs of a body rebelling against its master. Rather, these responses have cognitive content.[30] A smile is not a meaningless spasm of facial muscles, caused by a glance in the same way that eating too many dried fruits can cause a stomach cramp; it is directed at the other's glance.[31] It reflects the knowledge of what that glance means – that the other finds us sexually interesting – and a judgment that this interest is welcome. The blush is not a meaningless rush of blood to the cheeks, but shows that one cares what the other thinks of her. It is, as Scruton says, "a kind of involuntary recognition of my accountability before you for what I am and feel."[32] It may be precisely to learn whether our feelings are important to another that we try to make eye contact in the first place.[33]

The sexual pleasure to be had from involuntary responses, then, is closely tied to the fact that it is, at least in part, an intentional pleasure, for it is through those responses that we can see the other's recognition of our intentions and whether she meets that recognition with interest or indifference, approval or rejection, excitement or disappointment, delight or disgust. The other's involuntary responses, in other words, may not fascinate us because they establish a relationship in which we have power, but because they give us something like an unmediated experience of her.[34] They give us a way to explore and learn about another person. Such exploration, moreover, far from being an intelligence-gathering exercise – acquiring information for the sake of using it later – may be an end in itself. Understood in this way, our preoccupation with involuntary responses need not be objectifying in the morally problematic senses noted above. Having imbued these responses with cognitive content, we do not reduce the other to a collection of inert body parts. What is more, we do not treat the other's body as a piece of property to be possessed and wielded. Rather, we treat it as interesting and significant because it is constitutive of a person whose subjective experiences interest us. There is still an attitude of permeability, of thinking of the other's feelings as responsive to us, but not the threatening attitude that those feelings are somehow ours to change as we please.

We may remain unconvinced that the other is treated as a fully autonomous being. The very fact that the desired responses are involuntary suggests that she is not altogether in a position of self-control, and that she has been degraded as a moral agent.[35] But we should hesitate to leap to that conclusion. We may, after all, acknowledge limits to our and others' self-control without thinking those limits are shameful, and without regarding the influence we have over others' physical and emotional states as a sign that we are somehow better or more fully human than they are, or as a sign that we in some sense have mastery over them. We may instead note that, as human beings, our well-being is subject to forces not altogether within our control, and that far from being a sign of weakness or a mark of shame, this lack of control over our feelings and their physical manifestation speaks to what it means to be a person.[36] Rather than (to use Nussbaum's phrase) "hide from our humanity," rejecting the idea that we can be both competent moral agents and embodied creatures with frailties, cares, and turn-ons, we would do better to embrace our physical selves, our softness, and our receptiveness to others and to the wider world.[37]

Scruton, in fact, argues that it can be through sexual desire that we begin to appreciate persons as embodied moral agents.[38] And Nussbaum suggests that our own autonomy may flourish when we come to accept our embodiment; that we will be readier to enjoy the pleasures and intimacies of sexual life, to exercise our sexual autonomy, if we cease to treat our sexual responses as degraded or undignified.[39] With this in mind, Nussbaum tentatively argues that the kinds of sexual play in which lovers frequently engage – focusing attention, for example, on each other's genitals, attributing personalities to them, and even naming them – need not be degrading at all. It may seem, in such cases, that one lover has reduced the other to a body part – indeed, that it is the body part and not the person that interests her. But that ignores the fact that we are able to attribute independent personalities and identities to our partner's body parts only because they respond involuntarily. That can be a source of delight because it teaches us something about our partner that even she may not have known, or knew only as a spectator. Taken in this spirit, there is nothing mocking or degrading in this kind of play and, in the idea that we can share delight in a body that is at once our own and yet responsive in ways we cannot always anticipate, we may well find it reassuring.[40]

We are still some way from being able to conclude that sexual activity need not be objectifying in a morally problematic sense. Even if we see another's body as constitutive of personhood – rather than as a thing to possess – there may still be instrumentalization to the extent that we see that person as a thing to be used, and not as a being capable of meaningful touching in return. It can be a wonderful thing when two people feel free to explore and enjoy each other as embodied creatures. It is another matter altogether when one person explores and enjoys the embodied personality of someone who is not free to reciprocate. In the latter case, the asymmetry of power between the two parties – one permeable and vulnerable, the other inscrutable and in control not just of the self but of the other – transforms the nature of the act.[41] It suggests that one's vulnerability to the other is indeed something shameful, that my amusement at your involuntary responses is at your expense and not a pleasure we can share as equals. What may yet be missing is a sense of trust, a sense that I do not regard you only as a specimen, amusement, or toy – as something to be consumed or studied – but as someone to whom I am, in a sense, open.

Our experience of seduction and flirtation confirms the difference that this kind of mutuality makes to us. The reaction we have to another's seductive glance or touch or kiss depends in no small part on our perception of it as involuntary. We may delight in a double take, or a smile that seems too broad to be calculated, or an absent-minded hand on our arm. If we imagine the same look or smile or hand, this time rehearsed or consciously aimed at us, we may find it decidedly less pleasing or attractive. We are more likely to find it pathetic, ridiculous, or predatory. Ovid observes that the art of seduction requires one to at least project an image of powerlessness in the face of one's own desire for the other.[42] Along similar lines, Scruton remarks: "[T]he caress and the glance must not reveal premeditation … truly arousing conduct is that in which the awakening of the woman seduced is made to seem like a mutual self-discovery, so that she seems, in her own eyes, to be responsible for what he feels."[43] It is ordinarily because we have a sense of mutual vulnerability, permeability, and powerlessness that we are able to experience sexual activity (broadly construed) with another as an experience of intimacy and connectedness, a sense that our embodied selves are connected in a way neither of us can control. In how you experience me, you reveal something about yourself that is fascinating to me. My fascination, in turn, reveals something about me, giving you something new and provocative to dwell upon. And so on. As much as anything else, we are excited by the experience of ourselves in a "cooperative enterprise, in which I and the other evolve within each other's perspective, changing for each other and through each other, with a constant and reciprocal anticipation of our mutual intentions."[44] In that context, our permeability, and the loss of what we might perceive as autonomy, ceases to strike us as threatening and instead becomes something wonderful and liberating.

Mutuality as Shared Socio-economic Standing

Sexual objectification may be benign in the absence of spontaneity – that is, it may be harmless or positive in a well-established relationship as well as in a budding romance. The experience of ourselves as part of a cooperative enterprise allows us to find fulfillment in the loss of our autonomy. That experience may emerge spontaneously, but it need not. Two people who have been intimately involved with each other for a long period of time may, for example, set aside a specific time for lovemaking, or fall into a habit of caressing each other at bedtime.[45] There is nothing spontaneous in this sexual touching, and their mutual caresses may reflect little by way of wonder. Because the pair know in advance, without having to say so, that they are committed to each other, their touching can convey an attitude of tenderness toward each other.

In "Objectification," Nussbaum suggests on several occasions that the background relationship between the parties can affect whether we see a particular instance of touching as instrumentalizing. In her discussion of Lydia and Brangwen in D.H. Lawrence's *The Rainbow*,[46] Nussbaum observes that it is not only symmetry and mutuality of desire in the moment that matters, but also the degree of mutuality in their relationship generally.[47] In an attached footnote, discussing Constance and Mellor in Lawrence's *Lady Chatterley's Lover*, she suggests we can infer some degree of mutuality from their socio-economic parity: "[A] working-class man in England of that time," she remarks, "is roughly comparable in social power to an upper-class woman."[48] Inasmuch as each is not in a position to dominate the other through the exercise of social power, we have one reason to conclude that neither engages in the mere use of the other. Likewise, Nussbaum notes that Lydia's "higher class origins and her property give her a rough parity" with Brangwen.[49]

As this suggests, in determining whether mutuality exists, it is necessary to look not only at the immediate circumstances surrounding the sexual activity in question, but also at the wider relationship between the parties (assuming one exists) and their relative social standing.[50] A street prostitute, driven by desperate need,[51] may appear to objectify her client just as surely as he objectifies her. (Indeed, clients frequently want prostitutes to simulate an experience of intimacy, or even a limited form of authentic intimacy.)[52] But any reciprocity is purely superficial: both know that it is only she who must trust him. He may do what he pleases, and needs only to suspend his disbelief in her genuine interest.[53] It is for this reason that, although Nussbaum refuses to regard prostitution as inherently objectionable, her defence of the practice is grounded in the fact that it is at least hypothetically possible for there to be rough socio-economic parity between clients and prostitutes, and for there to be regulatory mechanisms in place that could, as it were, level any power imbalance between them.[54] For their part, Gardner and Shute likewise make the point, albeit in a footnote, that what they see as the objectionable nature of prostitution is in part tied to an absence of regulation and employment protection – in other words, to sex workers' vulnerability to their clients' domination.[55]

Likewise, a sexual encounter between partners in a long-term relationship may be pernicious rather than nurturing. We may, on close inspection, find that he does not take her seriously as a person with ends of her own, and that she remains only because she believes she has no other options. Under those circumstances, we may be inclined to see his pleasure at the involuntary responses he provokes as just one more way in which he exercises power over her and mocks her autonomy (even without necessarily being aware that he is doing so).[56]

Mutuality as Shared Plans

So far, it seems that broader mutuality is important primarily because it guarantees that the parties in a relationship are in a position to give meaningful contemporaneous consent. But consider this passage:

> [I]nstrumentalization does not seem to be problematic in all contexts. If I am lying around with my lover on the bed, and use his stomach as a pillow there seems to be nothing at all baneful about this, provided that I do so with his consent *(or, if he is asleep, with a reasonable belief that he would not mind)*, and without causing him pain, *provided, as well, that I do so in the context of a relationship in which he is generally treated as more than a pillow*. This suggests that what is problematic is not instrumentalization per se, but treating someone primarily or merely as an instrument. The overall context of the relationship thus becomes fundamental.[57]

In her parenthetical remarks, Nussbaum makes it clear that somewhat instrumentalizing conduct can be benign even if the person used is asleep at the relevant time, and therefore in no position to offer conscious, "active" consent. The moral touchstone under those circumstances is not *my* consent, but your (good faith) belief that, if I was awake, I "would not mind." What is striking about this is not only the suggestion that your use of me can be morally benign when I am not able to give ongoing consent, but also that, in the example provided, it would be obvious to you that I, being asleep, am unable to give consent in a robust sense. This suggests that mutuality, in the context Nussbaum describes here, cannot find its significance in the fact that it guarantees that the parties are able to give contemporaneous consent – since, presumably, its moral importance would in that case also hinge on whether it was actually given. (It is difficult to see how else it could matter.) Furthermore, the example suggests that conduct can be non-instrumentalizing even where there is no symmetry or mutuality between the parties at the moment the touching occurs: obviously, I cannot be fascinated by you while I am asleep and oblivious of you.

Many would intuit that it cannot always be morally objectionable to touch one's sleeping partner.[58] Those intuitions get hazier when we imagine the touch as sexual, but even here much depends on how broadly we construe "sexual": a kiss on the neck or squeeze of a thigh might be regarded as a sexual (or sexualized) signal of intimacy and affection, and intuitively it seems to make a moral difference that the couple have one kind of relationship rather than another. Indeed, there is arguably a sexualized dimension to Nussbaum's own example of using her partner's stomach as a pillow. Whether we think so or not, the fact that Nussbaum seems to allow for something other than active, ongoing consent in a paper that is centrally about sexual objectification deserves some attention.

The first point we can make about the passage is that, although Nussbaum loosens her grip on consent, she does not relinquish it altogether. Contemporaneous consent is not necessary, but the touching in question must still fit within the range of expectations that the touched individual would have, given the relationship with the objectifier. Since we are still supposing a degree of rough socio-economic parity, moreover, these expectations should not be seen as impositions by one person upon another (along the lines of "you can expect me to abuse or humiliate you"). We should instead see them as the expectations both individuals have of how feelings of intimacy or affection can be conveyed in their relationship given how each thinks it appropriate to do so. In a sense, we can say that the touched individual has given consent – not consent to the act of touching itself, but to the norms that govern and define the relationship.

But what about the fact that there seems to be no mutuality in the moment? Even here, we should be careful. The mere fact that our partner is sleeping does not mean that we are entitled to do whatever we want for whatever reason we want. In an intimate relationship, norms determine not just what kinds of physical touching are permissible, but under what circumstances, for what reasons, and with what attitudes. Those norms do not vanish when one's partner is unable to enforce them any more than the criminal law vanishes when there is no police officer nearby.

Within the context of a long-term relationship in which the parties respect each other as ends in themselves, a given sexual episode may be decidedly one-sided and yet mutual in the relevant sense. My ends may be wrapped up with yours, such that my well-being does not just provide you with reasons for action – for we could say that the well-being of others, no matter who they are to us, should motivate us in one way or another – but partially determines what other life-defining goals you pursue (and vice versa).[59] You may reject a home and career in another city because my well-being depends on being close to my friends and family, or on pursuing a career or an education that I can only have here. Our relationships with others (for example, with friends who might otherwise be suitors, or with in-laws who would otherwise be strangers) may be limited and defined in part by our relationship with each other. Against this backdrop of shared plans, it will often make less sense to ask whether your unsolicited interest in my embodied personhood is tender rather than predatory. The way we have constructed our life together presupposes our loyalty to each other as autonomous beings,[60] and can give sexual touching – even when it is one-sided or unexpected – a significance it does not have for people involved in more transient or exploitive relationships.[61]

The fact that our plans – our past and future – are shared seems to make a moral difference in another sense. Two people, in the course of exploring each other's embodied selves and becoming more intimate, learn how each responds to certain kinds of touching and learn how each expresses feelings of attachment to the other. Over time, they become able to recognize how each expresses tenderness and loyalty to the other.

They come to share a common language of intimacy.[62] To be sure, they may be unable to readily articulate how they are able to recognize those feelings, just as we may be unable to explain how we know what other expressions and gestures mean in other contexts in our lives. For my purposes here, it is enough to note that people recognize signs of tenderness from their partners, that some of these signs are sexual in nature, and that, within the context of a relationship characterized by loyalty and mutual respect, there may be nothing problematically objectifying about certain kinds of sexual touching.

Furthermore, the idea that loyalty might make a moral difference is not so far-fetched. In other contexts where the asymmetrical intimacy between adults might otherwise be regarded as troublingly objectifying, the fact that a duty of loyalty exists is often thought to cure the moral problem. Consider many (perhaps all) fiduciary relationships.[63] A doctor or dentist may need to feel around tender areas of her patient's body, provoking involuntary winces and cries in the process, so that she may arrive at a diagnosis. The patient may, in fact, be unconscious and unable to speak up for herself. A lawyer or therapist may need to elicit from her client information so upsetting that it provokes tears or a flush of indignation.

It is certainly possible for their conduct to be objectifying, and in troubling ways: a lawyer may treat her client as nothing more than a repository of evidence, just as a doctor may fail to take seriously (or utterly ignore) her patients' subjective experience of their ailments or injuries, focusing entirely upon their bodies as sources of diagnostic information.[64] But these would (at least in many circumstances) be unprofessional courses of action. We would not tend to think of doctor-patient or lawyer-client relationships as inherently immoral, in spite of both their often objectifying nature and the asymmetry of power built into them.[65] The reason can be found in an observation frequently made with respect to fiduciary relationships; namely, that the fiduciary owes the beneficiary a duty of loyalty.[66] Doctors and lawyers are expected to engage in what might otherwise seem like objectifying behaviour only insofar as they are compelled to do so out of a disinterested concern for the well-being of their patients and clients; i.e., because a medical treatment or litigation strategy, appropriate for the needs of the patient or client, cannot be formulated without the intrusion. The sober manner and environment in which these examinations take place, to say nothing of the duty of confidentiality,[67] moreover, are expected to convey the professional's attitude that her intrusion into the viscerally personal affairs of the patient or client is neither frivolous nor undertaken for personal amusement or gain. The duty of loyalty, in other words, removes or mitigates the vulnerability, and sense of shame, that the beneficiary would otherwise endure.

We can also get a rough sense of the difference mutuality makes to the moral calculus if we consider the comparison David Sussman draws between seduction and torture.[68] In both seduction and torture, Sussman argues, the object experiences a loss of autonomy and control. Whereas the loss of control by the object of seduction may be experienced as ultimately liberating and deeply satisfying, however, that experienced by the object of torture could not. The difference, as Sussman shows, can be attributed to the absence of mutuality in torture. There is nothing like a fiduciary relationship between torturer and victim. Quite the contrary, the torturer's attitude to her victim is marked by hatred, contempt, or, at the very least, an attitude of profound indifference toward her well-being.

Conclusion

Nussbaum's analysis of objectification, above all else, stands for the proposition that context matters. We cannot make moral judgments about sexual touching without considering the circumstances in which it takes place. In particular, we must ask whether there is mutuality in one or more senses of the word. As the above analysis suggests, the fact that sexual touching occurs within the context of an intimate relationship characterized by mutual respect and loyalty makes an important moral difference.

CHAPTER 6

Exit, Voice, and Mutuality

Introduction

In chapter 5, I examined Martha Nussbaum's understanding of instrumentalization – wrongful objectification – and found it closely wrapped up in various ideas of mutuality. I found that mutuality can exist even where one party to sexual touching is asleep and therefore in no condition to subjectively consent. There seems to be room in Nussbaum's treatment of instrumentalization to recognize such a thing as implied consent.

That conclusion will alarm many people. The mere fact that a set of sexual norms is accepted in a given relationship, most of us intuit, cannot end the analysis. Sexual assault law, as I have shown, is intended to combat pernicious and objectifying gender norms. The very fact that many people accept those norms is what makes it so important for the law to step in. The objective of the offence would be utterly defeated if, instead, acceptance of traditional sexual norms was generally treated as a defence. If we are to accept something like implied consent, we need to be able to draw sensible boundaries around it.

My task in this chapter is to draw those boundaries – or at least to help us find them. To a large extent, I simply pick up where the preceding chapter left off. But, here, I want to scrutinize Nussbaum's treatment of mutuality and implied consent in light of the work of a feminist theorist who is skeptical of her work: Clare Chambers. She argues that, in determining whether we should defer to an individual's decision to live according to a certain set of norms, we should ask whether it is autonomous in any meaningful sense, and whether those norms effectively harm her. My aim is to show that, even on Chambers's terms, we can recognize a role for implied consent. Moreover, Nussbaum's own treatment of mutuality suggests that the two are not so far apart. By using Chambers's work, I hope to give somewhat more content to the idea of mutuality. In the process, I also hope to show how a doctrine of implied consent, if accepted, could be contained.

Nussbaum and Second-Order Autonomy

In speaking about autonomy, Chambers shows, we must distinguish between first- and second-order autonomy.[1] She explains:

> Second-order autonomy applies to the manner in which an individual comes to have a particular way of life or comprehensive conception of the good. One is second-order autonomous if one actively and willingly chooses one's way of life free from compulsion or influence that would obscure that choice ... First-order autonomy applies to one's attitude to the rules and norms that are part of a way of life. One is first-order autonomous if one leads a daily life in which one questions rules and norms and actively chooses how to respond to them. One may be first-order autonomous and follow rules, but only if one considers the rule and decides that it is a good rule to follow.[2]

To illustrate the distinction, Chambers frequently discusses the decision to enter a convent or the army. So long as one is not under undue pressure to make such a choice, it can straightforwardly be second-order autonomous. But having entered the convent or army, one is under considerable pressure to obey any number of rules or commands with which one disagrees. In that sense, there is an absence of first-order autonomy.[3] First- and second-order autonomy, then, can (and often do) come apart.

Political liberals like Nussbaum and John Rawls place a heavy emphasis on second-order autonomy.[4] It falls to the state to create the conditions under which citizens, with wildly different comprehensive conceptions of the good life, can all live "according to their own lights."[5] They must have the ability to choose their own ways of life. That being the case, it is not the proper role of the state to force people away from ways of life in which their day-to-day choices are constrained – in which, in other words, they lack first-order autonomy. This is because Nussbaum, like many others, regards the subjective experience of choice as a factor that can make a given hardship morally just.[6] There is all the moral difference in the world between fasting and starving.[7] Likewise, there is no moral comparison between the pain I experience during a visit to the dentist and that experienced by Dustin Hoffman's character during the dental drill scene in *Marathon Man*.[8] Unabashed state paternalism – by which individuals are prevented from making their own decisions about how to live – fails to give due regard to the significance of choice in living the good life.[9]

We get an oblique sense of Nussbaum's commitment to second-order autonomy in her discussion of objectification. There, she observes that, within the context of an intimate relationship defined by mutuality, it is possible to engage in touching – possibly including sexual touching – that is not accompanied by contemporaneous consent and yet does not amount to impermissible instrumentalization.[10] The sleeping person "used" as Nussbaum's "pillow" plainly does not have any first-order autonomy: he has no opportunity to decide whether Nussbaum should have access to his body. Nussbaum, though, does not regard that as morally problematic in itself. This is arguably because their relationship is defined by a set of norms in which that sort of touching is permissible and legitimate. The context in which the touching takes place, Nussbaum suggests, makes it morally acceptable under the circumstances painted. We might say, following Chambers, that Nussbaum's analysis privileges the second-order autonomous decision of the sleeping party to have an intimate relationship defined by norms in which this sort of touching is legitimate. The absence of first-order autonomy is, in light of that decision, morally acceptable.

Chambers and the Problems with Second-Order Autonomy

But is it? Here, it is worth considering Chambers's analysis of second-order autonomy, since it sheds light on why Nussbaum's approach is troubling in some circumstances. Chambers argues that Nussbaum is far too quick to dismiss concerns about first-order autonomy. Chambers is not deaf to the fact that choice matters – that having control over our lives is a large part of what makes them fulfilling[11] – and takes the view that there are limits to how far the state can properly prevent us from making choices that undermine our first-order autonomy. But she claims it is possible to reject paternalism (at least as a blanket proposition) and still think that there is room for the state to prevent some self-harming activities. This is because of the role that social norms play in our second-order decision-making. Chambers notes that "people do not make choices in a vacuum."[12] "Social norms," she observes, "set out what may be chosen, and place conditions on what must be done in order to receive certain benefits."[13] Individuals may be under considerable social pressure to conform to those norms, and may not be aware that alternative courses of action are possible or realistic. We should not be too quick, for this reason, to treat decisions as truly autonomous in a morally important sense.

Examples abound. Women who live in certain communities may be expected to marry and produce offspring. Men may be discouraged from pursuing careers in nursing or childcare. Women who want to pursue certain career paths may be expected to conform to particular standards of beauty – requiring at the very least the wearing of make-up and feminine clothing,[14] but possibly also dieting, medication, body-shaping devices, or surgery. Workplace norms may require women of colour to style their hair in particular ways, and to avoid styling it in others.[15] Professional football players, or members of the military, may be expected to quietly tolerate verbal, physical, and even sexual abuse and humiliation with a stiff upper lip as part of a masculine locker room or barracks culture – or to respond with physical violence.[16] Corporate culture may expect men and women to work long hours, even at the expense of family life.[17]

As these examples suggest, the social norms that influence our decision-making can often "reflect and perpetuate inequality."[18] Members of racial "minorities" are discouraged from appearing "too ethnic" in professional settings. Women generally are expected to conform to standards of beauty and behaviour which tacitly (sometimes explicitly) reinforce the idea that they are primarily objects for the sexual gratification of men. Insofar as they do – because it is too dangerous or too much trouble to push against the limits imposed by the culture, or simply because it never occurs to them that alternatives exist – they inadvertently send the message that the social norms are not constructions, but reflect the natural order of things.[19] This, in turn, encourages people to hold others (and themselves) to them. They become collaborators in a system of inequality.[20] (I return to this idea in chapter 7.)

Furthermore, many decisions are arguably only coherent when viewed in light of a system of norms reflecting inequality. The choice to wear make-up could, in principle, be explained away as a mere whim: the expense can be low; injury (typically) does not result; and it can be removed safely and painlessly. But what about something like breast-enlargement surgery? As Chambers says, this procedure is costly, dangerous, and in an important respect irreversible.[21] Arguably, the fact that so many women subject themselves to it can be explained only with reference to a system of norms in which women are treated as objects of male gratification, and in which opportunities are denied to those who fail to conform.[22]

Nonetheless, Chambers does not claim that the state should block second-order decisions merely because they are influenced by social norms – even when they reflect inequality. We should also ask whether such decisions are harmful: "[S]ocial norms are sometimes harmful. If [an individual] is to follow a social norm, [she] may be required to harm herself. The harm may be physical, mental, or material. It may also be social – it may require the individual to lower her status relative to that of others. In other words, a social norm may reflect and perpetuate inequality. In some cases a norm may be both harmful and unequal, in that it may require some people but not others to harm themselves."[23] As this passage indicates, Chambers does not use "harm" in the narrow Millian sense.[24] For her purposes, it is enough to show that the practice in question is harmful to the individual herself; it is unnecessary to establish that it will also harm others.[25] At the same time, she insists that the harmfulness of the practice must rise to a certain pitch.[26] Furthermore, although harm to others is not a necessary condition for prohibiting the activity, it is a relevant consideration. In particular, the fact that a decision will help to reinforce an unjust social norm that, as it were, pollutes the atmosphere in which others must make first-order choices, counts as a harm. In recognizing this sort of free-floating social harm, Chambers's approach has some affinity to Joel Feinberg's "legal moralism" and to the Supreme Court of Canada ruling in *Butler*.[27]

Once the concept of harm enters the equation, we are able to distinguish between different first-order decisions, even when all are informed – and made sensible – by the same pernicious gender norms. We can, for example, distinguish between wearing make-up and having breast-enlargement surgery.[28] As I observed earlier, the physical and material costs attached to the former are vastly less than those of cosmetic surgery. The fact that women wearing make-up reinforces gender norms is a relevant factor for Chambers's purposes, but even with that in mind the harm is relatively trifling.

Chambers's approach, then, does not lead to the conclusion that the state can prohibit any notionally harmful activities it likes. It may, however, support the view that the state can and should restrict many more practices than Nussbaum supposes. In making that argument, Chambers co-opts Nussbaum's reasoning. Nussbaum claims that the state is entitled to ban female genital mutilation notwithstanding the fact that the practice is part of a religious and cultural way of life, and even when it is practiced upon adults provided with full information about the procedure.[29] She appeals to a number of reasons: it is (a) irreversible; (b) entails lifelong consequences for health and (c) sexual functioning; and (d) reflects a phallocentric view of sex and sexuality.[30]

Chambers claims that this argument for prohibiting female genital mutilation commits Nussbaum, whether she likes it or not, to the view that many other social practices should be banned. In particular, she claims that breast-enlargement surgery, on Nussbaum's analysis, should be prohibited since all of the four reasons she cites apply just as well to it.[31] Now, it is not at all clear that this is true. Chambers's argument that breast-enlargement surgery will irremediably compromise sexual functioning is fleeting and unconvincing.[32] And the physical, psychological, and social harms associated with female genital mutilation are so extreme that Nussbaum's opposition to it hardly tells us anything about the acceptability of other social practices.[33] For my purposes, though, any disagreements between Nussbaum and Chambers about the limits of deference owed to second-order autonomy are less important than their agreement on what factors make deference broadly appropriate.

Influence and Disadvantage

In deciding whether the exercise of an individual's second-order autonomy can justify lack of state regulation over first-order decision-making, Chambers suggests that a variety of considerations should bear on our analysis. These broadly fall into two categories: influence, and harm (or "disadvantage").[34] "The influence factor," Chambers notes, "aims to capture the idea that individuals may be encouraged, by their social context, to make [certain] choices."[35] There is no escaping social pressure of one kind or another – our world, and our lived experience of it, is shot through with social norms of varying weight and gravitational force. But that does not mean that we should give up on the idea of autonomy. As Chambers and others observe, it only means that we should put the idea in context and treat autonomy as a continuum rather than a zero-sum game.[36]

The second factor is disadvantage. This takes into account "the simple fact of differences in advantage that the differently choosing groups receive."[37] "The greater the difference in disadvantage," Chambers notes, "and the more enduring and less reversible that disadvantage, the more we should worry."[38] The use of the term "disadvantage" rather than "harm" reflects the fact that, as we saw earlier, what counts as a harm will often depend on whether it was chosen in any meaningful sense. Harm and influence, then, are closely bound up with each other. The use of the term disadvantage represents an attempt to disentangle it from the category of influence so that each can do illuminating analytical work. At the same time, we should not make the mistake of treating influence and disadvantage as hermetically sealed compartments. As the above quotations suggest, the disadvantageousness of a practice is partly a function of the degree of influence that is brought to bear on the individual, in that it will affect its reversibility. Likewise, we may become suspicious that social pressure is doing an inappropriate amount of work when we consider the nature and scope of the disadvantage suffered by a person.

Influence: Exit and Voice

Having committed oneself to a "way of life," we should ask whether, and to what extent, the individual is free to abandon it. To use Hirschman's language, we should ask whether there are opportunities for "exit."[39] As Leslie Green observes, the ability to exit a way of life is significant insofar as it serves a protective function and an expressive function.[40] It is protective inasmuch as the individual is able to exercise "a form of self-defence" – she may abandon a state of affairs in which her interests are harmed.[41] But it can also be expressive, inasmuch as leaving a way of life sends a message to those left behind that their practices are objectionable.[42] Green remarks: "Underneath the idea that no one can be required to accept a particular way of life lies, I think, the familiar notion of personal autonomy. The fundamental reason for thinking exit necessary is to fulfill the protective and expressive functions that enhance the capacity for a self-directed life, including the capacity to form, revise, and pursue our ends."[43] Green is not alone in treating the right of exit as an important safeguard of individual autonomy[44] – indeed, he and others often proceed on the basis that it is an essential safeguard. This is, however, a problematic conclusion. Even if there is no formal barrier to leaving a way of life – say, for example, a religious community – such an option might be all but inconceivable to those who are part of it. That way of life may so inform an individual's perception of what life paths are open to her that she is, practically speaking, trapped in it.[45] Indeed, even if there is an awareness of her notional opportunities for exit, there may be unacceptable costs attached to such a choice. Shachar notes: "The 'right of exit' argument ... obscures the very real hardships of leaving one's identity group (economic hardship, lack of education, skill deficiencies, or emotional distress, for example), and suggests that an injured insider, because she is maltreated in intragroup spheres, should abandon the very centres of her life, family, and community."[46] Hirschman also makes this point. He is primarily concerned with explaining the circumstances under which the deterioration in quality of a firm's product – a "repairable lapse"[47] – would be addressed by the firm. He argues that one way in which this could occur is through the exit of customers (who cease to buy the product) or members (who leave the firm). Hirschman, though, does not focus exclusively on the commercial context. He also turns his attention to other "basic social organizations" responsible for delivering public goods – including "the family, the state, or the church."[48] As Chambers observes, Hirschman – anticipating Shachar on this point – makes the point that the exit option will frequently be unavailable in the context of those institutions.[49]

Even if there is no realistic right of exit, there may be another option: "voice."[50] This refers to individuals' ability to influence the norms that govern a practice or set of social practices by expressing their preferences to others participating in it. Exit and voice are both complements and substitutes for each other.[51] They are complementary insofar as a person's decision to abandon a way of life may, as Green suggests, serve as a profound criticism of the practices and norms of those still engaging in it.[52] In that sense, it serves the expressive function I noted earlier.[53] Indeed, the connection goes even deeper: the very fact that someone is able to leave a way of life gives others a reason to take her complaints seriously, and may therefore make it unnecessary for her to actually exercise her power of exit.[54] Hirschman observes: "The chances for voice to function effectively as a recuperation mechanism are appreciably strengthened if voice is backed up by the threat of exit, whether it is made openly or whether the possibility of exit is merely well understood to be an element in the situation by all concerned."[55] So voice can be made more effective merely because a right of exit exists. But that is not to say that the absence of the latter entails an absence of the former. Voice can also serve as a substitute for exit.[56] So long as there are effective channels through which individuals can express dissatisfaction with the norms and practices constituting a way of life, it may be unnecessary for members to exit.[57] Indeed, if it is too easy to abandon a way of life, there may be no incentive for members to go through the (often considerable) trouble of complaining about their conditions and trying to transform social norms. Individuals have an incentive to complain, and make their preferences known, only if they are sufficiently invested in the organization or way of life – in Hirschman's words, if they are sufficiently "loyal" to it – that it is worth their while to try to change it.[58]

For this reason, Chambers suggests it may be appropriate to have "equality tribunals."[59] In the context of cultural groups, she notes, "exit is inevitably extremely costly and difficult, and ... the difficulty of exit could not really be lessened without undermining the very concept of a cultural or religious group to which people develop strong attachments."[60] With that in mind, she argues, individuals should be able to take complaints to a body, outside the group in question, that can authoritatively determine whether the norms constituting its way of life are consistent with principles of equality.[61] This would allow people to make second-order autonomous decisions to enter or remain part of a way of life, while also ensuring that they can exert ongoing influence on its norms and practices – i.e., that they have a voice.[62]

It is, of course, possible that someone might "choose" not to approach such a tribunal for the same reasons they might "choose" not to exit the way of life altogether: the possibility of change may strike people as so unthinkable that they do not attempt to speak to (or through) an arbiter.[63] On that basis, Chambers observes, "it is quite proper for the state to engage in advertising or education campaigns informing individuals of their new rights."[64] There may be considerable social pressure on individuals not to approach equality tribunals. Tellingly, though, Chambers takes the view that equality tribunals may still be preferable to a right of exit. As Hirschman observes, there is less likelihood of social change when those who are least satisfied with the norms and practices constituting a way of life simply leave it.[65] If they stay, and become dissenters, they can "weaken[] the unjust norm" in question, "improv[ing] the situation for others."[66]

In drawing attention to Chambers's argument about equality tribunals, my point is not to endorse it in all (or even most) respects. Its importance lies in the fact that voice can sometimes provide sufficient guarantee of second-order autonomy, even where there is, practically speaking, little power of exit.

Disadvantage

In assessing the disadvantage sustained by individuals who have committed themselves to a particular way of life, a number of factors are germane. Most straightforwardly, we should examine the extent to which the norms and practices constituting that way of life require someone to take non-trivial risks with her physical or psychological well-being.[67] Thus, as I observed above, Chambers distinguishes between women wearing make-up and women having cosmetic surgery in large part because the latter is far more invasive and dangerous than the former.[68] She also suggests that material disadvantages count in the analysis. Thus, social norms that require women to forego an income of their own and instead become full-time housewives are relevant harms.[69] This is not only because of the financial opportunity costs in themselves, but because of the loss of autonomy and independence they entail. Chambers notes: "[W]omen who choose to become full-time housewives rather than chasing corporate careers will not just suffer the disadvantage of a lower income. They will also be significantly disadvantaged by their financial dependence on others, which will leave them less able to make autonomous choices or to resist future oppression from the person on whom they are dependent."[70] As we saw in the discussion of influence, the loss (or diminution) of a power of exit does not necessarily leave an individual utterly exposed to the whims of others. We need to consider as well whether an individual has room to exercise voice. But Chambers's point remains valid: leaving oneself exposed to oppression or exploitation can and should be treated as a freestanding harm.

Chambers regards status harm as a valid consideration as well – in particular, the effect of norms on the social standing of the individual as a member of a social class. She states:

> Social norms ... can be characterized not only by the actual physical harm they inflict upon the individual, but also by ... their "status harm." An individual suffers status harm when she follows a norm that portrays her as inferior ... Physical harm and status harm need not coincide. It would be possible for a woman to respond to sexually objectifying appearance norms in a way that caused no physical harm but did bring her status harm, perhaps by wearing certain clothes or makeup.[71]

As this passage suggests, we should not be quick to assume that social norms are harmless merely because they do not cause physical harm. The fact that they reinforce the public perception that members of vulnerable groups – including the individual herself – should not be taken seriously in certain roles, or are something other than full members of the political community, is reason enough to conclude that they do cause harm.[72] As I show in chapter 9, this line of reasoning is echoed in the work of Catharine MacKinnon and in the recent work by Jeremy Waldron on hate speech.

Finally, Chambers's analysis strongly suggests that the (ir)reversibility of a harm is an important consideration. We can be more comfortable with people experimenting with their autonomy, even when doing so gives rise to certain disadvantages, if the costs of that experimentation can be contained or reversed later. But if those costs are irreversible, or if they can be reversed only by sustaining other further costs, then we may become nervous at certain kinds of experimentation. Thus, Chambers notes the irreversibility of breast-enlargement surgery: "breasts which have had implants removed do not return to their original appearance."[73] Furthermore, once one has breast-enlargement surgery, one is effectively committed to more surgery later to maintain the implants.[74] The surgery can lead to additional serious health complications, and may interfere with the detection of breast cancer.[75] The fact that the surgery cannot be easily undone, and may lead to a series of health issues throughout life, are reasons Chambers cites for concluding that a commitment to individual autonomy does not require the state to permit the practice.

This reasoning does not only apply to physical or psychological harms, but to material harms. Returning to the example of the housewife, Chambers states: "[W]omen who choose to eschew paid work will find that choice, and the consequent disadvantage, difficult to reverse. It is difficult to return to the workforce after prolonged absence, and almost impossible to reach a level of career success open to those who have not had such an absence. The choice, therefore, causes *enduring* disadvantage."[76] At times, admittedly, she seems to suggest that irreversibility is not so significant. She seems to take issue, for example, with the claim (attributed to Nussbaum) that the irreversibility of female genital mutilation makes a moral difference in itself. Chambers replies: "[Female genital mutilation] is irreversible ... but so are most tattoos, male circumcisions, abortions, precautionary mastectomies or hysterectomies, and many sterilizations. The irreversibility of even a bodily procedure does not in itself suffice as a reason to ban it."[77] We should not, however, make too much of this passage. Chambers's point, here, is only that we cannot appeal to irreversibility alone as a basis for preventing people from engaging in certain practices. In determining whether a practice should be prohibited, we need to consider whether the choice to engage in it has been influenced by social norms that impose harms of one sort or another. Most of the counterfactuals she mentions are medical procedures that cannot be viewed as physically harmful. Perhaps more to the point, they do not obviously reflect pernicious gender norms and do not seem to reinforce those norms – to impose, that is, status harms – in the way that breast-enlargement surgery does.

Influence in Intimate Relationships

With the above in mind, we can already make a few general observations about the factors that should guide us in deciding whether the decision to enter or remain in an intimate relationship (an exercise of second-order autonomy) should preclude the state from ensuring that there is subjective consent during each and every sexual encounter (an exercise of first-order autonomy). Consider the right of exit. This should not be understood narrowly. As Newman observes, one could be said to exit a community or way of life in a number of different senses.[78] Thus, it matters whether and to what extent one had the option not to be involved with someone in the first place. Depending on the religious or cultural tradition in which one is ensconced, one may have more or less freedom not to be engaged or married, and more or less freedom to choose one's partner(s). The barriers to being un- or disentangled may be formal or informal. They may involve higher or lower degrees of social pressure, with greater or lesser social sanctions applied to those who violate social norms. This first point reflects the fact that, for those embedded in certain ways of life, marriage is not, properly speaking, a choice but a *fait accompli*.[79] A right of exit may refer to the power of a person to walk away from a way of life in which remaining unmarried is not an option.

But this is not the only sense in which a right of exit could be important. It also matters whether and to what extent the decision to marry or become the intimate partner of another person gives rise to social pressure to provide sexual access. There is, of course, no reason in principle why one should entail the other. Plainly, though, many religious and cultural traditions tie institutions of marriage to reproduction.[80] Many insist that women have a duty to provide sexual services for their partners.[81] To a degree, this is true in Western culture too, where there is a widespread expectation that one will marry for love,[82] and that romantic love can and should be expressed sexually.[83] At least since the sexual revolution, there is frequently a (sometimes subtle) suggestion that women who are uninterested in sex must be psychologically damaged in some way.[84] These ideas, often internalized by men and women, can exert considerable influence on women's decisions over whether to permit sexual touching – and particularly intercourse.[85] In this sense, a right of exit refers to women's power to abandon a particular set of sexual expectations within their intimate relationships.

Finally, it matters whether there is social pressure on those already involved in intimate relationships not to leave them. This pressure can take many forms. It may be religious, in that some traditions may preclude (or at least strongly discourage) divorce. It may be economic.[86] An individual who has no formal educational or employment qualifications may likewise be discouraged. A person who leaves her partner may face social stigma in her family and wider community, ranging from dirty looks and occasional insults to outright ostracization. Depending on the size and location of the community, this may make it all but impossible to leave. If the relationship is one in which children are involved, there may be additional pressure on one or both parties to sustain it. Finally, and most obviously, a person may be effectively compelled to remain in an intimate relationship through implicit or explicit threats of violence.[87]

Each of these points goes to exit in one sense or another, and all make a difference as we determine whether the decision to adopt a set of sexual norms within an intimate relationship deserves deference and respect by the state. They are "structural" features of the relationship.[88] But we also need to consider voice. Again, we should not assume that someone in an intimate relationship can have a voice only if a narrow set of conditions holds. She may be able to effectively express her preferences and complaints about a system of sexual arrangements within an intimate relationship in many ways.

Plainly, we will want to consider whether the internal dynamics of the relationship are such that the parties take each other's preferences as valuable and important in themselves – whether they take expressions of dissatisfaction as reasons to continue or discontinue a course of action. Suppose, for example, that a woman touches her partner (whether sexually or not) in a certain "time, place, or manner,"[89] and discovers that it is not welcome. Does she treat her partner's expression of non-consent on a particular occasion as a reason to exercise more care in the future? Is each open to discussing sexual matters with the other, such that they both have an opportunity to air complaints and get a better understanding of each other's physical and sexual boundaries, inhibitions, and turn-ons? Is there, alternatively, a tacit understanding that sexual matters should not be talked about, or that it is inappropriate for one or another party even to have sexual preferences? How closed is the conversation – does it take place against a normative backdrop in which certain sexual roles are presupposed? Is there room, in that conversation, to contest those norms?[90]

The fact that the conversation might now be closed is problematic even if both parties began as full and equal participants. It is important that we have room to decide for ourselves whether and when a set of sexual norms should be terminated or changed. No one wants to be held to her choices too rigidly.[91] Having made certain choices early in my life, I may eventually cease to regard them as *my* choices in any meaningful sense. The person who made those decisions – those plans – I may conclude, bears no relation to the person I am now. If the point to respecting autonomy in the first place is to secure the sense of well-being that comes from experiencing a life as self-authored,[92] we need to acknowledge the significance of the fact that I can become alienated from my past selves.[93]

Joseph Fishkin, in *Bottlenecks*, notes the importance of "flexibility" while discussing the phenomenon of "job-lock."[94] He states: "Job lock, whatever its cause, closes off different pathways through which people could proceed from their current position in the economic structure to pursue their idea of a better life."[95] This is problematic because of its impact on workers' autonomy – "the state of affairs in which a person is able to exercise her own judgments about her own ends, goals, and paths in life, and actually pursue them."[96] In much the same way, I am proposing here that to truly own choices and commitments in the sexual arena, there must be room to abandon them.

All of these questions go to whether the culture of the intimate relationship in issue is such that any expressions of complaint or preference will be heard. As the earlier discussion of exit and voice suggested, in determining whether a person has a voice in her relationship, it makes sense to pay attention to her opportunities to assert independence. Where one party depends on the other – for, say, her social standing, her economic means of subsistence, or her spiritual fulfillment – or where she is regularly subjected to threats of physical violence, we should be suspicious of her ability to negotiate on level terms, or even of her willingness or freedom to express preferences at all.[97] Nor should we be oblivious to the possibility that, in a relationship marked by disparities of wealth or social standing, one or both parties may come to believe that one is owed the other's deference. The ability to exit a relationship should inform the analysis of voice.

Furthermore, as Chambers's discussion of equality tribunals suggests, we should not assume that voice must be expressed privately – in principle, it is possible for preferences or complaints to be expressed through public or semi-public mechanisms. For example, the parties to a relationship might agree to have their disputes arbitrated or moderated by a third party, such as a counsellor, friend, family member, or religious figure. In determining whether this creates a genuine opportunity for voice, we would need to consider the values and norms guiding the arbiter or moderator – otherwise, the process threatens to become less about settling grievances and more about reinforcing a culturally dominant set of values, possibly at the expense of the weaker party in the relationship. It may, in short, foreclose rather than facilitate discussion.

As Chambers's discussion also shows, we should pay attention to not only the scope of the conversation occurring within a given relationship – the extent to which it permits or encourages the parties to talk about sexual issues and question prevailing norms – but also the extent to which such a conversation takes place in the wider community in which that relationship is situated. Chambers observes that those within a sufficiently closed culture may find the idea of challenging dominant social norms inconceivable.[98] With that in mind, she argues that there is a role for government in educating its citizens about the availability of alternative ways of life.[99] Whatever we think about that claim, she is certainly right that the absence of dissenting views in a culture can make it impossible for some individuals to have a real voice in determining which norms apply to them.

One could plausibly argue that much of my discussion of exit and voice presupposes that there is a still more fundamental question at the bottom of both: does the relationship permit or promote the exercise of critical thinking and reflection by each party?[100] At various points I have suggested that there can be no meaningful right of exit or voice if one is unable to get sufficient critical distance from the dominant norms and practices that constitute one's way of life. It is unsurprising that this kind of factor should loom large in the analysis. After all, the point is to determine the extent to which the state should defer to the second-order autonomous decisions of individuals in the absence of first-order autonomy. And what is first-order autonomy, if not the active questioning of rules and norms?[101] Naturally, the more room the parties have for critical reflection and active choosing, the less concerned we will be.[102]

That said, we should be careful not to assume that people and relationships embedded in religious and cultural traditions that are not our own must lack the ability to critically reflect on their circumstances or on the norms that govern them, or that they must be in a state of false consciousness. In *Remembrance of Things Past*, Marcel Proust frequently remarks upon people's tendency to see others as though they are automatons, lacking in self-awareness ("I imagined, like everyone else, that the brains of other people were lifeless and submissive receptacles with no power of specific reaction to anything that might be introduced into them").[103] We treat them – from what Strawson coins the "object-ive" rather than "reactive" point of view – as problems to be managed, or people to be saved, rather than as people with whom we can engage in reasoned debate about the good life.[104] And, to be clear, Chambers does not suggest that some individuals are free of the influence of social norms and pressures – these are inescapable.[105]

With this concern in mind, Nussbaum observes that we should be careful not to assume that certain religiously informed practices, like polygamy, are inherently more damaging to women than monogamy: there is a risk of exaggerating the faults of those practices and minimiz-ing those of secular traditions to which some of us may be more sympa-thetic.[106] Love takes many forms.[107] We may be all too willing to presume that people with radically different ideas about how to live, or how to express love for others, must be confused about what it means to live a good life or what love means. The same can be said for sexual fulfillment. People have different motivations for engaging in sexual activity. What matters is not why they engage in it – whether for pleasure, to express or achieve an emotional connection with a partner, or for spiritual rea-sons – but that conditions exist in which they can critically reflect on what they are doing, express their sexual preferences in relative freedom and under conditions in which those preferences will be taken seriously, and protect themselves if their sexual preferences are not respected.

Harmful Sexual Norms

This brings us to harm.[108] In determining whether the state should defer to an individual's decision to hold herself to a set of sexual norms, we should consider the extent to which those norms result in physical dis-advantage. Do the norms in question permit unexpected kisses on the cheek? Bites on the neck? Can affection be expressed through the touch-ing of breasts or other body parts? Do the norms permit penetration while one is asleep?[109] These are very different kinds of touching that entail very different kinds of physical harm, ranging from the trivial to the profound. These differences matter a great deal in deciding just how much deference we owe the parties involved.

We should also be concerned with status harm. On this point, we could say that any sexual norms suggesting that women are passive sexual objects, or providing standing consent to any form of sexual touching, reinforce to some degree the idea that women are entitled to less respect as persons – just as the use of make-up arguably entails status harm even though it involves manifestly less physical harm than breast-enlargement surgery. But status harm is no more all or nothing than physical harm. (If it were, Chambers would be committed to the view that the state can forbid make-up, a conclusion she resists.)[110] Again, the nature of the touching makes an important difference to the status harm it entails. The fact that one has permission to engage in relatively superficial acts of touching (e.g., an unexpected kiss on the cheek) hardly signals – on its own, at any rate – that one party is merely an object for the sexual gratification of the other. By contrast, as the permission becomes more sweeping, ostensibly authorizing more kinds of sexual touching in the absence of contemporaneous consent, it becomes less possible to escape the conclusion that one party is simply an instrument. The ability to do whatever one wants, when and how one wants, with another person's body is difficult to square with the idea that both are equal partners in the relationship.

This last point ties closely into the earlier discussion of voice. The very fact that both parties have the opportunity to shape the norms that govern their relationship is itself both a sign and a symbol of the mutual respect they have for each other as persons. It follows that we should be more suspicious of arrangements in which the opportunity for one party to complain or express preferences about sexual norms is lacking or severely diminished – where, e.g., permission extends to being touched sexually while asleep, or where it permits advanced sexual touching in the absence of a clear signal of contemporaneous consent. By contrast, one can have an arrangement of implied consent that nonetheless gives both parties extensive opportunities to exercise their voices and shape the sexual interaction taking place and the norms that will govern them in the future.

Finally, we should consider reversibility. Here, too, the nature of the touching matters. Some forms of touching will entail no (or vanishingly small) health costs. Others may entail more long-term physical effects. But separate and apart from the physical harms attached to the touching, we should consider the reversibility of the status harms caused by a given set of sexual norms. To what extent will those norms send the message to both parties that one has a degraded standing in the relationship, thereby making it impossible (or inconceivable) for her to change them later, and perhaps compromising her voice in other aspects of the relationship as well?

Nussbaum on Mutuality

We have now seen a wide range of factors that can be brought to bear on whether the sexual norms within an intimate relationship warrant deference by the legislature. To what extent are these considerations reflected in Nussbaum's treatment of instrumentalization and mutuality? As I discussed in chapter 5, Nussbaum is content merely to sketch out certain aspects of her analysis – her concern is more with showing the importance of context in assessing the general moral defensibility of objectification than with dwelling on the precise circumstances under which we can say that mutuality exists. But what she does say gives us some valuable clues.

First, recall Nussbaum's suggestion that the socio-economic parity between Mellors and Constance in *Lady Chatterly's Lover* is an important guarantee of mutuality.[111] It gives us insights into the nature of their relationship – i.e., whether it is one-sided or exploitive (however unintentionally) rather than mutual and cooperative. That point is closely bound up with the common-sense idea that we should consider the parties' relative power to exit the relationship in question when assessing the degree of influence to which they are subjected. To that extent alone, we can see some reinforcement of the importance of rights of exit in Nussbaum's analysis of mutuality.

Nussbaum also notes, in her discussion of Lydia and Brangwen, that Lydia's "higher class origins and her property give her a rough parity with him."[112] That point is worth exploring for a moment. After all, it is far from clear that Lydia had much social power in England. She had only just arrived when her first husband died.[113] Her father was dead.[114] Her mother "had married a German merchant and gone away."[115] When Lydia met Brangwen, she was a housekeeper – not a position with great social standing, as he himself appreciated – and he was a successful landowner.[116] So we need to look a bit closer at Nussbaum's suggestion that there was parity between them.

One point to consider is that Lydia's grew up the daughter of a land-owner. We are told that "[i]n Poland, the peasantry, the people, had been cattle to her, they had been her cattle that she owned and used."[117] We are given the sense throughout that she is comfortable with exercising power on her own behalf. (Indeed, Brangwen frequently mistakes her aloofness for lack of interest until, two years into their marriage, he has an epiphany that she might simply be lonely.)[118] There is also the difference in their age and life experience: she is six years older than he, has suffered the death of two children and her first husband, and knows other cultures and languages.[119] She is mysterious to him – Lawrence emphasizes Brangwen's sense that she is apart from him, a separate, distinct, unknowable individual[120] – and may even slightly intimidate him.

All this gives Lydia voice. What she says to Brangwen, and does not say, matters to him. And that is partly a function of the rough socio-economic parity between them. Even stripped of her financial resources (as she seems to be), she has the bearing, intelligence, and force of will of someone who was raised and educated as a landowner's daughter.

The significance of voice to Nussbaum's analysis of objectification has been brought out by Rae Langton.[121] She suggests that, although Nussbaum herself does not explicitly claim that silencing is one of the ways in which human beings can be treated as objects, it can be added to the list without doing violence to her broader analysis. Langton cites Catharine MacKinnon's observation on the effects of pornography: "Pornography makes [women's] speech impossible, and where possible, worthless. Pornography makes women into objects. Objects do not speak. When they do, they are by then regarded as objects, not as humans."[122] MacKinnon's views about pornography are, for my purposes here, less interesting than the fact that Langton quotes them. The passage suggests that the person who is silenced is effectively treated as someone lacking in autonomy – she is powerless to assert her will. Her subjectivity, if it is not denied, might as well be, for she is treated as something with nothing to say (worth listening to). She is also considered fungible with non-persons – with things that are inert in an important sense. She is, after all, treated as something other than a living, dynamic consciousness with which one might actively engage in conversation or debate; her words are simply treated as something to be managed, patiently endured (like noise), or manoeuvred around.[123]

My point is that Langton's idea of silencing as a form of objectification can be accommodated into Nussbaum's cluster-concept. It is possible to silence someone without engaging in all forms of objectification – notably, instrumentalization – but there is little doubt that it may be easier to use someone else as a tool when she has no way to express her intentions and desires. In that respect, the presence of voice is plainly significant.

Second, consider Nussbaum's pillow example.[124] Earlier, I noted that, in determining whether the parties both have a meaningful voice in fashioning the normative arrangements between them, we should consider whether they treat each other's preferences as reasons to engage or not engage in forms of touching. Nussbaum suggests that the moral defensibility of using her sleeping partner as a pillow in part depends on whether she has a belief about her lover's preferences. What is more, it must be a reasonable belief – it is not enough to be careless with his preferences. This is underscored by her suggestion that her use of her lover in this way must take place in the "context of a relationship in which he is generally treated as more than a pillow."[125] His preferences count.

There are a number of other circumstantial matters of interest in the example. Nussbaum, like Chambers, places some importance on the lack of physical harm (or discomfort) caused by placing her head on her lover's chest. That ties into the point that strikes everyone who encounters the example: its apparent triviality. This is nothing like Gardner and Shute's "pure case of rape" – in which a woman is raped while she sleeps and never discovers or suspects that it happened.[126] In the pure case, the assailant is a stranger; the norms that govern their relationship are entirely different from those that could conceivably govern those of intimate partners. Even if the assailant was the woman's long-term partner, though, the act did not involve mere sexual or sexualized touching, but penetration. Questions of physical pain and injury arise that are simply non-starters in Nussbaum's example. As I noted earlier, drawing on Chambers's analysis, this makes an important difference to our intuitions about the defensibility of state deference. This is not only because physical harm matters in and of itself, but also because the nature of the touching seems to tell us something about the relative status of the parties, and therefore about their ability to exercise voice. It also seems to cause (or reinforce) status harms in the relationship.

In chapter 5, I suggested that the idea of loyalty may subtly inform Nussbaum's pillow example. It is worth thinking, again, about how this idea ties into the broader framework for assessing mutuality that I have set out in this chapter. In talking about loyalty, the overarching theme was that the autonomy and preferences of one's partner are taken as reasons for action – indeed, sometimes as reasons to take steps of profound personal significance. (The examples are legion: either partner may decide, for the sake of the other, to move to another city or country, to live in a house or an apartment, to abandon or adopt a religious community, to have children, or to pursue or abandon educational or employment opportunities.) That strongly suggests that both parties have a voice in determining the sexual norms of their relationship.

In my discussion of loyalty, I observed that we can learn something from professional relationships in which one party has fiduciary duties to the other. Plainly, a lawyer or doctor can fulfill her fiduciary obligations without being loyal in any deep sense of the word. She is, however, held to a set of legal and professional standards that provide a measure of assurance to clients and patients that they will not be exploited in spite of their vulnerability.[127] In other words, an external mechanism exists to which the powerful party is accountable, and to which the weaker party can appeal. What is more, the standards to which professionals are held tend to require the fiduciary to be responsive to the beneficiary's preferences and complaints – to treat them as agents whose autonomy is worthy of respect. Lawyers obviously have an ethical duty to take their clients' instructions seriously, but they also have more mundane responsibilities, such as returning their clients' phone calls on a timely basis.[128] Doctors are expected to listen to their patients and address their questions and concerns in a compassionate and respectful way.[129]

Conclusion

Though Chambers seems to adopt a more skeptical posture to exercises of second-order autonomy than Nussbaum, she would not necessarily reject a narrowly conceived doctrine of implied consent to sexual touching. Where there is ample room for exit and voice in a relationship, and where the sexual norms within it permit touching that entails little or no physical or status harm, there is good reason for the legislature to defer to the parties – namely, out of a concern for their sexual autonomy. Going forward, I will identify intimate relationships that satisfy these criteria as those characterized by mutuality.[130]

Naturally, the cases in which these criteria would most obviously be satisfied are also unlikely to reach the courts at all. This simply reinforces the fact that my concern is with the law's expressive function – with the idea that the law should not label conduct that is blameless (or insufficiently blameworthy) as criminal whether or not offenders are convicted, prosecuted, or even investigated. For now, it is worth considering the fact that we can recognize a doctrine of implied consent without concluding that all intimate relationships should be treated as law-free zones. We can and should draw moral lines to distinguish between those sexual norms that the criminal law should respect and those it should not. In determining which is which, we should apply the criteria set out above.

CHAPTER 7

What Is Stereotyping?

Introduction

In chapter 2, I argued that the offence of sexual assault targets wrongful sexual objectification – i.e., the treatment of a person as a mere instrument of sexual gratification. That offence was closely tied to the creation of the 1983 rape shield provisions; in particular, those restricting the admissibility of evidence from the complainant's sexual history. As I have discussed, rape and sexual assault are facilitated by widespread social norms concerning how women and men are "supposed" to act. Men are expected to be sexually aggressive. Women are expected to be sexually submissive. Women should, so the norm goes, entertain expressions of sexual interest as quasi-commercial offers, but resist them insofar as they want to maintain the value of the (sole) commodity they have to sell: their sexuality, indeed their virginity.[1] Their sexual integrity is expected to be so valuable to them that they will refrain from the use of judgment-impairing substances and from "leading men on" with "seductive" clothing, and will use all their physical strength to resist an attack.

The Supreme Court of Canada rejected the defence of implied consent was rejected in *Ewanchuk* in large part because it was understood to rest on gender stereotypes. McLachlin J. (as she then was) stated:

> [S]tereotypical assumptions lie at the heart of what went wrong in this case. The specious defence of implied consent (consent implied by law), as applied in this case, rests on the assumption that unless a woman protests or resists, she should be "deemed" to consent ... On appeal, the idea also surfaced that if a woman is not

modestly dressed, she is deemed to consent. Such stereotypical assumptions find their roots in many cultures, including our own. They no longer, however, find a place in Canadian law.[2]

To use the language of David Archard, the defence of implied consent – at least, as the court understood it in *Ewanchuk* – presupposed that women are "disposed submissively to surrender to the sexual advances of active men."[3] The majority did not dwell on the connection between its approach to implied consent and honest but mistaken belief in consent, and the need to dispel these norms. L'Heureux-Dubé J., however, devoted much of her opinion to the role of gender stereotypes in the lower court rulings. Nothing in the majority opinion takes issue with her reasoning or is obviously inconsistent with it. In suggesting that it is an error of law for proto-defendants to infer consent from silence, passivity, or ambiguous conduct, the majority proceeded on the basis that Parliament's intention was to use the law of sexual assault to (among other things) address pernicious gender stereotypes.[4] Moreover, the majority in *Hutchinson* explicitly grounded its interpretation of section 273.1(1), in part, in the idea that Parliament had that very goal.

The Supreme Court has signalled on other occasions that it is concerned with gender stereotypes. In *Seaboyer*, L'Heureux-Dubé J. stated:

> The woman who comes to the attention of the authorities has her victimization measured against the current rape mythologies, i.e. who she should be in order to be recognized as having been, in the eyes of the law, raped; who her attacker must be in order to be recognized, in the eyes of the law, as a potential rapist; and how injured she must be in order to be believed. If her victimization does not fit the myths, it is unlikely that an arrest will be made or a conviction obtained. As prosecutors and police often suggest, in an attempt to excuse their application of stereotype, there is no point in directing cases toward the justice system if juries and judges will acquit on the basis of their stereotypical perceptions of the "supposed victim" and her "supposed" victimization.[5]

L'Heureux-Dubé J. was writing in dissent, but the majority in *Seaboyer* was no less concerned about the role of gender stereotyping in sexual assault trials. In declaring that sexual history evidence was categorically irrelevant to the issue of consent in sexual assault, McLachlin J. (as she then was) explicitly rejected the use of "myths and stereotypes."[6] And the perception that the majority decision in *Seaboyer*, which struck down the 1983 rape shield provisions governing the use of sexual history evidence, would reinforce stereotypes provided the impetus for Bill C-49, which ultimately gave rise to section 273.1(1) of the Criminal Code.

More recently, in *Hutchinson*, the Supreme Court remarked:

> The definition of "consent" in s. 273.1 was part of a parcel of amendments added to the *Criminal Code* in 1992, intended to address Parliament's concerns about sexual violence against women and children and to promote and ensure the full protection of s. 7 and s. 15 *Charter* rights ... The centerpiece of the revisions was a new provision narrowing the defence of honest belief of consent. An accused who chooses to rely on the defence of honest belief of consent is required to take reasonable steps to ascertain that the complainant was consenting. Parliament's intention was to "overcome the apparent unwillingness by some to let go of the debunked notion that unless a complainant physically resisted or expressed verbal opposition to sexual activity, an accused was entitled to assume that consent existed" ... Section 273.1 therefore signalled that the focus should be on whether the complainant positively affirmed her consent to the "sexual activity in question."[7]

The passage suggests that the interpretation given to section 273.1(1) in *Ewanchuk* was informed by the fact that Bill C-49 also narrowed the defence of honest but mistaken belief in consent. In devising the reasonable steps requirement in section 273.2, Parliament ostensibly signalled that consent could only refer to a state of mind of the complainant at the time of the sexual activity. The point of section 273.2 was to undermine a stereotype about women, namely, that they are sexually passive and submissive. By denying a defence to criminal defendants who rely on this stereotype, Parliament would send the unequivocal message that such thinking is unacceptable. If that is the purpose of the section, though, then Parliament could not have intended to allow a defendant to argue that the complainant *actually* consented to sexual activity notwithstanding the fact that she did not agree to the touching at the time it took place. That, the court implicitly reasoned, would reinforce the very stereotype that section 273.2 ostensibly meant to undercut.

One cannot disentangle sexual assault law from the aim of abolishing gender stereotypes. That aim informs the *Ewanchuk* court's rejection of implied consent in the sexual sphere. It is, however, far from clear that an appropriately modified version of the defence would need to rest on stereotypes at all. Stereotypes, I will show, entail a certain way of thinking about persons as naturally possessed of particular predispositions and character traits based on their membership in a given group. But it is (at least in principle) possible to say that a person has given implied consent to an activity without supposing that she has a natural predisposition to engage in it. That possibility should give us pause as we consider whether a doctrine of implied consent must rely on gender stereotypes.

Or so I will argue. The argument proceeds in four parts. First, I take as my starting point Lawrence Blum's philosophical analysis of stereotypes. His concern, and that of many thinkers, is not with idiosyncratic beliefs about the traits of discrete groups, but with beliefs informed by social norms. I suggest that social norms can guide a person's conduct in at least two distinct ways. They may affect the balance of reasons for accepting or rejecting a social practice. Alternatively, they may undermine the sense that it is possible or feasible to change or abandon that practice.

Stereotypes, I suggest, frequently operate in the second sense: they affect what we regard as possible. I develop this point in the second part of my argument, where I engage with the work of Catharine MacKinnon, Sally Haslanger, and Rae Langton. Pervasive gender norms, they note, encourage the view that traits commonly observed among the members of a given groups are not simply conventional habits, but naturally embedded. As I argue in the third part, this is what makes stereotypes so damaging and wrongful – they create the impression that it is pointless even to discuss giving the members of stereotyped groups greater opportunities and roles in our community. They treat individuals as inert objects with no meaningful subjectivity of their own. This suggests, however, that one does not commit the wrong of stereotyping merely by treating others in a manner consistent with a stereotype. The question, ultimately, is whether individuals are treated as autonomous entities whose capacity to reject stereotypical modes of behaviour is respected and taken seriously. It may well be wrongful simply to act in a manner consistent with a stereotype, since doing so threatens to reinforce it for others. But, I argue fourth, it is not the kind of wrong targeted by the offence of sexual assault.

Stereotypes, Social Norms, and (Non-)Conventions

In his philosophical study of stereotypes, Blum notes that they share two defining characteristics. First, they are false – or, at best, misleading – generalizations about a group.[8] Second, they have "rigidity or fixedness."[9] Blum explains:

> This fixity or rigidity [of stereotypes] is not an attribute of the generalization itself, but of the way it is held by the individual cognizer. One part of this mode of cognizing is that members of the stereotyped group are regarded as fundamentally the same … Another dimension of the fixedness is that the cognizer tends to be resistant to evidence of the falsity or misleadingness of the generalization. When presented with evidence contrary to the generalization, he characteristically fails to revise the generalization appropriately.[10]

To hold a stereotype is to "ha[ve] some cognitive investment in the association between the target group and the [stereotypical] characteristic in question."[11] This does not mean that holders must consciously endorse the generalization.[12] They may simply make an association between a group and that characteristic.[13] Thus, according to Blum, many holders of stereotypes do not, strictly speaking, believe that members of the target group generally possess the characteristic in issue – if, that is, they can only "believe" a proposition that has been articulated, formulated, or made vivid in some sense, such that it could be accepted or rejected. One can make an association without ever having had the generalization crystallized in that way.[14] Indeed, this is not unusual: "The way that cultural stereotypes circulating in the wider society come to take hold of individuals is not primarily through being put to individuals as explicit generalizations that the individual is invited to endorse."[15] Rather, an individual comes to accept the stereotype because she is rarely, if ever, called upon to question it – the culture presupposes its correctness.[16] Thus, one may hold a stereotype without realizing it: "An individual can discover that she holds a stereotype by reflecting on her behaviour, or by finding herself holding expectations of members of a group that she did not realize she held; she might find himself [sic], for example, surprised that an Asian student wants to study literature, and, reflecting on that, realize that she held the stereotype that Asians are only interested in math and science."[17] It is unnecessary, for my purposes, to precisely track the line between belief in Blum's narrow sense and mere association; it is enough to observe the division in the ranks of those who hold a stereotype. Some hold it explicitly and consciously: they endorse the proposition that members of a given group generally possess a particular trait. Others do not. They associate the group with the trait, and therefore hold the stereotype, but would not necessarily endorse the generalization (even to themselves) if confronted with it as an express proposition. Some would, but many hold the stereotypical association simply as a matter of convention – i.e., because others hold it.

Blum's concern – and that of most feminists and others concerned about pernicious gender and other stereotypes – is not with individuals who "construct ... purely personal, idiosyncratic stereotype[s] of a group."[18] Rather, the concern is with the effect of "stereotypes as culturally salient entities."[19] As Blum observes: "Normal, unpathological individuals absorb stereotypes from the world around them just because they live in that world, not because of their specific personality traits."[20] Our focus is on stereotypes as social norms.[21] In understanding how they persist, and how they affect targeted groups, it is helpful to return to H.L.A. Hart's discussion of the practice theory of rules.[22]

Hart notes that a rule exists in a social group when (a) deviation "from the regular course" is treated as a "lapse[] or fault[] open to criticism, and threatened deviations meet with pressure for conformity";[23] (b) "deviation from the standard is generally accepted as a *good reason*" for criticism;[24] and (c) at least some members of the group have "a critical reflective attitude to this pattern of behaviour."[25] On this last point, Hart states: "What is necessary is that there should be a critical reflective attitude to certain patterns of behaviour as a common standard, and that this should display itself in criticism (including self-criticism), demands for conformity, and in acknowledgments that such criticism and demands are justified, all of which find their characteristic expression in the normative terminology of 'ought,' 'must,' and 'should,' 'right' and 'wrong.'"[26] To take a simple example, it is (or was) a social rule that men must remove their hats when entering a church – and not simply a habit of people behaving in this way.[27] Men who did not remove their hats would be regarded as people who had done something wrong (if not morally or legally wrong), and would be pressured to conform, albeit in perhaps subtle ways. Moreover, there would be a contingent in the community who, critically reflecting on the rule, would argue that it is appropriate for people to conform with it – say, because it is a sign of reverence, humility, or respect for God or the church, because it is rude to block the view of the person sitting in the pew behind them, or simply to avoid rocking the boat. Those who engage in critical reflection on the rule need not agree on why it ought to be followed.[28] Indeed, one can have the "internal point of view" for no other reason than that others follow the rule: "[S]ome rules may be accepted simply out of deference to tradition or the wish to identify with others or in the belief that society knows best what is to the advantage of individuals. These attitudes may coexist with a more or less vivid realization that the rules are morally objectionable."[29]

A social norm can exist in a community despite the fact that many, even most, members regard it as arbitrary and morally problematic.[30] The consensus can persist, in other words, as a result of convention, not a belief or conviction that it would be right to behave in this way in the absence of any pre-existing practice.[31] To the extent that is the case, the mere fact that people act in accordance with the norm can reinforce it: those who follow or enforce a rule for conventional (or other) reasons will, whether intentionally or not, encourage their peers to follow and enforce it for conventional reasons. The norm is self-sustaining.

Why can the fact that others follow a given rule encourage us to do so? Sometimes, even though we recognize that the norm could be otherwise and perhaps improved upon, our interest in coordination makes it appropriate to defer to the existing practice.[32] When we reason in this way, we consciously recognize the practice as historically contingent and malleable. We see there is nothing natural or immutable about it, but decide that the need for our community to have a uniform response to a collective action problem justifies the status quo. As we critically reflect upon the practice, we see it for what it is.[33]

But sometimes the pervasiveness of a practice, or interlocking network of practices, can warp our reasoning by convincing us that it is not historically contingent or socially constructed, but natural and immutable. We may be convinced, in that case, that there is no point in deliberating upon the merits of a practice, in challenging it, or in creating conditions under which people could more easily escape or shape it. We may conclude that there is no harm in treating certain groups of people in certain ways, or imposing certain expectations upon them, because they want to be treated in this way – or that, at any rate, we are reasonable in expecting them to be content with the situation. Or we may think that the costs attached to transforming the practice in a meaningful way are unrealistic in light of the small number of people expected to deviate from the norm.

In a sense, the person who thinks in this way is just reasoning from convention: she is moving from the observation that many people act in a certain way to the conclusion that she should continue to act in that way and impose those standards of conduct on others. But the resemblance between the two modes of thinking is purely superficial. The first kind of conventional reasoning treats the widespread nature of a practice as one factor to be weighed in determining whether it ought to be sustained. The second treats the practice as a basic, immutable fact about the world – one that narrows the parameters of what it is possible or realistic to do. For someone employing this form of reasoning, it may not even make sense to ask whether the practice ought to be sustained – or no more sense than asking whether there ought to be unicorns or laws of physics.

When practices are used to inform reasoning in the second sense, they serve an epistemic function: they are cited as evidence that a proposition about the world is objectively true.[34] In the context of (cultural) stereotypes, the widespread nature of certain practices is used to justify the belief that members of a given group share a particular characteristic or set of characteristics simply by virtue of their membership. The person who holds a stereotype accepts (on some level) that she ought to expect a certain characteristic (including kinds of behaviour) among the members of a particular group.[35] She will treat members who do not conform to her expectations as exceptions to the rule, and not as evidence that she ought to cease to apply the norm to that group.[36] It is in this sense that, as Blum notes, stereotypes are "resistant to evidence of the falsity or misleadingness of the generalization":[37] those who do not conform will be treated as deviants,[38] and not as representative members whose conduct is informative about the characteristics of the group as a whole.

MacKinnon and Haslanger on Objectivity and Objectification

Like many other theorists, MacKinnon argues that gender is a social construction. One is a man or a woman not by virtue of any intrinsic features, but by virtue of a set of social norms defining what it means to be one or the other. To be a man is to have a certain kind of role in a social system that includes women, and vice versa. In that respect, being a man or woman is no different from being a landlord or a major league baseball player. Just as it would make no sense to speak of landlords in a social system that did not recognize ownership, property, or tenants, or third basemen in one that did not recognize baseball, shortstops, or home runs, so it would make no sense to speak of men or women in the absence of a particular set of social relations.[39] Gender is a "relational or extrinsic property of individuals."[40]

MacKinnon argues that gender, by definition, is hierarchical. She states: "[S]exuality is gendered as gender is sexualized. Male and female are created through the eroticization of dominance and submission. The man/woman difference and the dominance/submission dynamic define each other."[41] Haslanger summarized MacKinnon's view in these "blunt" terms: "One is a man by virtue of standing in a position of eroticized dominance over others; one is a woman by virtue of standing in a position of eroticized submission to others."[42] To excel as a woman, to behave in a way constructed as feminine according to existing gender norms, is to adopt a submissive posture. Likewise, masculinity entails dominance. These traits are eroticized in the sense that one who is submissive is regarded (both by others and herself) as an "object for the satisfaction of the dominant's desire."[43] Objectification, on this view, is built into the very idea of what it means to be a woman – to be a woman is to be someone capable of being converted into an instrument for the gratification of men. Haslanger notes: "[I]n MacKinnon's terms, the social category of women is that group of individuals who are viewed functionally as objects for the satisfaction of men's desire, where this desire is conditioned to find subordination stimulating, and where men have the power to enforce the conformity of those they so perceive to their view of them."[44] In this account, two points are worth observing. First, objectification requires a particular kind of attitude: it requires one to see women as instruments for men to use. Second, it requires one to have the power to enforce gender norms of femininity or submissiveness.[45]

MacKinnon has written at length about the connection between objectivity and objectification:

> The stance of the "knower" ... is ... the neutral posture, which I will be calling objectivity – that is, the nonsituated distanced standpoint ... [This] is the male standpoint socially ... [The] relationship between objectivity as the stance from which the world is known and the world that is apprehended in this way is the relationship of objectification. Objectivity is the epistemological stance of which objectification is the social process, of which male dominance is the politics, the acted out social practice. That is, to look at the world objectively is to objectify it.[46]

Her point is not just that there is "something wrong with knowledge as it is traditionally pursued and understood," but that "women are actively hurt" when men and women pursue knowledge in this way.[47] As Langton notes, this view may be somewhat "overstated,"[48] but in an important sense it is right – by "objectively" describing the existing state of affairs in the world, one effectively enforces objectifying gender norms. Haslanger states:

> Objectification is not just "in the head"; it is actualized, embodied, imposed upon the objects of one's desire. So if one objectifies something, one not only views it as something which would satisfy one's desire, but one also has the power to make it have the properties one desires it to have. A good objectifier will, when the need arises – that is, when the object lacks the desired properties – exercise his power to make the object have the properties he desires. So if one does a "good" job in objectifying something, *then*

one attributes to it properties which it in fact has. Thinking alone doesn't make it so, but thinking plus power makes it so.[49]

Haslanger, like other feminist philosophers, wants to make a tricky but important point: the fact that gender is socially constructed does not make it less real. Gender norms are historically and culturally contingent, and therefore malleable. But they are not illusions. One cannot undo a norm simply by telling people to ignore it. Norms are, after all, the standards by which others judge us and by which we judge ourselves, and so they exert a real pull on decision-making and behaviour. This leads, however, to a troubling conclusion: the person who sees women as sexual objects captures something that is objectively true. Given how gender is constructed in our culture, we can reasonably expect women to behave like sexual objects.

This conclusion, in itself, does not mean there is anything wrong with taking an objective epistemological stance. In principle, one could describe a culture's social norms without endorsing them, taking the position, we might say, of the uncommitted observer – the social scientist observing a social system from a position of critical remoteness.[50] As Haslanger notes: "[W]e may allow that there is *something* accurate about an (ideal) objectifier's view of things; moreover, one need not be an objectifier in order to acknowledge such claims as accurate or, more generally, to make accurate claims oneself."[51]

Often, though, it is not the position of the non-participant observer that is adopted. Frequently, one does more than describe the social norms in play – one applies them, holding others to standards of femininity or masculinity. By participating in a social system in which men and women can objectively be expected to conform to certain norms, without challenging those expectations, one does not just describe a state of affairs – one effectively makes it true. Now, one might do so in full awareness of the fact that gender is socially constructed, and that one is reinforcing that construction. But it is far more likely that the objectifier labours under an illusion; namely, that the state of affairs he observes is natural, not contingent.[52] This, Haslanger suggests, is far more troubling:

[T]he point that men view women *as objects* is not simply the
point that men view women as something to use for their pleasure,

as means and not ends. To view women as objects is to view women as a (substantial) kind; it is to view individual women as having a Woman's Nature. As the objectifier sees it, it is distinct- ive of this (alleged) kind that those features he finds desirable or arousing in women are a consequence of their nature, and so under normal circumstances women will exhibit these features ... [I]t follows from this view that women who fail to have those features men find desirable should be considered as deviant or abnormal. And if women are to develop in accordance with their nature, we should provide circumstances in which they will have those features. From the point of view of the objectifier, his view of women captures their individual nature; MacKinnon aims to unmask this illusion: "See: what a woman 'is' is what you have *made* women be."[53]

The objectifier who sees women as submissive and passive by nature, Haslanger seems to say, engages in a deeper form of objectification. He does not see the objectified person as a person whose subjective desires and interests are being overridden or manipulated or ignored; in an im- portant sense, he treats her as something without subjective desires or interests. To use Nussbaum's language, the objectified person is treated as something that is wholly inert and lacking in subjectivity, and that has no meaningful autonomy to act contrary to the wishes and desires of the objectifier.[54] She is more completely an instrument to be used.

This belief that women are sexual objects by nature is also pernicious because, as I suggested earlier, it implies that it is pointless even to talk about whether existing practices and gender norms should be trans- formed.[55] Haslanger remarks:

Once we have cast women as submissive and deferential "by nature," then efforts to change this role appear unmotivated, even pointless. Women who refuse this role are anomalies; they are not "normal" observers, and so their resistance, recalcitrant observations, and even their very efforts to speak may be ignored. Strangely, against this backdrop it is of no help to insist that women are rational agents capable of freely deciding how to act, for then it simply appears that women, by nature, rationally choose their subordinate role. As a result, there is even less motivation for social change.[56]

In claiming that women are submissive by nature, the objectifier can point to "observed regularities" in existing social practices. But this is a false move. We can conclude that women are submissive by nature, rather than as a result of contingent social forces, only if we suppose that the objectifier has a privileged vantage point from which to observe women's behaviour, and that he himself has not affected their behaviour (i.e., by observing it). It depends on a claim of "aperspectivity."[57] Haslanger concludes: "The norm of aperspectivity ... functions to mask the power of the objectifier, thereby reinforcing the claim that the observed differences between men and women are a reflection of their natures. By this move the objectifier casts gender differences as asocial and amoral: We aren't responsible for things' natures, so morality has no foothold. And because we cannot change something's nature, there is nothing to be done about it anyway."[58] Ultimately, the objective stance, insofar as it is used to support the inference that women are submissive and passive by nature, is problematic because it is not really objective at all: it entails projection and "wishful thinking."[59] The objectifier uses the individual as a screen onto which he projects his sexual fantasies and desires.[60]

Stereotyping and Voice

MacKinnon and Haslanger's work on the connection between objectivity and objectification is significant because it gives us a sense of what makes gender stereotypes both so intractable and so pernicious. Indeed, their intractability is in large part what makes them so pernicious. Haslanger's analysis shows that gender norms equating femininity with submissiveness and passivity are especially difficult to dislodge to the extent that they are commonly understood to reflect women's nature. This is tied to the fact that, in characterizing or treating women as naturally submissive, one engages in a deeper form of objectification, regarding them as essentially unresponsive to arguments about how men and women ought to live and behave toward one another. By contrast, as we saw in the earlier discussion of conventions, we can accept that men and women typically conform to objectifying social norms without suggesting that there is anything fundamentally wrong with a person who does not – certainly without concluding that such conformity is unreflective, automatic, or amounts to a failure of rationality. When we perceive conformity as a phenomenon driven by rational calculation, as the product of a chain of reasoning rather than a natural limit on deliberation, we open up possibilities for discussion, debate, and change that were foreclosed.

The problem with seeing submissiveness or passivity as a natural, immutable character trait among women generally has much to do with the basic wrongness of stereotyping: it assumes that certain ways of relating to women are non-starters, and so rules out the possibility of engaging with them as individual persons.[61] Women are, on this manner of thinking, unable to autonomously engage with or react to certain ideas or courses of action – i.e., those that treat them as something other than passive entities. Individual women who insist that they are active sexual agents are to be managed or humoured, not taken seriously.[62] Notably, Blum argues that the wrongness of stereotyping is bound up with how it forces individuals into static categories:

> Stereotyping involves seeing individual members through a
> narrow and rigid lens of group-based image, rather than being
> alive to the range of characteristics constituting each member as
> a distinct individual. Independent of the particular stereotype I
> might have of a group, all stereotyping involves this masking of
> individuality ... Stereotyping, *unlike generalizing in an open, revisable fashion*, views individual members of the group only through
> a constricted, group-based lens.[63]

Blum focuses here on the extent to which a stereotype involves treating people as interchangeable – on its tendency to fungibilize human beings. But the tenor of his argument suggests that the actual problem is quite different. Blum indicates that the difficulty with stereotyping is that it cannot be revised in light of new evidence. What individual members of the stereotyped group say or do is taken as uninformative – their behaviour is treated as either confirming the stereotype, or an exception that proves the rule. In either case, the individual is pathologized – regarded as an inert mechanism lacking in subjectivity. The difference between one who conforms to social norms and one that does not is simply that between being a mechanism that functions and one that does not.

Denise Réaume also discusses what it is that makes stereotypes so problematic. In a passage cited with approval by a plurality of the Supreme Court in *Quebec v. A.*,[64] she observes:

> Once this construction of a group has set in, others are likely to treat members of that group disadvantageously out of an honest belief that this merely reflects their just deserts or even simply because that is how everyone treats them, without ever thinking about the insult involved. They may even understand their conduct, as with certain traditional sexist practices, as a positive effort to accommodate the "natural weaknesses" of the stereotyped group. However, neither the absence of contempt as a subjective matter nor well-meaning paternalism prevents the use of stereotype from violating dignity. To be denied access to benefits or opportunities available to others on the basis of the false view that because of certain attributes members of one's group are less worthy of those benefits or less capable of taking up those opportunities can scarcely fail to be experienced as demeaning because it *is* demeaning. The message such legislation sends is that members of this group are inferior or less capable, and such a message is likely, in turn, to reinforce social attitudes attributing false inferiority to the group.[65]

Again, the wrong of stereotyping is closely tied to the way in which members of stigmatized groups are treated as having natural inclinations and limitations that make it not only acceptable but desirable to treat them in disadvantageous ways.

Viewed in this way, Blum's argument is not that stereotypes fungibilize, but that they treat individuals as inert, lacking in subjectivity, and to an important extent non-autonomous. To put the matter another way, the problem with stereotypes is not that they treat individuals as fungible, but that they treat them as fungible with things rather than with persons. This squares nicely with Nussbaum's understanding of fungibility. As she observes, it may be morally acceptable to treat human beings as fungible insofar as they are all treated as autonomous, rational agents.[66] Moreover, Blum recognizes that the wrongness of stereotyping cannot be boiled down to a failure to respect persons as individuals. He notes that "[t]reating or seeing others as individuals is not always a required or appropriate standard of conduct." [67] (This point is developed at length in Schauer's work on the subject.)[68] Like Nussbaum and others, Blum draws on the commercial sphere to illustrate that it can be – and often is – morally acceptable for people to treat each other as more or less anonymous agents.[69] In that context, diversity among persons is thought irrelevant – buyers and sellers are expected not to care about each other's motives for engaging in the transaction in question.[70] Notably, though, it is the nature of the social practice – the conventions that constitute and structure commercial transactions – that lead people to regard this kind of fungibilization as acceptable, and not the belief that all consumers or all sellers have a common nature that makes certain relations immutable. (Indeed, people commonly observe that impersonal commercial relationships can metastasize into friendships, even if they do not often do so.) Concerns about inertness, lack of subjectivity, and lack of autonomy, then, do not straightforwardly apply here, as they do when we are talking about stereotypes.

In chapter 6, following Chambers, I argued that in determining whether the state is entitled to intervene in a way of life, we should examine the extent to which the norms constituting it are harmful and leave room for the harmed individual to exert influence over their development. In my analysis in this chapter, I have suggested that, when social norms constituting a way of life are thought to reflect a natural order rather than a constructed one, we will have greater reason to conclude that the harms they cause are more pronounced and that inhabitants have less influence over them. As I have noted, norms that are perceived to be grounded in the natural inclinations of men and women are more likely to be regarded as beyond the bounds of rational discussion and debate. Effectively, a person who is disadvantaged by such a norm will be utterly robbed of voice. Even the power of exit will be circumscribed, since an individual who regards a state of affairs as natural may see no point in trying to escape from it. But the fact that a norm is taken to reflect a natural state of being does not only affect an individual's degree of influence. By encouraging the sense that one's life options are curtailed or narrowed – perhaps radically – stereotypical lines of thinking can cause harm.[71]

The connection between objectification, projection, and silencing has been brought out on a number of occasions. Recall MacKinnon's suggestion: "Objects do not speak. When they do, they are by then regarded as objects, not as humans, which is what it means to have no credibility."[72] Langton, drawing in part on this idea, proposes that silencing should be added to Nussbaum's cluster concept of objectification.[73] She notes: "Speech is a distinctive capacity of persons, just as distinctive perhaps as autonomy and subjectivity."[74] To project one's sexual fantasies onto women effectively denies their subjectivity, treats their sexual availability as an inert fact about the world, and constrains their sexual autonomy.[75] Haslanger, for her part, states: "Women who refuse [the] role [projected and imposed upon them] are anomalies; they are not 'normal' observers, and so their resistance, recalcitrant observations, and even their very efforts to speak may be ignored."[76]

Reinforcing Gender Stereotypes as a Criminal Wrong

Our concern with gender stereotypes is grounded chiefly in the idea that submissiveness and passivity should not be attributed to women as natural characteristics. We are less concerned with behaviour that conforms to gender norms insofar as it reflects an appreciation of a person's individual values and rational decisions. It is, quite simply, one thing for a man to proceed on the basis that a particular woman must want his sexual advances because that is how women are or what wives do. It is quite another for him to proceed on the basis of considered reflection about that person's individual desires, as informed by free and open discussions between the two – discussions in which social norms are understood as constructions from which they can depart without deserving (even quiet) criticism. In the former, the man reasons on the basis of projected desires and stereotypes. He denies the other's subjectivity and restricts the field of what is possible for her. In the latter, he does not. He treats conformity (or lack thereof) to social norms as a matter to be considered and potentially rejected by a rational, autonomous person. The decision to conform, once made, can be revisited or revised at any time.

It is, of course, far from obvious that many discussions about the appropriate boundaries of sexual touching, even in the context of intimate relationships, are so free and open. In chapter 6, I set out a (non-exhaustive) list of factors to consider when determining whether both partners in an intimate relationship can be said to have a meaningful voice. Whether or not those conditions exist often or at all is an empirical question – one I will not even attempt to answer. In principle, however, we can draw a moral distinction between norms grounded in wishful thinking and gender stereotypes, and those that treat the individual's autonomy and personhood as a lodestar.

Not everyone will find this distinction compelling. Beyond the empirical question that I am leaving open, there is a further problem. As I have shown, those who treat gender norms as natural often do so based on the evidence provided by their own eyes: they regard the sheer pervasiveness of conformity to social norms as a reason to infer that they have a natural foundation. Even if one conforms to widespread gender norms on the basis of rational reflection and discussion rather than stereotypical thinking, one may nonetheless encourage others to project their desires onto women.[77]

On this basis, one could shift the argument against conforming to gender stereotypes. There may be no criminalizable wrong done to the woman who has ostensibly been treated as a passive sexual object. But even if that is so, we might say that a wider social harm results when men and women reinforce gender norms. If we emphasize these "externalities," then it no longer matters *why* men and women conform to gender norms – the mere fact that they do encourages others to believe that women are naturally and immutably passive, and that men are naturally dominant. We might, again following Haslanger's analysis, draw a distinction between objectifiers and collaborators.[78] Objectifiers understand women's passivity as a natural (and desirable) state of affairs. Collaborators need not. By giving objectifiers a (spurious) reason to believe that women are naturally passive, however, collaborators contribute to a state of affairs in which pernicious gender norms are sustained. In that sense, they also could be said to engage in a kind of wrongdoing.

It is fair enough to regard this as the kind of wrong that the law can properly address. MacKinnon and Langton, after all, focus on the role of projection in sustaining objectifying gender norms by way of arguing that pornography causes social harm and can therefore be targeted by criminal and civil sanctions.[79] This reasoning informed the Supreme Court's decision in *Butler*.[80] In upholding the constitutionality of the criminal obscenity provisions, the court took the view that the impact of violent and degrading pornography on wider social norms – and not merely, or even mainly, on the participants themselves – could ground criminalization. The court cited with approval the following passage:

> The clear and unquestionable danger of [violent pornography] is that it reinforces some unhealthy tendencies in Canadian society. The effect of this type of material is to reinforce male-female stereotypes to the detriment of both sexes. It attempts to make degradation, humiliation, victimization, and violence in human relationships appear normal and acceptable. A society which holds that egalitarianism, non-violence, consensualism, and mutuality are basic to any human interaction, whether sexual or other, is clearly justified in controlling and prohibiting any medium of depiction, description or advocacy which violates these principles.[81]

We might also look to hate speech provisions. Jeremy Waldron, who was influenced by MacKinnon's analysis, argues that their primary purpose is to provide "assurance" to members of vulnerable minority groups that they have the basic social standing in the community to engage in activities that will allow them to flourish and thrive.[82] Hate speech undermines that assurance by sending the message that the extent to which minority groups can participate in the community is a matter of public debate.[83] The mere fact that it erodes social norms of equality is reason enough to use civil and criminal sanctions to suppress it. In the same way, we might say that those who reinforce gender norms erode or prevent norms of equality from coalescing, undermining women's assurance that they will be treated as fully autonomous beings, and so reach a pitch of wrongfulness that warrants criminalization.

In subsequent chapters, I refer back to the arguments of MacKinnon and Waldron when addressing the claim that a degree of overbreadth in the criminal law can be permissible and even desirable. The claim I am addressing here is quite different: it is not whether we can permissibly apply this offence to cases it was not intended to catch, but whether it actually targets those cases. It is an argument, in other words, about how it is appropriate to interpret the offence.

Could we say that the offence of sexual assault targets mere surface conformity with gender stereotypes – that it treats this kind of behaviour as per se unreasonable? It is tempting. As I noted in chapter 2, the offence was created partly to address widespread objectifying social norms. This answer, though, is not sufficient in itself. As I have shown, it was thought important to relabel rape as sexual assault in order to emphasize that the crime is one of violence. We can safely regard a case in which the defendant sexually touches another person on the basis of a stereotype, in which he treats her as little more than a screen onto which to project his fantasies, as one of violence. It is by no means so clear-cut that we have a case of violence when the defendant acts on the basis of a set of norms developed in collaboration with the individual who has been touched, and on the reasonable basis that she continues to endorse those norms.

One could reply that in such a case there *is* an act of violence – just not one directed at the person who has been sexually touched. The act of violence, one might say, is directed at women as a class, who are harmed when gender norms that encourage non-consensual sexual touching are proliferated. But that treats the individual who has been touched as though she is complicit in the wrong, rather than the victim of it.[84] After all, if the wrong lies in spreading pernicious gender norms, then both parties are implicated in it – each has encouraged the other to act in a manner consistent with gender stereotypes. Yet that is surely an absurd result.[85]

The central issue in a sexual assault trial is not whether the defendant had skewed attitudes about women, but whether he sexually assaulted one woman in particular. This is why consent is always a (negative) defence, whether or not the acts to which the complainant consented were demeaning or degrading – if the offense of sexual assault was only, or even mainly, concerned with addressing pernicious gender norms, we might well restrict what consent can legally mean much further than Parliament has. After all, as the court in *Butler* observed, the appearance of consent can reinforce degrading gender norms even more than the portrayal of acts unaccompanied by the pretence of consent.[86] The fact that consent matters even when any third-party observer would conclude that the complainant is allowing herself to be used sends a strong signal that the core wrong the offence of sexual assault targets is the wrong done to the complainant specifically and not to women generally.

The Story so Far

At the outset of this chapter, I observed that the Supreme Court rejected the doctrine of implied consent in large part on the basis that it relies upon stereotypical assumptions about women. That is not – or at least need not be – true. Where a claim of implied consent rests on the suggestion that women generally are predisposed to sexual passivity or submissiveness, it does indeed depend on stereotypical reasoning and must be discarded. But where it rests on the claim that this person had, through an exercise of her autonomy, adopted a set of norms in which she played a sexually passive or submissive role, a defence of implied consent no longer relies on stereotypes about women. Rather, it rests on an appreciation of that individual's sexual autonomy and unique subjectivity.

This view fits neatly alongside the conclusions reached in the preceding chapters. I have shown that some acts of sexual touching can be construed as non-instrumentalizing, even where they occur in the absence of contemporaneous consent. This is particularly so where they take place in the context of an intimate relationship marked by loyalty and mutuality. I have suggested that conditions of mutuality will exist where both parties have an ongoing opportunity to shape the sexual norms that govern their relationship – i.e., where each has a meaningful voice in determining how it is appropriate for the other to engage in sexual touching. I have also argued that, even if the law is not required (as a matter of principle) to defer to all such normative arrangements between couples – assuming that conditions for mutuality have indeed been satisfied – the case for deference is strong when the sexual touching in question gives rise to only trivial harms.

There is nothing novel in the idea that the law should carve out a space within which private norms can dictate whether touching, unaccompanied by contemporaneous consent, constitutes wrongdoing. That idea finds expression in the doctrine of implied consent. In chapter 3, I showed that the doctrine of implied consent, in the context of assault simpliciter, reflects the value that our society places on our ability to engage in social practices and activities in which we are unable to control others' physical access to us. With appropriate modifications and limits, reflecting the fact that sexual objectification is rife in our culture, that reasoning can apply in the sexual assault context as well.

Finally, the language of section 273.1(1) did not preclude recognition of an appropriately modified defence of implied consent in the sexual sphere. In chapter 4, I claimed that "voluntary" in section 273.1(1) can be understood to refer to not only present intentions but also future-directed intentions – that the Criminal Code can be read in such a way that it recognizes the significance of the complainant's planning agency. This is turn reflects the fact that a right to sexual autonomy can encompass the right to give up control – at least to some limited extent – over others' sexual access to her body. In relying upon another's decision to cede her control to some degree, I have argued here, it is by no means obvious that one engages in stereotyping. That conclusion brings us full circle, for the wrongs of stereotyping are tied up with the wrongs of objectification.

CHAPTER 8

Context and the Marital Rape Exception

Introduction

Parliament's abolition of the marital rape exception as part of the 1983 legislative reforms to the law of rape and sexual assault was rightly proclaimed a victory for women's equality and sexual autonomy. In her foundational work on sexual assault law, Christine Boyle gently suggests that it would be difficult to recognize the doctrine of implied consent, in the sexual sphere, without resurrecting the marital rape exception in some form.[1] In a subsequent work, she remarks:

> Should there be some form of implied consent exception to *Ewan-chuk* for ongoing intimate relationships? The criminal law cannot treat such relationships as falling outside the law of sexual assault without resurrecting some form of presumption of consent from marriage or other ongoing relationship, thus making people in such relationships sexually touchable, irrespective of their wishes, until they actively withdraw consent. It seems plausible that people in relationships do touch each other in the absence of communicated consent, and without taking reasonable steps, but placing the risk of non-consent on the person touching is consistent with respect for the sexual autonomy and physical integrity of persons in relationships, and particularly for wives, a group with the historical experience of disrespect.[2]

Boyle articulates a valid concern, namely that the doctrine of implied consent, if applied to the sexual assault context, would effectively give men a right of sexual access to their partners. There is a reasonable argument that the institution of heterosexual marriage, as well as the norms that constitute the social practice of engaging in a long-term intimate relationship, has traditionally been informed by misogynistic values that treat women as sexual instruments to be used by their partners.[3] If the doctrine of implied consent would require us to give a legal stamp of approval to wrongfully objectifying arrangements between intimate partners, then we have a compelling reason not to recognize it in the sexual sphere. It also suggests that, when Parliament crafted section 273.1(1), it intended to abolish the doctrine of implied consent.

I have three broad replies. First, even if we conclude that the doctrine of implied consent should be available, it does not follow that it should be available for all spousal relationships or all forms of sexual touching. Different intimate relationships, including marriages, may be governed by very different normative arrangements formed under very different conditions. The criminal law is not required to defer to all of them – possibly not even most of them. The mere fact that two people are married settles nothing. Indeed, we find in the case law on section 273.2(b) a number of examples of marital relationships in which the norms constituting them were unable to legitimate the sexual touching in question. This goes some way to explaining why courts have tended to treat the fact that sexual touching occurred in the context of a marital relationship as irrelevant when determining whether, per section 273.2(b), the defendant took reasonable steps to ascertain consent. When we examine the norms that governed the particular relationships in issue and the defendant's domination of the complainant in crafting them, these are simply not the sort of cases in which the complainant could be said to have exercised meaningful sexual autonomy in any sense. These cases serve as a reminder that formal relationship status is not the issue; the issue is whether the complainant regarded herself and her partner as governed by a set of norms that can properly be said to reflect her autonomous will.

Second, the legislative history of Bill C-49 is, at best, equivocal as to whether Parliament intended to rule out the limited form of implied consent I have discussed here. The Supreme Court of Canada emphasized that Bill C-49 reflected the intention of Parliament to give women greater control over others' sexual access. That is true as far as it goes.

When we examine the legislative history of sections 273.1(1) and 273.2(b), however, a number of points are striking. In particular, Parliament's focus was overwhelmingly on rape rather than sexual assault in all its forms. Furthermore, it was often remarked – by the minister of justice, among others – that the legislation was not intended to change sexual and gender norms in any radical fashion. Finally, debates tended to dwell on the legislation's impact on sexual activity between strangers or acquaintances. There was virtually no discussion of sexual activity between members of an intimate relationship – what there was focused on marital rape. These observations may not rule out the possibility that Parliament intended to abolish implied consent in all cases, but they should give us pause.

Third, scholars who are critical of the doctrine of implied consent nonetheless treat the fact that the defendant and complainant were in an intimate relationship as morally significant. The above passage by Boyle suggests strong misgivings about recognizing the doctrine of implied consent in the sexual assault context. But she also suggests that some forms of what we would otherwise describe as sexual touching should be construed as something else when they are undertaken in the context of an ongoing intimate relationship – and that the doctrine of implied consent can apply to them. Effectively, she opens the door to implied consent as a defence to some sexual touching. She simply goes about it by adjusting what it means to engage in sexual touching.

The Plasticity of Intimate Relationships

In chapter 6, I argued at length that the law should defer to normative sexual arrangements that govern intimate relationships only when they were made under conditions of mutuality. The mere fact that an intimate relationship exists is irrelevant. That is no less true when the relationship in question is a marriage. Indeed, we should not automatically assume that marriages are intimate relationships at all.[4] People may marry for any number of reasons.[5] The history of marriage is dominated not by unions arranged by two individuals motivated solely by love, but by unions arranged by parents or the wider community for some sort of economic or political end.[6] It is hardly unusual, today, to hear long-term couples speak of getting married to secure some tax or pension benefit.

Some may have their marriages arranged by their parents and follow through on them to avoid a social stigma. Some may go to Las Vegas and marry on a whim. Even those who get married out of love may ultimately stay married for reasons that have nothing to do with affection for their spouses, including the threat of lost pension benefits; the financial and emotional cost of dividing assets, mementos, and pets; the sheer bother of having to explain the problems in one's relationship to friends and family; and the desire not to subject one's children to the trauma and upheaval of a separation.[7]

For many people, intimate relationships (including, of course, many marriages) are different from other relationships in part because there is a sexual component. We should not, however, be quick to assume that they do: the mere fact that two people label themselves a couple, or that they are married, means little or nothing by itself. People carry on intimate relationships in different ways – consider the long-distance relationship – and we should be wary of assuming that, merely because a woman has involved herself in an intimate relationship, she is participating in a social practice in which any sexual touching (or form of it) is reasonable or expected.[8] In determining whether the social norms that define and govern a relationship make it reasonable for the parties to it to engage in certain forms of sexual touching – even in the absence of express consent – we should not be lazy and try to make labels do all of the analytical work for us.

One could object that I am simply not talking about implied consent anymore;[9] that the doctrine only makes sense if a social practice has a single, incontestable set of rules. But I am not sure why we would want to adopt such a premise – still less why we must. Return, once again, to the hockey context. Imagine that players agreed beforehand not to check one another. It is inconceivable to suppose that, if one player checked another, a defence of implied consent could still be raised on the basis of how the game is usually played by other people. Likewise, suppose the players did not say anything beforehand but, over a period of weeks and months, a convention emerged in which players understood they would not check each other. Again, it is impossible to imagine that a defence of implied consent would succeed. Now consider the matter from the other direction. Suppose a group of people regularly decide to play a contact version of basketball – or, over time, a convention emerges – whereby a degree of roughness is treated as legitimate and acceptable.[10] In that case, it seems that implied consent should be available as a defence to assault, at least insofar as some kinds of forcible touching are permissible. The point to the implied consent inquiry is not to fetishize a particular version of a given social practice, or to reify it, but to make it possible for people to engage in activities that give them satisfaction but that are incompatible with a requirement for contemporaneous consent.

The doctrine of implied consent, if it applied to sexual assault, would no more require us to rely on labels of "partner" or "marriage" than it requires us, in the ordinary assault context, to rely on labels of "hockey" or "basketball." The inquiry at all times is on the norms of the practice in which the parties in question were actually engaged – not on the norms of some other, privileged version of the practice in which someone else might have engaged. In asking whether an intimate relationship features the sort of norms that could make it reasonable for someone to engage in sexual touching in the absence of contemporaneous consent, we must look at what the parties have actually said to one another in the past, and what conventions have built up over time in their relationship.

To a point, the implied consent cases themselves conceal the degree of control that participants can have over the norms to which they are subject. After all, such cases tend to wind up in court precisely because the defendant's touching (at least arguably) failed to meet even minimum standards of conduct. They may involve a professional hockey player, bound by clear and express rules, swinging a stick at the head of an opponent.[11] They may involve a parent, with no medical training, circumcising his own child.[12] They may involve a doctor touching his patient in a way that cannot be explained with reference to standard medical practice.[13] In such cases, we encounter the limits of implied consent.

Those limits are important, particularly in the context of practices in which there is a fiduciary relationship at work. We are right to worry that parents and doctors will exploit their children or patients.[14] But focusing exclusively on the limits of implied consent distorts the fact that the law gives parents, doctors, nurses, therapists, and teachers (as well as others engaged in the caring professions) considerable discretion when deciding how to carry out their responsibilities with particular children, patients, and students. That is not a failing of those practices. Rather, it reflects the fact that at least some of us, some of the time, want to be cared for – to be raised, treated, nursed, educated – by individuals who are somewhat free to express themselves authentically and spontaneously; that is, who are able to foster a sense of intimacy.[15] Relatedly, it also reflects our interest (again, at least some of the time) in not being treated as if we were interchangeable with others. People often seek this kind of closeness and intimacy in the professional or commercial sphere. It would be strange if we could not also seek it in our personal and sexual lives.[16]

Case Authorities on Section 273.2(b)

The case law on section 273.2(b) is by no means settled as to the significance of the fact that the sexual touching in question occurred in the context of an established relationship between the complainant and defendant. There are good reasons for this. First, most if not all professional relationships do not and cannot have norms legitimizing sexual touching; lawyers, doctors, massage therapists, teachers, professors are all categorically barred by professional norms from sexualizing their relationships with their clients, patients, and students. Many non-professional relationships are also defined by their non-sexual nature – for example, those between family members and certain kinds of friends. So in most cases where the complainant and defendant have a defined relationship at all, it will either make no difference to the reasonableness of the steps taken, or it will suggest that those steps were less reasonable than they might otherwise have been.

It is in the context of intimate relationships that one could most credibly argue that the defining norms make the need to ascertain consent to sexual touching less demanding or even non-existent. But, and this is the second point, there are relatively few cases in which the Crown has sought to prosecute defendants for sexually assaulting their long-term partners.

There are, however, at least two cases in which the significance of the defendant's marital relationship with the complainant has been discussed at length. Neither supports the conclusion that it has significance in itself. That is, for reasons I raised above, the appropriate conclusion: we cannot determine the norms constituting an intimate relationship simply by applying a label to it; nor can we determine whether or not the relationship is defined by mutuality and respect. Those questions must drive the inquiry. Ultimately, then, I enlist these cases to show that a doctrine of implied consent does not commit us to a result that is flatly at odds with our current approach to, and intuitions about, "reasonableness" in the context of section 273.2(b).

There are signals that relationship status can indeed make a difference to the reasonableness of the steps taken by the defendant. At the same time, there is clear confusion as to when and how it matters. In *V. (R.)*,[17] the trial judge remarked:

> [W]ithin the confines of a viable marriage, the Crown must prove beyond a reasonable doubt that the conduct of the accused was subjectively outside the norms of tolerated behaviour in that particular couple's sexual relationship within their marriage. In other words, it is my view that the Crown must establish not that the complainant said "no" on that particular occasion, but that in the context of the parties' entire marital relationship, and in the context of that particular situation, her saying "no" differed from the way they historically interacted for a sexual purpose and that the accused, thereby, should have known from such different behaviour that her "no" or her rejection of the accused's advances was different from the way the parties interacted sexually in the past.[18]

On this basis, the trial judge acquitted. The Crown appealed, arguing that "a criminal assault occurs whenever there is physical sexual touching of one partner by another in an on-going marital relationship without obtaining express consent in advance to the touching."[19] The summary conviction appeal judge, Thomas J., rejected the Crown's position as untenable, "erroneous in principle and ... offend[ing] ordinary common sense,"[20] and awarded costs against it.[21] The Ontario Court of Appeal, though it dismissed the appeal from Thomas J.'s decision, disagreed with his reasoning, as well as that of the trial judge. In an unpublished endorsement, the court stated:

> The trial judge and the summary conviction appeal judge made serious errors of law. On the complainant's story, the defence of mistaken belief in consent was not available. Merely because there was a viable marriage does not itself give rise to a defence of

mistaken belief in consent in the face of the complainant's unequivocal statements to the respondent that she was not consenting to further sexual relations. There was no burden on the Crown
to disprove the defence merely because the parties were married.
Nor could it be said that there could be any implied consent in
those circumstances.[22]

The court of appeal is quite right. The mere fact that the complainant
and defendant are married is neither here nor there. By itself, that does
not even give rise to a prima facie case that the defendant's belief in consent was normatively justifiable – i.e., reasonable. This question, as I have
said, cannot be resolved by looking at labels. It can be resolved only by
considering the norms governing the relationship between the complainant and defendant, whatever label we happen to apply to it.

At times, the trial judge in *V. (R.)* seems to make something very like
this point – he refers, after all, to "the norms of tolerated behaviour in
that particular couple's sexual relationship."[23] But consider the facts
of this case. The defendant and complainant had been having marital
trouble for a number of weeks. (Indeed, the complainant testified they
had been having "communication problems" for several years.)[24] They
were sleeping in different beds. The complainant suspected infidelity
on the part of the defendant. On recent prior occasions when the defendant had broached the subject of sex, the complainant was obviously
uninterested.

Under these circumstances, there is no reason to believe that their
relationship was defined by norms legitimizing sexual touching in the
absence of express authorization. At the very least, the trial judge appears to have treated the norms of the relationship as static – as though,
having once had such norms, they must persist over time. (That may be
the upshot of the trial judge's suggestion that one must look to the "entire
marital relationship.") But even if we suppose that the relationship between the complainant and defendant had ever been constituted by the
sort of norms capable of legitimizing the defendant's conduct, it would
be inappropriate to proceed on the basis that they are unchanging.[25]
Such an approach would be incompatible with respect for the complainant's sexual integrity, and would do nothing to advance her autonomy.

Both parties must be free to renegotiate the terms on which their relationship is conducted.

The limits of implied consent in the context of intimate relationships are further brought out in *R. v. T. (W.A.)*, a decision by Moreau J. of the Alberta Court of Queen's Bench.[26] In that case, the defendant was convicted of ten counts of sexual assault over an eighteen-month period. The complainant had been his wife at the time of the offences. The defendant argued that, on each occasion, he had an honest belief in consent. He placed a great deal of reliance on the suggestion that, in his sexual relationship with the complainant, he tended to initiate while she was typically passive, expressing her consent through "body language." In rejecting that claim, Moreau J. relied in part on out-of-court remarks from the defendant himself in which he described the sexual touching as "rape." She also rejected the defendant's claim that the complainant had communicated consent. In reaching that conclusion, Moreau J. pointed to several factors. Here, it is worth setting out Moreau J.'s reasoning at length:

> On [the defendant's] own testimony she was silent despite his
> questioning, "Does this feel good?" "Can I proceed?" He acknow-
> ledged in [out-of-court statements] that he was pressuring her
> to have sex. He also knew that she did not want to have sex in
> the majority of their encounters as he stated that he could count
> on one hand the number of times they had good sex during the
> period of the indictment and that she initiated sexual contact very
> infrequently. He stated that he had to learn her body because she
> didn't talk about what she liked and didn't like; he had to learn
> her body language and "learn intimately what her body language
> meant." He acknowledged however, that she was silent before and
> during the intercourse he characterized as "pity sex." Similarly, he
> stated that with respect to the "rape sex," her initial refusal would
> eventually be followed by consent *through her body language* ...
> [A]t one point in the spring of 2008 she started expressing her lack
> of consent in an aggressive fashion. I find in the context of their
> sexual relationship that the aggressive stance she adopted was
> consistent with a decision on her part that she would no longer

permit him to ignore her passive lack of response to his unwanted advances which were preceded by her verbal refusals to have sex.[27]

Under these circumstances, Moreau J. held, the defendant was at the very least reckless in proceeding as he did. In the picture painted throughout Moreau J.'s judgment, there is a striking lack of mutuality in the relationship between the defendant and complainant. On the findings reached by the trial judge, the defendant engaged in sexual touching even though he knew the complainant generally did not want him to touch her in that way. The fact that he regularly got away with behaving in this fashion in no way suggests there was a social norm legitimizing that conduct. Indeed, the very fact that the defendant referred to this kind of sexual conduct as "rape sex" indicates an awareness that what he was doing was illegitimate – that he was not approaching sex with his partner on equal terms, or from a place of loyalty. He was simply using the complainant as a means of gratifying his own sexual urges. We get no sense of the touching as anything other than instrumentalizing within Nussbaum's meaning of the term.

Moreau J. continued with these remarks:

> If an accused acting honestly perceives his sexual partner's conduct to be ambiguous or unclear, he or she must abstain or obtain clarification on the issue of consent. As in all cases, within the marital relationship the circumstances surrounding the allegations must be carefully scrutinized to determine whether the words or actions of the spouse could honestly have been misinterpreted as positive communications of consent. The existence of a marital relationship, however, does not entitle a spouse to assume consent unless otherwise advised.[28]

Janine Benedet, commenting on the decision, stated: "[T]he mere existence of ... a [spousal] relationship does not give an air of reality to ... [an honest belief in consent]. Rather, the accused must explain how the prior relationship lays a foundation for a belief in consent on the occasions at issue."[29] Both passages are quite right. Again, the fact that the defendant and complainant in *T. (W.A.)* were married is all but irrelevant. The question is whether their relationship was, by mutual consent, governed

IMPLIED CONSENT AND SEXUAL ASSAULT

by a set of norms capable of legitimizing the defendant's touching. It was not.

The Limits of the Legislative Debate

One looks in vain for any sign that Parliament meant to dictate how women exercised their sexual autonomy in the context of intimate relationships. Rather, four aspects of the legislative debate over Bill C-49 leap out. First, one of the central objects of the legislation was to enhance the sexual autonomy of women – protecting not only women's right to restrict sexual access but also their right to determine the shape of their sexual lives. Second, the emphasis was overwhelmingly on rape, not on "lesser" forms of non-consensual sexual touching. When relatively trivial forms of sexual touching were mentioned at all, they were dismissed as falling outside the practical scope of the offence of sexual assault – meaning that the consent provision was not intended to apply to them. Third, the stress was overwhelmingly on "date rape" and not on sexual touching within long-term intimate relationships. Finally, and closely tied to the first three points, there was considerable emphasis on the idea that Bill C-49 was not intended to fundamentally change the way in which sexual negotiations take place.

Bill C-49 and Sexual Autonomy

Introducing Bill C-49 for second reading, the minister of justice took the *Seaboyer* decision as her point of departure.[30] Kim Campbell observed that "[b]oth the majority of the Supreme Court of Canada and the dissenting opinion supported the underlying philosophy and aims of the [old section 276]."[31] She noted that, although section 276 "reached too far in its attempt to correct past wrongs," the *Seaboyer* majority had "recognized that sexual assault complainants must be protected, that improper fishing expeditions should be a thing of the past."[32] The need to provide "appropriate protection for the complainant, specifically in relation to the use of his or her sexual history" was "the driving force behind [Bill C-49]" – its "central feature."[33] Campbell described the effect of the sexual history provisions in these terms: "The proposed provision follows from the first principle outlined by the Supreme Court of Canada.

The fact that the complainant has engaged in other sexual activity with any person, including the accused, should not lead to the inference that the complainant is more likely to have consented to the sexual activity in question, nor should it lead to the inference that the complainant is less worthy of belief."[34]

In addressing the use of sexual history, the aim was to protect complainants from needlessly invasive and humiliating lines of questioning and make it less likely that stereotypes would illegitimately figure into the fact-finding process. Ultimately, the hope was that more victims of sexual assault would come forward, and that their rights would be vindicated. Thus, Campbell remarked: "[The sexual history provisions] are essential to protect victims from embarrassment, to preserve their privacy and dignity and to encourage their co-operation in prosecutions."[35] Moreover, the preamble to Bill C-49 included this passage: "Whereas the Parliament of Canada wishes to encourage the reporting of incidents of sexual violence or abuse, and to provide for the prosecution of offences within a framework of laws that are consistent with the principles of fundamental justice and that are fair to complainants as well as to accused persons."[36]

In one sense, then, the sexual history provisions looked backward – they offered support to women whose rights to sexual integrity and autonomy had already been violated. But they were not purely procedural in nature. They also reflected a substantive conviction about the nature of sexual consent in the law. After all, the claim by Campbell and others was not that evidence of sexual history was being withheld from criminal defendants in spite of its relevance to issues of consent, but that such evidence is not typically relevant in the first place. They echoed the point made in *Seaboyer* – i.e., that consent on prior occasions, in particular with third parties, should not be taken, at least as a matter of law, to tell us anything about an individual's willingness to engage in sexual activity in the here and now.

The reasons for taking this approach, as conveyed by Campbell, are closely tied to the value of sexual autonomy. Discussing the sexual history provisions, she stated: "All men, women and children must have autonomy over their own lives and more specifically, their bodies. They must have the right to make decisions about their lives including their sexual lives without the fear that those decisions will later be subject to unfair scrutiny and misinterpretation."[37] The fact that a woman's sexual choices could be later used against her, Campbell suggested, unfairly burdened her exercise of sexual autonomy. For women to have a genuine right to explore their sexuality, the law would need to combat stereotypes and prejudices that might otherwise chill its expression. That is an important point – all the more striking for being made by a minister of justice – for it underscores that rape shield legislation was designed not only to preserve the sexual integrity of women, narrowly understood, but also to advance their autonomy in the wider sense of that word. By giving women the assurance that their sexual choices could not be "unfair[ly] scrutin[ized] and misinterpret[ed]" at some point in the future, Parliament aimed to embolden them to exercise their autonomy. Unsurprisingly, the importance of autonomy loomed large in the minister of justice's discussion of the new definition of consent: "No one can deny that every person has the right to make decisions about their body, including whether or not to engage in sexual activity."[38]

The Emphasis on Rape

The concern among members of Parliament was not on non-consensual sexual touching tout court, but on sexual assault approaching the level of rape. Consider the comments of the Honourable Dawn Black, a prominent supporter of Bill C-49. On second reading, she stated:

Some men do feel threatened by this proposed law. As one male lawyer put it, he feels that the law makes seduction a crime. This particular comment is very instructive. What some men might call seduction many women know as rape. Men who respect women have nothing to fear in any shape or form from this law. *Only men who force themselves on women*, who do not care what women feel or think, *who think that they have some God-given right to have sex with any woman that they choose and at any time.* Those are the men who can be prosecuted under this law and it is about time.[39]

Shortly after, she said:

When a man forces his penis into a woman without her consent that is rape whether it is a teenager or an adult male. No one is ever going to be convicted for a kiss on the cheek. If cases involving penetration cannot even come to court we are fooling ourselves to think that someone might be convicted for something like kissing and hugging.

We must not forget that most sexual assaults are not reported including debilitating assaults. People who think that the courts will be full of kissing cases are attempting to ridicule a very, very serious matter.[40]

Black plainly contemplated that the offence of sexual assault, and the new consent provision she advocated, would be used only for especially grave forms of sexual assault – non-consensual sexual touching encompassing or approaching rape. Later, while the bill was in committee, she made this clear again. During an exchange with Philip Bryden and John Westwood, Black remarked: "I think when you made your presentation, a lot of what you said, a lot of the language you used, was very love-laden language. For instance you made comments about two people drunk, making love, but we're not talking about making love here; we're talking about sexual assault and rape. We're not talking about making love. I think that's really clear in the bill."[41] Bryden observed that Parliament is "defining what constitutes sexual assault" – that "sexual assault" is nothing more than a term of art, an empty vessel into which one could (in principle) pour any content one likes.[42] That being the case, he and Westwood suggested, Black and others could not simply stipulate that Bill C-49 would not cover lovemaking (whatever that means) or hand-holding. Without more fleshing out, the legislation could well cover more kinds of sexual touching than Black anticipated. She replied: "Are you saying to us that you think there are going to be charges laid under this legislation when someone holds hands?"[43] Other remarks are to similar effect.[44]

These remarks are telling. They suggest that, so far as at least some parliamentarians were concerned, the new definition of consent was not intended to extend to all forms of touching, even on the assumption that they could be construed as sexual. There was little drive to make this clear in the legislation because it was thought that prosecutorial or judicial discretion would resolve any potential overbreadth problems. This attitude is suggested in the comments of another member of the legislative committee, the Honourable Rob Nicholson: "My guess is that what would happen in the court is that there would be a higher standard – for holding someone's hand there wouldn't be a very high standard – that as the activity became more intimate, the courts would examine the facts to conclude whether there in fact was agreement or consent. So it might sort itself out, and I think that's what may happen in a number of these things."[45] Other comments likewise suggest that parliamentarians did not intend to craft a consent provision that required explicit, contemporaneous consent to all forms of sexual touching. The Honourable Mary Collins, minister responsible for the status of women, made this point quite clear during the second reading of the bill:

> Sexual assault means all sexual assaults that run from the near simple, if I can put it that way, sexual touching up to the more violent crimes of sexual assault and rape. There may be aspects of the law and procedure that are going to have to be thought through for all of the various types of sexual assault, not just rape.
>
> [Black] placed very heavy emphasis and appropriately so on the offence of rape/sexual assault that is the most serious, that is the most heinous, that is justifiably the major target of the Criminal Code. There are other sexual assault offences. I feel we have to make sure that when we deal with this bill that we keep in mind that we are dealing with all types of sexual offences. I have a feeling, as I read the bill, as I listen to colleagues, that maybe not all of that has been thought through.[46]

As we have seen, this problem was not addressed – but only, it seems, because it was understood that judges and the Crown would use their discretion to narrow the effective application of the law.

The Lack of Focus on Intimate Relationships

The discussion in the House of Commons hints that, at least so far as many of its members were concerned, Bill C-49 was primarily intended to address the problem of date rape – not to address how people involved in intimate relationships would govern their sexual lives. Black focused on criticisms that the bill would effectively criminalize "seduction."[47] There is nothing in her comments to suggest a preoccupation with relatively trivial sexual touching between long-term intimate partners. Indeed, she took the view that, practically speaking, acts of non-consensual "kissing and hugging" would be unlikely to be prosecuted at all.[48] This observation was not made by way of suggesting that they should be prosecuted, but rather to counter claims of overbreadth. During second and third reading of Bill C-49, various members of Parliament remarked upon the problem of date rape.[49] No one discussed how or whether the new law should apply in the context of intimate relationships.

We should keep in mind that parliamentarians often had a fuzzy, common-sense notion of sexual assault when we consider certain passages in the legislative debates and committee hearings. Toward the end of the legislative committee hearings, for example, there was some discussion as to whether there should be a special warning that consent could not be attributed or presumed on the basis of certain characteristics – i.e., "on the basis that they were persons of colour, or ... workers in the sex trade, or ... lesbians, homosexuals or disabled."[50] That motion was defeated in committee and again on the third reading.[51] This was (at least in part) out of concern that a provision that hived off some characteristics would inadvertently send the message that one could imply consent from others – particularly, marital status.[52] Nicholson remarked: "[I]f we say consent cannot be implied or presumed if you're in this particular group, are you suggesting that there is another category in which we might be able to presume or imply consent? For instance, do we say we imply or presume consent between married people necessarily?"[53] Later, Black expressed some doubts about removing the word "all" from section 273.2(b). She noted that "men who are accused of sexually assaulting women" might be able to argue that they had an honest but mistaken belief in consent merely because they had taken "a trivial reasonable step."[54] In making that point, Black observed that sexual assault complainants traditionally have not been "taken seriously by our criminal justice system," and explicitly pointed to the old marital rape exception.[55]

Some members of Parliament, offering support for Bill C-49, tied their endorsement to broader concerns about the perceived rise of casual sexual touching outside of intimate relationships. Collins, for example, expressed concern at the attitude of many teenage boys:

There were comments like "I want to have sex before I am 16." A lot of their lives seem to revolve around that and that was what was important to them.

It was not a meaningful relationship with young women. It was just sort of physical sex without thinking about the implications of that with a partner. Obviously we have to address those issues. We know that people have hormones when they grow up, but how do they direct those kinds of virtues in fair and productive relationships between young men and women?[56]

Rightly or wrongly, there is simply little to suggest parliamentarians were preoccupied with the sexual norms that govern intimate relationships.

The Conservative Bent of Bill C-49

Finally, there was repeated assurance given in Parliament that Bill C-49 did not purport to redefine intimate relationships in Canada. Introducing the bill at second reading, the minister of justice stated: "Consent is defined as the voluntary agreement of the complainant to engage in sexual activity. *This definition is the ordinary, common sense meaning of consent.* As a matter of law, conduct that falls short of a voluntary agreement is not consent."[57] These remarks exhibit a tension that remained unresolved throughout the debates on Bill C-49. Campbell wanted to present the bill as a transformative cultural moment in which the government purported to educate the public about the true meaning of consent. Certainly, many (though not all) of the witnesses who appeared before the Legislative Committee on Bill C-49 emphasized its educative role,[58] as did a few members of Parliament during the House debates.[50] But members of Parliament sometimes expressed skepticism at the idea that men and women would have serious difficulty adjusting to the new law, and some witnesses took the view that Bill C-49 was not coping with a problem of widespread ignorance so much as a problem of under-deterrence.[60] Campbell and others frequently insisted that the bill did nothing more than carry common-sense understandings of sexual consent into the criminal law. Appearing before the legislative committee, the minister of justice stated: "The bill does not seek to impose a new code of sexual morality on Canadian society. It does not seek to remake the dating habits and sexual relationships of Canadians. It does not, for example, require that consent be overt, unequivocal, or given in advance nor does it outlaw sex after a few glasses of wine. Bill C-49 is intended to reflect Canadian sexual reality."[61] She echoed these sentiments during the third reading of the bill,[62] as did others.[63] During the committee hearings, many of the witnesses' remarks were made in relation to the third part of Bill C-49 – that affecting the defence of honest but mistaken belief in consent. As the bill was originally worded, criminal defendants wanting to use the defence would have needed to show that they had taken "all" reasonable steps to ascertain the existence of consent.[64] This gave rise to considerable debate at the committee stage over whether the bill would impose criminal liability for negligent sexual touching, or would shift the onus of proof to the defendant.[65] It does not much matter for my purposes whether there was any merit to these arguments. What matters is the mere fact that they were made; that they reflected a concern that Bill C-49 was intended to radically change social norms governing sexual negotiations between men and women, and that "slow learners" would be convicted on the basis that they were insufficiently enlightened.[66] Notably, Don Stuart argues that section 273.2(b), as it was then worded, might offend section 7 of the Charter by making the offence of sexual assault something other than one of subjective mens rea.[67] To avoid that kind of constitutional problem, he suggests, Parliament would do better to create a separate offence of "negligent sexual assault."[68] Ultimately, the word "all" was removed precisely to circumvent some of these objections and concerns.[69] At the same time, Stuart's suggestion to create a second-tier offence of negligent sexual assault was rejected for the very reason used to justify discarding the offence of rape ten years before: the concern that people would not take seriously the need to take greater care.[70] It would continue to fall to prosecutors and sentencing judges to distinguish between different levels of moral blameworthiness.[71]

Summary

When we examine the legislative debates, we get no sense that Parliament turned its mind to the circumstances under which the state should block women from making certain choices vis-á-vis how to govern their sexual lives. It was primarily concerned with stranger and acquaintance rape – i.e., with cases in which there was no plausible basis for inferring that the complainant had adopted a set of norms by which the defendant could legitimately engage in sexual touching in the absence of contemporaneous and express consent. In these contexts, it is clear that the defendant's belief in consent must be based solely on myths and stereotypes about women's sexual proclivities generally. To the extent that parliamentarians considered sexual assault in the context of intimate relationships, it appears they were preoccupied with penetration – with the very kind of intrusive sexual touching that, as I discussed in chapter 6, even a modified defence of implied consent would rule out. Quite simply, the legislative debates on Bill C-49 do not state whether the language of section 273.1(1) necessarily precludes a modified defence of implied consent.

Implied Consent by Another Name?

I began this chapter with a quotation by Boyle. She has wrestled with the idea of implied consent in the sexual assault arena more than any other Canadian scholar over the last thirty years. Her position is instructive. After the 1983 reforms, she expressed uncertainty as to whether the courts would recognize the doctrine of implied consent in the context of sexual assault, and expressed some misgivings about its extension.[72] She did not, however, claim that its use was inherently problematic:

> It will be very interesting if the courts do develop the notion of implied consent. That development will tell us a great deal about "societal" views on what is supposed to be acceptable sexual behaviour. This will be very treacherous ground. A narrow doctrine may have to develop, based possibly on each particular situation, but there is surely no room for a general rule that we all consent to some level of sexual touching, no matter how prevalent it has been in the past. It is vital that consent either be expressed or implied from facts that are present in a particular context rather than any assumptions about what is acceptable.[73]

Though Boyle argues that the doctrine of implied consent should not be used to give men any general right of sexual access to women, she recognizes that it could be useful in "particular contexts."[74]

Later, in a paper co-written with John McInnes, Boyle argues that sexual touching invariably requires active consent.[75] The footnote in which they develop this argument, though, is intriguing. Though they claim that active consent is required the moment that touching becomes sexual within the meaning of *Chase*, and that "'doing nothing' can never amount to consent," they also argue that "it is of course true that the means by which consent is communicated and the ease with which it is communicated will vary from case to case."[76] They remark:

> For example, the rubbing of the back of the complainant and the ensuing touching in *R.J.S.* is an entirely different thing than the same activity in the context of a sexual relationship of long standing: in the former context [touching] *probably reaches the Chase threshold at an earlier stage than it does in the latter*. If violation of sexual integrity is seen as the threshold test, there is increasing room for subtlety in the form by which the voluntary agreement to engage in sex can be expressed between two partners as their relationship becomes a long standing one. In our view the [Criminal Code] provisions do not import into the bedrooms of the nation the necessity of a cynical contractual regulation of sexuality in the form of written agreements, as certain commentators have fatuously suggested. They simply require a voluntary agreement.[77]

The suggestion, here, is that the relationship context is one factor that should determine whether we regard touching as sexual in the first place, and that there need not be active consent for every instance of intimate but non-sexual touching. In other words, one may give implied consent to touching that would in other circumstances satisfy the *Chase* test so long as it occurs in the context of a long-term intimate relationship. For all practical purposes, this will often be the same as arguing that the doctrine of implied consent can apply to sexual touching. Instead of arguing about the scope of implied consent, we are now arguing about the meaning of "sexual touching."

Boyle returns to this point in a subsequent (post-*Ewanchuk*) commentary on *V. (R.)*: "[M]any touchings in relationships may not be sexual at all, and so the doctrine of implied consent could apply. One can think of many examples: hugs, holding hands, comforting touches, emergency first aid, grabbing a spouse out of the way of approaching traffic."[78] With the possible exception of hugs, the examples hardly suggest that the sort of touching I described in the introduction to this book might be captured by implied consent. Intriguingly, though, this discussion occurs after Boyle acknowledges that the reasoning in *Ewanchuk* might require the conviction of "a wife who kisses her sleeping husband on the lips before going off to work."[79] She mentions no other point that could conceivably prevent such an absurd result. Though Boyle again expressly (and emphatically) rejects the idea of implied consent to sexual touching, the example she uses in that context is one of a man who approaches his wife from behind and rubs her breasts in order to determine whether she is interested in intercourse.[80] Without expressing a view on whether this kind of behaviour necessarily falls outside the scope of implied consent even if we recognize its application to sexual touching, it is telling that Boyle here uses an example that is less evocative of tenderness and affection than at least some of those I used in the introduction.

To some extent, Boyle provides an answer to the problem I raised in the introduction. But taking her approach seems to require us to revisit the Supreme Court's decision in *Chase*. There, the court made it quite clear that touching may be sexual whether or not the defendant's motive was sexual gratification.[81] On that reasoning, it does not obviously matter whether the touching was intended to test the waters or merely to display affection or playfulness. It is likely for this reason that we tend to see few cases in which a serious issue arises as to the sexual nature of the touching in question.[82] Indeed, one might speculate that it was precisely to avoid it becoming an issue that the court in *Chase* rejected an approach that would put the defendant's motives at the centre of the actus reus inquiry. It is therefore far from clear that Boyle's solution is any less radical than anything I propose.

Conclusion: What Does Implied Consent Really Entail?

Insofar as the doctrine of implied consent applies to the normative sexual arrangements in an intimate relationship at all, we may say that there is indeed a limited right of sexual access granted to the partners in it. But it is a right conferred by the parties themselves, and not by the doctrine.

The doctrine, properly understood, merely allows the parties to intimate relationships to authorize one another to engage in certain kinds of sexual touching in the absence of contemporaneous consent. It does not require any sort of authorization. The marital rape exemption, by contrast, proceeded on the basis that a woman necessarily consented to any and all sexual touching by her husband, no matter how instrumentalizing, for the duration of their marriage.[83] It effectively denied women's right to decide how they wanted to be touched sexually by their partners. Interpreted in light of its purpose – namely, to enhance sexual autonomy and expand the range of options that women have in deciding how to conduct their sexual lives without committing them to any particular sexual arrangement – the doctrine of implied consent simply bears no resemblance to the marital rape exemption.

Here, though, I want to pose a problem – one that has quietly loomed over my analysis and will now drive the remainder of the book. So far, I have noted the dearth of prosecutions – still less, successful prosecutions – of men who have engaged in non-consensual sexual touching of their intimate partners. In making the case for implied consent, my focus has been on instances where the sexual touching would strike many readers as relatively trivial – a kiss on the cheek of the sleeping spouse, an unexpected squeeze of a thigh under a restaurant table, an unexpected hug from a partner. I use these examples in an appeal to readers' intuitions. These are cases, I have supposed, in which readers can most plausibly assume an acceptance of sexual norms in which the various forms of touching described are legitimate even in the absence of contemporaneous consent.

But my claim has not been that people in spousal or dating relationships must give implied consent to these forms of sexual touching – or any others. What makes a relationship sexually intimate is not the fact that it is spousal or has any other label attached to it, but the set of normative arrangements and expectations that actually govern it. That is a point to which we must be continually alert, because – and here is the problem I want to pose – intuitions are not necessarily trustworthy.[84] Recall the observation I made in chapter 2: the point of the 1983 legislative reforms was, to some extent, to challenge existing social norms concerning how men and women should sexually interact. "Normal" rules of sexual engagement, reformers argued, entailed violence against women – precisely because, in our culture, to be a woman is to be some-one to whom it is appropriate to behave in a sexually aggressive fash-ion. Likewise, to be a wife or a girlfriend is to assume a social role in which one is expected to sexually satisfy one's partner. Consider this passage from the trial judge's ruling in *V. (R.)*: "[W]hen parties get mar-ried, they, by the very nature of the relationship, are consenting to en-gaging in sexual intercourse and consummating the marriage. Even after consummation, a marriage continues to imply that parties have joined together for various purposes including that of retaining or continuing their sexual relationship. A husband and wife's sexual relationship is just one means through which they communicate in the marriage."[85] There is ample evidence that, well after *Ewanchuk*, many members of the public, the police, lawyers, and judges continue to believe that a viable spousal relationship must involve some form of sexual touching – and of a par-ticularly invasive form.[86] Quite simply, there is good reason to believe that non-contemporaneous sexual touching is not taken as seriously when it occurs in the context of spousal or dating relationships.[87]

That's a problem – a big one. A sexual assault is no less an assault because it occurs in the context of a spousal relationship. It is no less a public wrong worthy of the criminal law's attention. I have tried to show that recognizing implied consent – with all the limits I have pro-posed built into it – in the sexual sphere would better reflect the ani-mating purposes of the offence of sexual assault. But if doing so simply reinforces the idea that men are entitled to sexual access to their wives and girlfriends just because they are their wives and girlfriends, then one may well wonder if I have articulated a sufficiently compelling reason to resuscitate the doctrine. If members of the public, the police, lawyers, and judges are going to assume that spouses or partners are in intimate relationships, and that these relationships presumptively entitle men to unlimited sexual access to their partners, then the doctrine will simply put women at risk. If they are too quick to see women exercising their voices in creating sexual norms, or too slow to spot instrumentalization when it takes place, then the doctrine will wind up effectively licensing too many wrongs. Is it worth it?

Maybe, in short, a degree of overbreadth is necessary to make the of-fence of sexual assault serve the purposes for which it was intended. I address this question in the next two chapters.

CHAPTER 9

The Value of Assurance

Introduction

I have argued that there is room to recognize a defence of implied consent in the sexual assault context provided we acknowledge two important provisos. First, the rules of at least some practices – in particular, intimate relationships and partnerships – are to be determined by the parties themselves rather than imposed upon them as objectively definitive of, or essential to, those practices. Second, there must be mutuality in something like Martha Nussbaum's sense of the word – a contextualized inquiry in which we must assess degrees of voice and harm in the sexual norms adopted by the parties. In the absence of those conditions, the suggestion that the defence of implied consent should be recognized in the sexual assault context loses its traction.

But these concessions will not satisfy everyone. The suggestion that a defence of implied consent could be available under any conditions will alarm many. Even giving defendants the opportunity to argue that a complainant gave implied consent to sexual touching is unacceptable, many will claim, as it badly undermines the assurance that women have (or should have) that they will not be subjected to non-consensual touching. Many may worry that leaving men an obvious loophole to exploit risks sending the message that they may treat women as sexual objects, and raises the fear that women in intimate relationships will again be treated as their partners' sexual property.

Now, the mere fact that some men wrongly exploit a defence, using it to earn an acquittal to which they are not entitled, does not mean that the law itself treats their conduct as permissible. But it is probably too much to expect the public to think in a nuanced way about the difference between permission and failed or incomplete enforcement.[1] We need to assume a degree of sloppy thinking. In any case, the fact that some men will game the law is a reasonable concern for women. They are entitled to proceed on the basis that others will not violate their sexual integrity – that they can explore the limits of their freedom, investigating opportunities for sexual and personal fulfillment, without trading away the law's protection. They are entitled to a degree of assurance that they will not be treated as sexual instruments, and that the law will vindicate them if they are.

At the same time, we need to remember – returning to the arguments in chapters 5 and 6 – that the existence of mutuality in a relationship makes an important difference to the moral and legal acceptability of sexual practices in which non-contemporaneous consent is regarded as legitimate. That a legal rule might be exploited by the undeserving does not change the fact that it also serves a genuine social purpose. Does the need for assurance justify the criminalization of objectifying courses of action among those involved in intimate relationships defined by mutuality? In this and the next chapter, I consider the significance of assurance as a justification for overbroad laws. In this chapter, I show that the need for assurance provides a valid basis for state legislative action. But, as I argue in the next, it does not follow that criminal offences, likes sexual assault, should be overbroad. Rather, it shows only that there should be substantive and procedural rules that allow the law to weed out undeserving criminal defendants without sending distorted messages to the public about the boundaries of wrongful conduct.

Waldron and MacKinnon; Hate Speech and Pornography[2]

In *Political Liberalism*, John Rawls described a "well-ordered society."[3] He states:

> To say that a society is well-ordered conveys three things: first …
> it is a society in which everyone accepts, and knows that everyone
> else accepts, the very same principles of justice; and second … its
> basic structure – that is, its main political and social institutions

and how they fit together as one system of cooperation – is publicly known, or with good reason believed, to satisfy these principles. And third, its citizens have a normally effective sense of justice and so they generally comply with society's basic institutions, which they regard as just. In such a society the publicly recognized conception of justice establishes a shared point of view from which citizens' claims on society can be adjudicated.[4]

Why is it not enough that "everyone accepts" the same principles of justice? Why is it also necessary that everyone "knows that everyone else accepts" those principles? Because, in planning our day-to-day affairs, it is often important to know whether others will treat us as equals. Even if the law formally permits an individual to engage in a certain course of action – to participate in the commercial or political sphere – the fact that executive or private actors might have different conceptions of equal treatment can burden the exercise of that freedom to the point where it is worthless or illusory. A Muslim person walking through airport security may receive no special scrutiny. A police officer who sees a black man driving an expensive automobile at night may not check his license plates for outstanding warrants. A hotel clerk may not refuse to check a gay or lesbian couple into a room. That one happens to have been treated with respect on one or another occasion does not change the fact that Muslims have special reasons to dread air travel, or that young men of colour must watch their step around police officers in a way that white people do not – that they must bear psychic costs not borne by others. It is, then, not enough that everyone is treated with dignity. They must be able to rely on such treatment on a day-to-day basis.

Jeremy Waldron draws extensively upon Rawls's discussion of the well-ordered society, and the importance of assurance, in his defence of laws prohibiting group libel.[5] To be full participants in a liberal democratic society, he argues, individuals must have some assurance that they have the basic social standing to engage in activities that will allow them to flourish and thrive. They must be confident that they can find meaningful work, get an education, seek high office or otherwise participate in the political sphere, honour their spiritual and family commitments – or do any of the other things that make a life fulfilling – and that they will not be treated as presumptively less worthy or deserving simply by virtue of their membership in a racial, religious, or ethnic group.

Waldron argues at length that people in a liberal democratic society cannot have the assurance that they will be treated with dignity if the physical landscape implies that their social standing is a matter for public debate. A billboard or pamphlet or full-page newspaper ad suggesting that Muslims are inherently committed to violence, or claiming that Aboriginal people should be kept out of predominantly white neighbourhoods because of the crime they would bring, or arguing that gay men should be barred from public schools because they are inclined to practice paedophilia, does not simply state an idea that can be answered with more speech. By affirming that they are not alone, such expressive acts embolden bigots to act on those views, and to present them as one of several equally valid ideological perspectives. Engaging racists or homophobes in debate does not resolve that problem, since doing so only presents their view as sufficiently reasonable to be taken seriously. Indeed, a virulent racist or homophobe may want to provoke a debate, if only to create the impression that it is perfectly normal to ask whether Muslim or homosexual people are sufficiently human to deserve the complete range of human rights. To an individual Muslim or gay person, just having that question on the table undermines the assurance that he or she will be treated like a social equal.

The way a society looks, then, does not just reflect or express its political health – it determines it. We do not need to wait and see whether a billboard or poster libelling a vulnerable group moves someone to discriminate against a member of that group before deciding whether its presence makes our society less just. We do not need to ask whether it reflects the bigoted opinions of many or only a few. A society heavily decorated with billboards and posters libelling vulnerable groups is less just, all other things being equal, merely because they are there.

On this point, Waldron says, Catharine MacKinnon's powerful arguments against pornography are instructive. She has long argued that pornography presents women as mere objects to be used for men's sexual gratification, and in doing so reinforces the way gender is socially constructed in our culture. The problem is not simply that pornography causes men to engage in individual acts of sexual violence.

Rather, MacKinnon claims, it pollutes the air we breathe, subtly (or not-so-subtly) leading us to think about women in ways that undermine their confidence in being treated as equals.[6] In doing so, it makes our society less just and more "disordered." Waldron suggests that hate speech can have much the same effect.

A recurring theme in MacKinnon's work is that pornography informs and reinforces gender norms by eroticizing female submission and passivity and sending the message that women exist as mere instruments to be used for male sexual gratification – and that for this reason it should be prohibited. Likewise, in *Butler*,[7] the Supreme Court of Canada suggested that material would be regarded as "obscene" within the meaning of section 163(8) of the Criminal Code, where it causes "harm" – meaning that "it predisposes persons to act in an anti-social manner as, for example, the physical or mental mistreatment of women by men."[8] The need to assure women that they will not be treated merely as instruments for men's sexual gratification was regarded as a sufficient basis for criminalizing certain kinds of conduct, even though doing so limited Charter-protected freedoms.

Waldron, too, concludes that the need to assure vulnerable groups that they will be treated with equal concern and respect can justify the use of the criminal law.[9] He refers to this passage from Rawls's *A Theory of Justice*: "[E]ven in a well-ordered society the coercive powers of government are to some degree necessary for the stability of social cooperation. For although men know that they share a common sense of justice and that each wants to adhere to the existing arrangements, they may nevertheless lack full confidence in one another ... [T]he existence of penal machinery serves as men's security to one another."[10] Leaving aside whether the coercive threat is credible, the substantive criminal law serves a valuable expressive function that can help to stabilize the liberal orientation of the community.[11] Waldron remarks: "[O]ne would expect that expressive function to be at the fore in a well-ordered society, particularly in connection with the public and visible assurance of just treatment that a society is supposed to provide to all of its members."[12]

There is some disagreement as to whether the sort of hate speech laws that Waldron is keen to defend would be adequate in providing the assurance and stability that the well-ordered society requires. Nussbaum draws upon Rawls as support for her more radical discussion of "political emotions."[13] She argues that it is not enough for a society committed to justice to bar people from libelling groups – it must encourage and foster emotions of love and compassion. Only this, Nussbaum claims, will give the well-ordered society "stability" – it will otherwise dissolve as people gradually lose confidence in their fellow citizens' commitment to equality values.[14] This view goes well beyond that expressed by Waldron, who is readier to rely on legal rights to guarantee equal treatment.[15] These two accounts, however, have much in common (on this point at least). Both take the view that it is not enough for the state to stand aside and allow individuals to libel vulnerable groups in the name of free speech – to simply protect the "negative liberty" of citizens.[16] It must also create and preserve conditions under which they reasonably feel free to exercise their autonomy.[17]

Brudner on Real Autonomy; Raz and the Hounded Woman

Alan Brudner likewise argues that it is not enough for the liberal state to protect negative liberty – in his words "formal agency."[18] It is, to be sure, important to protect citizens' ability to choose how to live and act.[19] But it is not sufficient. To borrow Brudner's example, one could choose to make a slave of oneself.[20] This would be a decidedly impoverished kind of freedom. If we truly take freedom seriously – if we want people to treat themselves as ends – we must insist on something more than the preservation of their ability to enslave themselves. We must also insist on the state protecting "real autonomy." On this model, "[f]reedom ... consists in actualizing the agent's potential for self-determination."[21] It falls to the state to protect those "agency goods" that are necessary for "realizing the agent's potential for acting from self-authored ends."[22] This means, among other things, guaranteeing life, bodily integrity, property ownership, an impartial administration of justice, and "laws and public services ordered to health, safety, and insurance against misfortune."[23] The state must protect "positive liberty."[24]

In a telling passage, Brudner remarks: "[I]f I am faced with a choice between death by starvation or stealing, any choice I make will exercise my capacity for freely choosing ends [formal agency], for it can always be said that I could have chosen otherwise than I did. But my choice will fail to realize my potential for acting from self-authored ends because the only available options are those that have been imposed on me by circumstances and that I would not choose were I empirically able to set ends for myself."[25] His point is straightforward enough. A person forced by circumstance to continually avoid one threat after another is not in a position to make effective use of her autonomy. She is precluded from pursuing life plans that she can be said to "own" in any meaningful sense.[26] Joseph Raz famously makes a similar observation in *The Morality of Freedom*, using the following thought experiment: "A person finds herself on a small desert island. She shares the island with a fierce carnivorous animal which perpetually hunts for her. Her mental stamina, her intellectual ingenuity, her will power and her physical resources are taxed to their limits by her struggle to remain alive. She never has a chance to do or even to think of anything other than how to escape from the beast."[27] Raz takes it as obvious that "the Hounded Woman" lacks an autonomous life. In explaining why, he notes: "All her choices are potentially horrendous in their consequences. If she ever puts one foot wrong she will be devoured by the beast."[28] In order to have real autonomy, she must have the opportunity to choose her ends under conditions of relative serenity, without fear that every misstep will be catastrophic. She must have the assurance that she will be buffered against, as it were, the slings and arrows of outrageous fortune.

For both Raz and Brudner, real autonomy is "a kind of achievement."[29] To have "self-authored ends," one needs a range of options.[30] That, in turn, requires one to "live[] in circumstances where acceptable alternatives are present."[31] Inasmuch as real autonomy is something of intrinsic value, so is having a wide variety of paths from which to choose, and the freedom to abandon one for another. Living in a tolerant society, then, is inherently good.[32] It is, moreover, a public good, inasmuch as (a) if any one person is to enjoy its advantages, then all must enjoy them; and (b) its advantages are "non-rivalrous" in the sense that one person's enjoyment of them does not diminish their availability for others.[33]

Raz does not say that the status of a good as a public good depends on the extent to which individuals subjectively enjoy the advantages from it. "[T]he degree to which they benefit," he says, "depends on their character, interests, and dispositions, and cannot directly be controlled by others."[34] Like Brudner, Raz proceeds on the basis that whether or not real autonomy exists is an objective question – not one that can be resolved simply by asking whether a person "feels" insecure and so decides not to pursue opportunities.[35] The question is whether one would *reasonably* feel vulnerable enough to treat certain courses of action as effectively foreclosed. Ramsay and others – notably, Jennifer Nedelsky – take the view that all people have "vulnerable autonomy."[36] But even if we disagree with that view, it surely is reasonable for members of historically disadvantaged and vulnerable groups to require a degree of assurance before exploring certain avenues. This may not make assurance itself a public good, because it is arguably a good that redounds upon individuals rather than the collective. It is, however, closely wrapped up with what makes a tolerant society worth having.[37] And so Waldron can plausibly make the argument that "[a] well-ordered society ... has a systemic and structural interest in provision of this public good – that is, in the general and diffuse furnishing of this assurance and the recognition of the basic dignity on which it is predicated."[38]

Four Defences of Overbreadth

Though people, particularly women, need some assurance that their sexual integrity will not be violated, many intuit that they also need some assurance that they can participate in social and sexual practices in which it is possible to surrender control. It seems inappropriate to define sexual assault in such a way that such practices are forbidden or impossible. The offence definition must recognize at least the possibility of implied consent. Otherwise, it will be overbroad – in the moral or political sense, if not the constitutional sense. That, at any rate, is what I have hinted at throughout this book.

But perhaps overbreadth is inevitable or necessary – or, to put the matter another way, perhaps it is impossible to craft a law that manages to both protect women and free them to explore sexual possibilities. By carving out a doctrine of implied consent, one could argue, we would create a new defence for those accused of sexual assault. It would allow such defendants to gain an acquittal even where the Crown proves that there was no (*Ewanchuk*) consent. Even if one accepts that the norms constituting a given intimate relationship are capable of justifying sexual touching in the absence of contemporaneous consent, there is no guarantee that implied consent will be argued only by deserving defendants.

Some defendants will attempt to use the defence even though it does not apply to their cases, and perhaps in full awareness of this fact. They will, we might say, attempt to game the law. Moreover, the risk that certain defendants and classes of defendant – notably, those intimately involved with complainants – will argue implied consent may dissuade police officers from investigating allegations of sexual assault, and may encourage Crown prosecutors not to lay charges in the first place. All this, one could credibly argue, will undermine the assurance that the offence of sexual assault can meaningfully protect women's sexual integrity.

The problem can be traced back to a theme that runs through this book: context sensitivity. The case for implied consent, I have argued, rests on the significance of affectionate or playful sexualized touching in the context of ongoing intimate relationships, and the understanding that this touching need not be objectifying in a morally problematic sense. These two points are arguably linked: the fact that touching occurs against a backdrop of mutual love and respect, Nussbaum claims, is a factor to consider when determining whether it is instrumentalizing. But how would the Crown prove beyond a reasonable doubt that the defendant and complainant were not involved in an ongoing relationship or that the touching in question was not driven by the desire simply to use another for sexual gratification?

It is a legitimate concern. The objectification inquiry requires a great deal of nuance and context sensitivity.[39] It requires us to pay close attention to, among other things, the background motivations of the person engaging in the touching, the relationship between the parties, and the attitude one has to the other's individuality. The Crown may not be well placed to adduce evidence on such matters. These difficulties of proof might allow those who engage in objectifying acts of sexual touching to avail themselves of the doctrine of implied consent.[40]

This argument takes on added force when we remember the observation in chapter 1 that the Crown tends not to prosecute those involved in intimate partnerships for what we might loosely describe as harmless sexual touching. The argument I am making in this book rests on the expressive function of the substantive criminal law – on the sort of message that the law sends to those involved in intimate partnerships when it denies that consent can ever be implied. Perhaps there are more urgent concerns; in particular, the fact that women are daily subjected to acts of sexual violence – violations of rights that may never find vindication in the criminal courts.

Given that exercises of police and Crown discretion already ensure that innocent persons will not be prosecuted or convicted, and that legislative recognition of a doctrine of implied consent would give undeserving defendants a weapon to exploit, one could argue that it is better to focus on protecting sexual integrity. Overbreadth, on this view, is unproblematic or even desirable in the sexual assault context.

This kind of argument has been made in a number of forums. In the remainder of this section, I focus on the arguments made by Cheryl Hanna, Elaine Craig, John Gardner and Stephen Shute, and Samuel Buell.

Cheryl Hanna: "Sex Is Not a Sport"

Hanna, writing about sadomasochism, has questioned the appropriateness of importing consent frameworks from the sporting context into the sexual sphere.[41] She observes that the notion of implied consent emerged out of the conviction that men should be allowed to engage in pursuits in which "manly" aggression could be given controlled expression.[42] Hanna notes: "The law clearly distinguished between those contexts in which men competed to enhance their manliness and those contexts in which their aggression went unchecked, or inspired runaway passion by the parties or observers."[43] The line between "civilized masculinity" and unchecked or unregulated violence, though, has shifted over time to reflect changes in social norms as to the circumstances under which aggression is acceptable. The trend, Hanna observes, has been "to confine the use of physical force to highly regulated contexts."[44]

Hanna does not object to physical aggression in itself. She objects to consent frameworks that license physical aggression in contexts where it is unregulated.[45] She writes:

> By limiting consensual violence to activities that take place within a regulated environment, the law not only serves the practical purpose of reducing injury, but it also theoretically shifts cultural norms of masculinity. There are no referees in a bar room brawl, no code of conduct, and no crowd control. Men can no longer use weapons, unless they wear protective gear. And women can now

get in the game. We find far less social value in violent physical competition than we did when dueling was legal, and it is no longer a manly duty to kill or be killed outside of the context of war. Although many argue that we are mired in a cult of violence, the law has at least served as a symbolic and practical check on natural human aggression in general, and violent male competition, in particular.[46]

Against this background, Hanna resists the suggestion that consent frameworks borrowed from the sporting context should be imported into the sexual arena. To do so, she argues, "would be to reverse the trend to confine the use of physical force to highly regulated contexts."[47] It would have "the unintended consequence of allowing people, mostly men, to use violence to satiate their sexual desires, redefining civilized masculinity within a sexual context."[48]

Again, Hanna does not suggest that physical aggression is inherently bad. Indeed, she explicitly expresses "ambivalence" about her conclusion.[49] Hanna acknowledges that, by restricting consent in the sexual sphere, the law effectively limits women's sexual autonomy: "[T]he law limits women's pursuit of pleasure through pain, thus prescribing normative behaviors that can be paternalistic and repressive. The current doctrine of consent assumes that no reasonable woman would or should consent to sexual activity that involves violent domination, just as it once assumed women had no right to play sports."[50] Hanna is writing about sadomasochistic sex in particular – suggesting that her concerns are only amplified when one adopts a model of consent in the sexual sphere that precludes much more than "pleasure from pain." She rejects transplanting the sporting model of consent not because she regards the loss of sexual autonomy as harmless, but because doing so would present too great a risk of undeserving defendants relying upon implied consent as a means of escaping criminal liability. She states:

> Would allowing consent in the s/m context undermine sexual
> equality? The law is intended to prevent the powerful from hurting
> the powerless; by criminalizing s/m that results in injury, the law
> arguably protects masochistic women from sadistic men who
> injure them in the course of non-consensual sexual relations,

effectively eliminating the "she likes it rough" defense. Thus, the law imposes normative standards of sexual conduct on men that are non-violent and non-dominating, again, civilized masculinity.[51]

Ultimately, Hanna rests her case on the need for overbreadth. Yes, she says, we interfere with women's sexual autonomy when we deny them the legal right to consent to certain kinds of sexual touching. But we could not recognize such a right to consent without giving those accused of sexual violence access to a defence that they could exploit – even when consent was not given. Since there is no way to ensure that men and women play by the rules in the sexual sphere, it is better, all things considered, to restrict the availability of consent altogether.

Elaine Craig: The Need for Over-Inclusiveness

Craig, in a recent paper, also makes this kind of argument.[52] She agrees with Nussbaum that an inquiry into the wrongfulness of sexual acts must be highly contextualized. It is, for example, no good to claim that sado-masochistic sex, or sex involving unconscious participants, necessarily violates sexual integrity or instrumentalizes one or both parties.[53] Taking that approach only reinforces a single set of sexual norms at the expense of individuals' sexual autonomy. At the same time, though, Craig insists that the criminal law should not require or permit a contextualized, case-by-case inquiry into whether certain sexual activities are morally acceptable. It would, for example, be wrong for the law to permit the sexual penetration of unconscious women, leaving it up to the individual factfinder to determine whether it involved wrongful objectification in a particular case. That, Craig argues, would leave too many women at risk of being raped, given the proliferation of pernicious gender norms in our culture. By foreclosing this kind of argument, one opens up the possibility that morally innocent defendants will be convicted. But, she concludes, this is simply the sort of Hobson's Choice that the law regularly confronts: whether to assure women that it will protect them, or to impose criminal sanctions only on conduct that is morally blameworthy on its own terms. It cannot do both.

According to this argument, although the offence of sexual assault is targeted at certain kinds of wrongful objectification, it must incidentally attack non-problematic behaviour in order to effectively hit the target. A (perhaps large) amount of overbreadth is necessary for the law to serve its various functions.

John Gardner and Stephen Shute's Modified Harm Principle

To a point, we can see the defensibility of overbreadth in Gardner and Shute's discussion of rape. As I discussed earlier, Gardner and Shute produced a thought experiment in which an unconscious woman was raped and never discovered that the violation had taken place.[54] The point of the experiment is to show that the core wrongness of rape does not lie in the harm it produces, but in the fact that the victim was treated as nothing more than an instrument of sexual gratification. In part, the experiment suggests a problem with the harm principle – it neglects the fact that acts can be criminally wrongful without producing any clear harm. But Gardner and Shute proceed to suggest that, even if we accept the harm principle, it does not preclude the state from criminalizing the "pure case of rape":

> [I]f the act in this case were not criminalized, then, assuming at least partial efficacy on the part of the law, people's rights to sexual autonomy would more often be violated. This would be a harm, not only to those people (if they were conscious and became aware of the rape), but also to a broader constituency of people (in our culture mainly women) whose lives would be then be even more blighted than at present by violations of their right to sexual autonomy, and, more pervasively still, by their justifiable fear of violations of their right to sexual autonomy. These blights are harms which the legal prohibition of rape, if it is functioning properly, helps to reduce. For the purpose of the harm principle that is all that is needed. There is no need to show, in addition, that a given rape caused, or was likely to cause, harm.[55]

Gardner and Shute claim that, even if a course of action is not in itself harmful, the harm principle allows it to be criminalized so long as other harms would result if it was not.[56] Non-consensual sexual penetration, on Gardner and Shute's view, can be harmless, and yet the fact that it is harmless does not provide an answer to charges that one has engaged in criminal wrongdoing. This is because we need to provide assurance to women that their sexual autonomy will not be violated – that they will not be treated as mere instruments of sexual gratification – and to that end will not allow claims of harmlessness to rebut allegations of rape in particular cases.

Now, although the harm principle is typically invoked in discussions of overcriminalization, it seems that what we in fact have here is really a defence of overbreadth.[57] Overcriminalization occurs when the state targets conduct that is not wrongful, or that is not the sort of wrong the criminal law should address, or that is already targeted by a pre-existing prohibition.[58] Overbreadth exists when the state targets conduct that is properly criminalized but does so with an offence defined in such a way that it will also catch other conduct.[59] Gardner and Shute plainly defend overbreadth. Even as they assume for the sake of argument that the pure case of rape is not harmful, they never doubt that rape generally is. To effectively address that harm, they argue, it would be at least open to the state to define the offence of rape in such a way that it covered the pure case as well – thereby dissuading those who would try to exploit a narrow definition.

Samuel Buell on Overbreadth and the Bad Man

Buell is much more explicit in defending overbreadth. It may be, he observes, too easy for offenders to evade sanctions for violating a given offence if it applied only to those who engage in the precise wrong that the offence was intended to target. For example, it may be that a course of action only amounts to the targeted wrong if the defendant had a particular state of mind. It may be difficult or impossible to prove, however, that the defendant had that state of mind rather than another. On that basis, we might prefer to widen the ambit of the offence so that it catches people with states of mind that are not culpable (at least in the relevant sense). The offence is overbroad. The overbreadth is justified, however, insofar as the targeted wrong is sufficiently serious, and the risk of evasion sufficiently grave, that it is the lesser evil.

Is this an unprincipled position to take? Not necessarily. To a point, we can find some support for it in H.L.A. Hart's *Concept of Law*. Hart observes that a member of the public might look to the criminal law for guidance in one of two senses. She might, like Holmes's bad man, look to the criminal law for no other reason than to find clues as to the circumstances under which she will be made to undergo sanctions. The person who adopts this attitude toward the criminal law does not believe that she does anything morally wrong merely because she violates one of its provisions. She may believe that a violation is imprudent, but even that attitude will depend on the perceived likelihood that disobedience will meet with prosecution and punishment. She might, however, adopt the attitude of Hart's puzzled man, who has internalized the prohibitions set out in the criminal law and looks to it to determine which courses of action are wrongful.[60] From that perspective, the criminal law imposes obligations, and neglecting them deserves opprobrium whether or not there is any genuine risk of prosecution or deprivation. Hart does not claim that any actual society is populated by "puzzled men,"[61] but he does suggest that, insofar as legal systems claim that citizens[62] have a duty to obey the law, they will invariably presuppose that the only appropriate attitude to their pronouncements is that of the puzzled man.[63]

With Hart's observations about the internal point of view in mind, Meir Dan-Cohen argues that the criminal law may feature two sets of norms: one directed at members of the public, and the other directed at legal officials.[64] Members of the public will be exposed to conduct rules purporting to guide their behaviour. They may not, however, be exposed to decision rules guiding the behaviour of legal officials as they decide whether they are entitled to arrest, prosecute, and convict members of the public for breaches of conduct rules. That information is valuable to members of the public only to the extent that they want to know if and when a given breach of conduct rules will meet with sanctions. Insofar as citizens are expected to be guided by conduct rules whether or not breaches are sanctionable, information about decision rules may be thought at best irrelevant and at worst corrupting, distracting, or confusing. For that reason, decision rules may be communicated to legal officials in such a way that they are not heard by citizens at large. There is, to use Dan-Cohen's language, "acoustic separation."

The use of acoustic separation means that some citizens – those whose attitude toward the criminal law resembles that of the bad man – may be guided away from courses of action in which they would otherwise engage on the basis of a mistaken belief that all violations of conduct rules are punishable. Dan-Cohen acknowledges that this use of vague language to discourage non-sanctionable conduct is a kind of manipulation – indeed, he describes it as "brutality" – but he hesitantly concludes that it does not represent a serious rule of law problem.[65] Since citizens are expected to look to the criminal law to guide them away from wrongful courses of action, and not simply to enable them to predict when they will be subjected to deprivations, they ought to interpret conduct rules in the widest sense possible. To adopt any other interpretive approach is to willingly engage in behaviour that one knows may be wrongful under the law.[66]

Dan-Cohen is not trying to make a case for overbreadth, but the reasoning that underpins his conclusion that acoustic separation is not a rule of law problem, has application to Buell's argument. If we conclude that citizens are blameworthy when they treat criminal prohibitions as nothing more than tools for predicting and evading sanctions, then Buell's qualified case for overbreadth can start to be seen as something more than a pure sacrifice of principle to efficiency. Insofar as citizens engage in conduct that gives rise to a reasonable concern that they are merely trying to evade the application of sanctions to what amounts to a serious public wrong, they have engaged in a criminal wrong. They have undermined our confidence that the offence in question will be treated as obligation-creating. We might say that the need for reassurance necessitates (or at least justifies) extending the offence so that it catches this conduct.

Conclusion

There is at least a reasonable case that the need to assure women that they will not be treated as mere instruments for men's sexual gratification of men can justify over-inclusive criminal offences. But, as the discussion of Nedelsky (and Hanna) suggests, we should exercise caution before resorting to overbreadth. Women need assurance not only that the law will protect their sexual integrity – but also that they will be in a position to exercise their sexual autonomy, even in ways that are not to everyone's taste. With that in mind, we should hesitate to rule out the possibility of implied consent altogether – especially if there are available alternatives to overbreadth. I consider that possibility in the next chapter.

CHAPTER 10

Overbreadth or Bust?

Introduction

In the preceding chapter, I considered the case for overbreadth. Under some circumstances, it may be impossible to define a criminal offence in such a way that it addresses only the targeted wrong without also making the offence practically unenforceable. Where the targeted wrong is sufficiently grave – as is the case with sexual assault – the only workable strategy may be to have an over-inclusive definition, relying on the discretion of police officers, prosecutors, and judges to ensure that those who have not engaged in the targeted wrong are not prosecuted or punished.[1]

The case for overbreadth is reasonable enough. It may indeed sometimes be the case that an offence must be defined in an overbroad fashion. But here a few observations are in order. First, the case for overbreadth is essentially one of legislative necessity. Elaine Craig does not deny that Parliament should generally seek to tailor criminal offences to address the wrongful conduct they respectively target, and only that conduct. She only reminds us that, to do their work, criminal prohibitions must be framed as rules rather than as open-ended standards, and that rules are invariably over-inclusive.[2] Cheryl Hanna accepts that there is a real "dilemma" over how best to protect women's sexual autonomy, and it is only with "ambivalence" that she concludes that an over-inclusive approach is best. Likewise, Samuel Buell points out that, when overbreadth is defensible at all, it is as a necessary evil.[3] John Gardner and Stephen

Shute treat overbreadth as defensible only insofar as it prevents harm.[4] None suggest that it is unproblematic.

Second, overbreadth is an answer only to one set of problems: those of under-enforcement. It solves difficulties produced by Holmesian bad men – people intent on exploiting loopholes in the law to avoid sanctions. But it creates new problems. Overbreadth is tolerable only on the assumption that administrative and judicial actors will exercise their discretion such that those whose conduct falls outside that targeted by the offence in question will not be prosecuted or punished. Thus, Buell draws particular attention to "agency costs" – the prospect of administrative actors using their discretion to chase after conduct that the legislature does not regard as wrongful.[5] There is an obvious risk that, with a change in policy, blameless individuals will be unfairly stigmatized and punished.

Leaving that risk aside, there is a more fundamental concern: that people who treat the criminal law as a source of obligations will take seriously the message that it is wrongful to engage in courses of action that, in fact, have been criminalized only to close an enforcement gap. This is the concern with which this book started. If we take the view that there is value in women being able to have certain kinds of intimate relationships, we should worry about an over-inclusive definition of sexual assault.[6]

Finally, the enforcement problems that overbreadth aims to solve do not (always) need to be addressed through an over-inclusive offence definition. They can be addressed by having a rebuttable legal presumption that, where the Crown proves that there was sexual touching in the absence of *Ewanchuk* consent, there was no implied consent. (In effect, implied consent would be treated as a positive defence.) On this model, it would not fall to the Crown to prove beyond a reasonable doubt that there was no implied consent; it would fall to the defendant to show that there was. In this way, we could address problems of under-enforcement without sending a distorted message to the public.

In this final chapter, I will explore the possibility of legally presuming the absence of implied consent, at least in the sexual assault context.[7] Throughout, my aim is modest – only to show that it is defensible and workable to shift the onus of proving implied consent onto the defendant.

Antony Duff: A Presumption of Unreasonableness?

As I have shown, there is a case for overbreadth. But do we really need to choose between having an overbroad definition of sexual assault and failing to provide assurance that women's sexual integrity will be sufficiently protected? Is the choice really so stark? Could we, rather than define sexual assault in an over-inclusive way, instead address the need for assurance with a presumption? The work of Antony Duff, here, is instructive.

Duff does not necessarily share the commitment of Alan Brudner, Joseph Raz, Peter Ramsay, and Jennifer Nedelsky to the idea of "vulnerable" or "real" autonomy. But he seems to embrace assurance as a value capable of justifying the creation of new criminal offences – particularly public welfare offences. It can also justify, under some circumstances, creating a rebuttable presumption of fault – i.e., imposing a reverse onus onto the defendant.

In *Answering for Crime*,[8] Duff defends regulatory offences, in which proof of the actus reus alone is sufficient basis for conviction unless the defendant can show that he acted with "due diligence."[9] There is in effect a rebuttable legal presumption that the defendant did not take "reasonable steps." Such offences are special, argues Duff, because they target courses of action that, although not inherently wrongful, are inherently risky.[10] In choosing to engage in that conduct, one takes on an obligation to assure the public that it is being undertaken in a safe fashion.[11] Thus, to borrow Duff's example, the factory owner whose machinery malfunctions and injures a worker must show that she exercised due diligence in maintaining it.[12] She may discharge that burden by presenting a written record of the steps she has taken, for example, the frequency with which the machinery is inspected and repaired. If she did not keep such a record, we might say that she has taken her chances with others' safety anyway. But having decided to embark upon an inherently dangerous occupation, Duff argues, the factory owner cannot complain of the need to assure her fellow citizens that she is doing so reasonably.

Duff identifies a further context in which it can be acceptable to presume that a course of action is criminally wrongful in the absence of proof of fault. A person "may be called to answer for ... sexually penetrating a non-consenting person without any reasonable belief that the person consented."[13] But, he says, it may be legitimate for the state to legally presume that there was no reasonable basis for forming a belief in consent once the Crown has shown that non-consensual sexual penetration took place.[14] The law can require the defendant to show that he took reasonable steps to ascertain consent. Duff states:

> D has a primary responsibility to refrain from non-consensual sexual penetration, and to make sure (when there is any reason for doubt) that his sexual activity is consensual. He will usually have to answer for failing to discharge that primary responsibility only if it is proved that he failed to discharge it – only if the prosecution proves *ab initio* that the penetration was non-consensual and that he did not reasonably believe it to be consensual: what he is called to answer for is sexually penetrating a non-consenting person without any reasonable belief that the person consented. However, when the context is such as to put him on notice that what he is doing might well constitute rape, *he incurs the secondary responsibility to make sure that he will be able to answer for his conduct* by doing all that he reasonably can to ensure that he is acting with V's consent: he can then be called to answer for sexually penetrating someone who was, for instance, unconscious; and if he cannot offer an answer which explains why he had good reason to believe that V did consent, the court can properly conclude that he failed to discharge not only his secondary responsibility, but also his primary responsibility – that he is guilty of rape.[15]

Duff does not use the language of assurance in explaining why someone may be called to account in the absence of proof that he did not reasonably believe that there was consent. But his discussion of "secondary responsibility" is revealing. By embarking upon a "risky" course of action, Duff says, one takes on an additional duty to make it possible to explain oneself later. Now, Duff cannot just mean that such proto-defendants have an additional incentive to give themselves a defence – they do, of course, but the mere fact that a defendant failed to exercise prudence in protecting himself from liability does not give us a reason to punish him. Duff's point is that the circumstances under which the sexual touching took place are such that it raises special concerns; that the defendant must assure us that he did not engage in such a risky course of action frivolously or capriciously.

The question is whether this duty to provide assurance could come into play with regards to other kinds of sexual touching. Importantly, Duff suggests it can. The fact that a person has sexually penetrated another in the absence of contemporaneous consent, he argues, is sufficient basis for requiring him to provide an account of himself.[16] By engaging in sexual penetration in the first place, he embarked upon an inherently risky course of action. It can properly fall to the defendant to show that he took reasonable steps to ascertain the presence of consent. Moreover, Duff observes, it will rarely be the case that the defendant could have reasonably believed that consent existed if it did not.[17] It is therefore safe to presume that, if the Crown can show that the defendant engaged in sexual penetration in the absence of contemporaneous consent, the defendant is unlikely to show that he proceeded reasonably anyway. Duff remarks:

> The reason for making [the presumption that the accused's belief was unreasonable] a formal matter of law would be primarily expressive: it would express our recognition of the fact that the non-consenting victim has been wronged, and of the stringency of the responsibility to ensure consent if there is any room for doubt about it – a responsibility such that a defendant who had discharged it would be able to offer appropriate evidence of having done so, by pointing to the very factors that gave reason to believe that V consented.[18]

There are two points I want to take away from Duff's analysis. First, and most straightforwardly, by drawing on the idea of assurance, Duff (whether he means to or not) connects his work to that of other jurists, philosophers, and theorists who likewise use it to explain why certain courses of action are civilly or criminally wrongful. Thus, as I discussed in previous chapters, Jeremy Waldron appeals to the idea of assurance when justifying hate speech laws. Likewise, Catharine MacKinnon implicitly appeals to it in explaining why the distribution of certain kinds of pornography is wrongful. And Nedelsky draws on the need to assure women of their sexual integrity as a reason why the reasonable steps requirement in the Criminal Code is valuable and important.[19] Duff makes a similar point: it is acceptable to put the burden of showing that the defendant acted reasonably onto him, insofar as his conduct raises special concerns he has an obligation to assuage.

Second, and relatedly, Duff emphasizes the expressive function of a reasonable steps requirement. Placing the burden on the defendant to show that he had a reasonable basis for proceeding as he did, Duff argues, sends an unequivocal message that non-consensual sexual penetration is a matter of concern for the state and the public. It is not a "private" matter, or an intrusion into citizens' "personal" lives. It is as surely an act of violence, as surely a concern for the state, as any public brawl.

Duff's focus is on the law of rape – hence his emphasis on sexual penetration. But it is possible to extend his reasoning to non-consensual sexual touching generally: whenever someone engages in non-consensual sexual touching of another person, we could say that the other has been wronged, that a risk has been taken with her sexual autonomy, and that we are entitled to require the defendant to explain why his belief in consent (assuming he had one) was reasonable. To a degree, that more or less tracks the Canadian law of sexual assault after the 1992 amendments: once the Crown has established that the defendant engaged in sexual touching of the complainant in the absence of contemporaneous consent, the defendant must adduce evidence to show he took reasonable steps to establish consent before he can argue that he had an honest but mistaken belief in consent.

I want to say, here, that once the Crown has shown that the defendant engaged in sexual touching of the complainant in the absence of *Ewanchuk* consent, there is a presumption that there was also no implied consent. My reasons broadly track those Duff articulates above. The fact that non-consensual (in the *Ewanchuk* sense) sexual touching took place gives rise to special concerns that the defendant engaged in the sexual instrumentalization of the complainant. The pervasiveness of objectifying gender norms, in conjunction with the physical, psychological, and social harms associated with sexual assault, create a particular need to assure the community – and women in particular – that the defendant's sexual touching occurred in a normative context capable of legitimating it. His conduct, we might say, is inherently dangerous.

The approach I adopt reflects the fact that sexual touching in the absence of contemporaneous consent – whether it takes place in an intimate relationship or not – is a matter of public concern deserving of the law's attention. The sexual sphere is one in which the prospect of instrumentalization is especially stark. It is hardly far-fetched to suppose that, when one person engages sexually with another, he should be ready to give an account of himself. When the defence is *Ewanchuk* consent, there are good reasons to place the burden on the Crown.[20] Placing the burden on the defendant to prove *Ewanchuk* consent would go too far in undermining the assurance of men and women that they can make use of their sexual autonomy free of undue state interference. But when the defence is implied consent, the concerns of instrumentalization are all the greater. The risks of convicting the morally innocent are also less pronounced.

Presenting the defence of implied consent as a positive rather than negative defence sends, as I have said, a powerful message about the significance of sexual touching as a matter of public concern.[21] By making the defence available at all, the criminal law underscores that men and women have the autonomy to decide how to conduct their own intimate relationships. In deciding just how far others may touch them in the absence of subjective consent, they adopt a position not unlike that of a public official exercising discretion.[22] The defence gives women the power to agree to arrangements in which they play passive sexual roles. But by placing the onus on the defendant, the criminal law also sends the message that it is – and we are – suspicious that such arrangements exist, at least insofar as they are characterized by mutuality. It is a suspicion grown from a long and depressing history of sexual objectification of women in our culture. The reverse onus sends the message that, whatever arrangements men and women make for themselves, they should discuss them rather than simply take them for granted. At the very least, they should proceed cautiously and respectfully with each other.

Canadian law has recognized other contexts in which it is considered safe to presume an element of the actus reus upon proof of something less or other than that element. Consider the (now struck-down)[23] offence of living off the avails of prostitution. Under the old law, the trier of fact was directed to presume that a criminal defendant who was living with a prostitute was living off the avails of prostitution in the absence of evidence to the contrary.[24] That presumption made sense because the mere fact that a defendant was living with a prostitute was enough to give rise to concerns that he was exploiting her – that, to use the language employed in *R. v. Downey*, the relationship was "parasitical."[25] This was especially so in light of the difficulties that the Crown would have in proving that the relationship was exploitive if the presumption was not in place, and given that the defendant would – if his relationship was truly non-parasitical – have little trouble adducing some evidence to that effect.[26] The public's need for assurance under the circumstances was sufficient to justify requiring the defendant to answer for his conduct. This was so even though it was by no means inherently wrongful to live with, or be habitually in the company of, a prostitute.[27]

For much the same reason, we might say that, on proof that the defendant was a school teacher sexually involved with a student, he may be called to answer for the sexual exploitation of a young person. This is so in spite of the fact that it may be, in principle, possible for there to be no exploitation under those circumstances. The mere fact that there was a teacher-student relationship, and that the defendant engaged in sexual activity with the complainant, would be enough to raise the specter of exploitation such that it would be reasonable to call the defendant to account for himself.[28]

In these and many other circumstances, we use rebuttable legal presumptions to partially relieve the Crown's burden in establishing a prima facie case of wrongdoing. We do so for reasons that at least bear a close resemblance to those offered by Duff. Even where conduct is not inherently wrongful, it can present a risk of wrongdoing sufficient to justify the sort of public concern and need for assurance that in turn makes it reasonable to expect citizens to answer for their behaviour in a criminal court.

Is There a Constitutional Problem?

Suppose we recognize a doctrine of implied consent, but as something akin to a positive defence requiring the defendant to discharge an evidentiary or persuasive burden. Would that pass constitutional muster under the Canadian Charter of Rights and Freedoms? There are good reasons to think it would. In what follows, I discuss a few of those reasons. This is a work of criminal law theory, not constitutional law, and so this discussion will amount to little more than a quick sketch. But it should suffice to show that a reverse onus is, constitutionally speaking, a credible option.

To start, we return to the observation that the offence of sexual assault targets wrongful objectification, and that no such objectification occurs where the doctrine of implied consent properly applies. Accepting those two points, we already have an overbreadth problem in the sense that "the law goes too far and interferes with some conduct that bears no connection to its objective."[29] The Supreme Court of Canada recently discussed overbreadth in *Canada v. Bedford*:

> Overbreadth allows courts to recognize that the law is rational in some cases, but that it overreaches in its effect in others. Despite this recognition of the scope of the law as a whole, the focus remains on the individual and whether the effect on the individual is rationally connected to the law's purpose. For example, where a law is drawn broadly and targets some conduct that bears no relation to its purpose in order to make enforcement more practical, there is still no connection between the purpose of the law and its effect on the *specific individual*. Enforcement practicality may be a justification for an overbroad law, to be analyzed under s. 1 of the *Charter*.[30]

Two points are worth making here. First, on this analysis, and accepting my premises on the purpose of the offence of sexual assault and the moral significance of implied consent, the offence plainly meets the test for overbreadth. The prohibition targets those who engage in wrongful objectification, yet applies to people who do not. But, and this is my second point, there is a possible section 1 justification for overbreadth: "enforcement practicality." This is the very justification Craig and Buell offer for having overbroad offences.[31] That justification only works, though, if the Crown satisfies the minimal impairment test set out in *R. v. Oakes*.[32] If there is a feasible means of addressing the enforcement problem, without excluding the doctrine of implied consent altogether, the limitation on section 7 is not justified. In this chapter, I've argued that a reverse onus on implied consent impairs the section 7 right to a lesser degree, while achieving the aims of overbreadth proponents.

Put simply, it is strange to suggest that a reverse onus should be swept off the table as unconstitutional if it would cure or replace a more serious constitutional defect. Even if overbreadth is not constitutionally fatal (again, given the premises I have set out), the reverse onus may be the more constitutionally desirable course. We should bear this in mind as we discuss the issues surrounding reverse onuses.

Since the Supreme Court's decision in *R. v. Whyte*, any reverse onus on the defendant is a prima facie violation of the presumption of innocence.[33] We can simply proceed on the basis that there would be an infringement of section 11(d) of the Charter.[34] Would it be justified under section 1? The objective, as I have shown, would be to assure women that those who engage in non-consensual sexual touching will not be able to secure an acquittal merely by raising a reasonable doubt as to the existence of a set of norms, within the context of intimate relations, legitimizing that conduct. That objective is pressing and substantial given the importance of the offence of sexual assault as a means of addressing the wrongful objectification of women, its role in protecting their rights to equality and sexual integrity, and the existence of gender norms that would make acquittals all too likely if implied consent was treated as a matter that needed to be disproved by the Crown.[35]

When the objective is formulated in this way, there is plainly a rational connection between it and the means chosen. We must then consider whether there is minimal impairment. Certainly, as I have shown, imposing any reverse onus impairs the presumption of innocence far less than would an overbroad offence definition.

Would the burden need to be merely evidentiary in order to pass the minimal impairment stage? That would depend on at least three broad considerations. (I do not suggest that this list is exhaustive.) First, we must consider how easy or difficult it would be for the defendant to obtain and adduce evidence going to the existence of mutuality and legitimizing norms. The more difficult it is, the more we can be satisfied with an evidentiary burden.[36] Second, and relatedly, we need to consider the circumstances under which it is reasonable to infer that a given set of norms existed at the relevant time. The mere fact that the defendant engaged in a form of sexual touching on an earlier occasion, or on several occasions, is only a speculative basis for concluding that the touching was legitimate within the rules constituting that relationship. Likewise, we should hesitate to infer that an intimate relationship is non-exploitive merely because the complainant had an independent source of income or social standing. The analysis is more subtle than that. Third, we need to take on board that triers of fact can be insufficiently alert to their own prejudices and biases.[37] They may be too quick to assume that intimate relationships generally are characterized by mutuality, or that they should or must involve norms that legitimize sexual touching in the absence of subjective consent. Under those circumstances, it may be unrealistic to expect the Crown to disprove the existence of mutuality or legitimizing norms once an evidentiary burden has been satisfied. That suggests a persuasive burden is appropriate. The more confidence we have that judges and triers of fact will approach questions of mutuality and normativity in a thoughtful, reflective way, the more confidence we can have that an evidentiary burden will suffice.

That leaves only the final step in the *Oakes* test: weighing benefits against deleterious effects. The drawback of the reverse onus lies in the risk of wrongful conviction – but for the reasons I have already stated, that is not such a concern. Leaving aside the use of police and prosecutorial discretion to limit the impact of the sexual assault provision on those who have engaged in non-consensual sexual touching in the context of intimate partnerships, we may be able to anticipate that the doctrine of implied consent will only rarely apply and, where it does, can be effectively used by the defendant. The benefit lies in the assurance that the reverse onus will provide women – particularly those in intimate relationships – that their sexual integrity will not be violated.

This is, as I noted above, an extremely quick run-through of the section 1 analysis we would undertake in justifying a reverse onus. My point has not been to state the case conclusively, but only to show why it is plausible and, therefore, why we should hesitate to see the implied consent debate as all or nothing. Our range of constitutional options is wider than that.

Conclusion

As I observed at the outset of this chapter, and throughout this book, my aim has been modest: to show that we can recognize a doctrine of implied consent in the context of sexual touching without undermining the symbolic and deterrent effect of the offence of sexual assault. The need to assure women that they will not and cannot be used as instruments for men's sexual gratification, and that their sexual integrity will be protected,

IMPLIED CONSENT AND SEXUAL ASSAULT

can indeed justify the use of extraordinary legislative measures. But the options are not exhausted by overbreadth. Parliament is also entitled to use legal presumptions to make implied consent a more difficult tool to wield for criminal defendants, while still conveying (through the offence definition) that normative arrangements, in which something other than *Ewanchuk* consent may be given, are legally possible. Perhaps that is not an acceptable substitute, but it falls upon critics to explain why.

Voice and Implied Consent

In *Men Explain Things to Me*, Rebecca Solnit draws a direct connection between the phenomenon of "mansplaining" and sexual violence against women.[1] The term refers to the presumption, typically implicit, that a woman must know less about a given topic than a man – no matter her wealth of experience or credentials and no matter his ignorance – just by virtue of her gender. At times, it can be vaguely comical, as in Solnit's anecdote of the man who insisted on telling her at length about a new book on Muybridge – a book she had written.[2] What makes that story funny is the way in which a man's illusions of intellectual superiority are instantly and publicly revealed for what they are: wishful thinking.[3]

If mansplaining could be boiled down to mere blowhardism, it wouldn't be so troubling.[4] But, as Solnit says, it is merely the tip of a very large cultural iceberg in which women are effectively and systematically silenced and treated as screens upon which men can project their fantasies of dominance and superiority: "It's the presumption that makes it hard, at times, for any woman in any field; that keeps women from speaking up and from being heard when they dare; that crushes young women into silence by indicating, the way harassment on the street does, that this is not their world. It trains us in self-doubt and self-limitation just as it exercises men's unsupported overconfidence."[5]

The assumption that any woman must know less than any man about any given topic is closely tied to the assumption that she cannot have anything meaningful or important to say for herself; that it falls to men to make sense of women's experiences, since they cannot or will not speak sensibly for themselves. It makes it possible for a man at a party to tell a successful philosopher about what she should read in her own field, but also for police officers, prosecutors, and newspaper columnists to dismiss reports of rape and sexual assault as "overblown" or "buyer's remorse."[6] It is what allows men like Brian Ewanchuk and Vittorio Flaviano to act as though a young woman's rejections and protestations are nothing more than lines in a script. As Solnit observes: "Having the right to show up and speak are basic to survival, to dignity, and to liberty."[7]

In the introduction, I made the commonplace observation that sexual assault law is, in large part, about protecting women's right to speak for themselves – and not simply to have words stuffed into their mouths. By now, I hope it is clear that reviving a modified version of the doctrine of implied consent can be regarded as one further step in advancing that project; a means by which women may be legally recognized as able to speak for themselves in deciding what norms should govern their intimate relationships. It gives legal effect and recognition to women's voices and, in so doing, treats them as something other than silent objects. In the better part of this book, I have explained how that could be true.

We should take seriously arguments that the law can protect women's voices only to a point. If recognizing a doctrine of implied consent, no matter how it is defined or structured, means putting them at the mercy of their partners and spouses, then perhaps it is necessary to accept the limits of the law in promoting their sexual autonomy and agency (at least in the here and now). But we should not assume that the law is so powerless or inflexible. Crafting the doctrine of implied consent in such a way that the burden falls upon defendants rather than complainants would seem to offer the protection we might hope to provide by abolishing it altogether, without having to restrict what women can do.

In the last chapter, I briefly alluded to one benefit of this approach – one that again ties into the importance of voice. At present, the law treats relationship status (on the surface, at any rate) as morally and legally irrelevant when determining whether a sexual assault has taken place. That encourages one of two equally radical and implausible positions: either that the sexual touching that frequently goes on in intimate relationships is, by and large, none of the criminal law's business; or that it is always and necessarily criminal. In practice, actors in the criminal justice system tend to act as though the former is true: except when sexual touching involves penetration (and often even then), we tend to see few prosecutions of intimate partners and spouses. Yet there is little public outcry. There is, I suspect, a common feeling that it would be unthinkable for the state to police the everyday sexual touching that goes on in intimate relationships – even (indeed, especially) if it was possible to do so. And so, for lack of a principled basis for distinguishing between sexual norms, we say nothing at all. Just as importantly, we inadvertently send the message that there is no urgent moral or legal reason for men and women to talk and listen to each other about their sexual preferences and rules of engagement. After all, if the norms don't matter, and if the law won't apply to them anyway, why bother?

By formally recognizing that mutuality makes a legal difference, the law of sexual assault may do more than capture a moral truth, though that is important in itself. By expressing the significance of voice, it may encourage men to respect it. Indeed, it may embolden women to *use* it. With that in mind, it is worth reopening a debate that, since *Ewanchuk*, has been closed.

Martha Nussbaum and Roger Scruton

In explaining why, employing Martha Nussbaum's analytical framework, we can conclude that sexual desire and sexual touching are not inherently objectifying in a morally problematic way, I draw periodically upon the language and analysis Roger Scruton provides in his important work, *Sexual Desire*.[1] This may seem curious for at least two reasons. First, *Sexual Desire* is quite conservative in its outlook, and Scruton reaches several deeply controversial conclusions concerning, among other things, homosexual sexual desire and activity and the proper role of women in society. Second, Nussbaum explicitly rejects much of Scruton's reasoning in *Sexual Desire*. To see why there is something to be gained from parachuting some of his claims into the framework she develops in "Objectification," it is helpful to take a moment to examine the precise nature of Nussbaum's criticisms and the extent to which she agrees with him – or, at any rate, expresses sympathy for some of his instincts and arguments.

In *Sexual Desire*, Scruton makes four broad claims, which Nussbaum subsequently describes as the Intentionality Thesis, the Particularity Thesis, the Romantic Thesis, and the Character Thesis.[2] The Intentionality Thesis, put bluntly, states that sexual desire is not a purely physiological or mechanical drive, but an intentional activity that can only be understood by examining the subjective experiences of one engaging in it. A person who desires another does not perceive the other as a mere phallus or receptacle, but as an intentional actor capable of recognizing the significance of gestures and touches, and of responding to them with gestures packed with a meaning of their own. From this first thesis,

Scruton proceeds to argue the Particularity Thesis: in perceiving the other as an intentional actor, one necessarily perceives him or her as a particular person, and not as a generic or fungible human being. This in turn ties into the Romantic Thesis: that the aim of desire is to move ever closer to the other – to receive and provoke ever more intimate and revealing intentional gestures and responses until the two partners have achieved a kind of union. Finally, the Character Thesis states that the natural extension of this union is the sharing of a way of life – i.e., marriage or something like it. The upshot of Scruton's argument is that sexual desire is immanently connected to erotic love and, ultimately, to marriage. Forms of sexual activity that drive a wedge between desire and love amount to "perversions," pernicious precisely because they erode the capacity of their participants to form truly loving human relationships.

Nussbaum takes issue with some of Scruton's argumentative moves. She accepts the claim that sexual desire involves an act of imagination in which the gestures of the other are imbued with significance. It may be, moreover, that one can only desire one person at a time – that one cannot desire without desiring someone. But even if one accepts that proposition, it is hard to know what to do with it. Don Juan may not desire more than one person at a time, but he is certainly capable of desiring different people in succession. Scruton would not claim that he cannot treat each of them as capable of reading his gestures and touches, and as capable of responding in kind. He acts intentionally – but does not seem to be especially particular. If the Particularity Thesis states nothing more than the proposition that, at any given moment, desire must be directed at a particular person, it is difficult to see how it can support the Romantic Thesis – still less, the Character Thesis. After all, the mere fact that one desires a person for a discrete period of time implies nothing about the depth of that desire. One may experience desire for another without being caught in the whirlwind of lust that Dante describes in *Inferno*.[3] Desire can be less spontaneous and more cool-headed and calculated than that, as when a long-married couple has a prearranged time for intimacy, or when college students hook up, or when two friends decide to confer benefits upon one another.

With these observations in mind, we have a sense of why Nussbaum concludes that "those who find that their experience of desire is plausibly captured by the Intentionality Thesis, but not by the Romantic and

Character theses, need not think that any effective argument in [Scruton's] book has shown that a commitment to the first implies a commitment to the others."[4] To the extent that Scruton's claims that certain sexual activities amount to perversions rests on the Romantic or Character theses, Nussbaum is able to reject those as well. Moreover, Scruton's arguments against homosexuality and female equality rest on additional arguments about the significance of gender. These arguments, as Nussbaum suggests, are also severable from his Intentionality and Particularity theses and, for our purposes, can be set aside.[5]

For my purposes, Nussbaum's critique of Scruton is interesting for what it does *not* reject. Critically, Nussbaum does not take issue with the Intentionality Thesis itself, or with some (albeit quite mild) version of the Particularity Thesis. But even more significant is the fact that she expresses considerable sympathy for the Romantic and Character theses, even if she does not think Scruton's argument can support them. Discussing the Romantic Thesis, Nussbaum states:

> Like many a romantic, I find [Scruton's] claim deeply appealing. I have the same difficulty Scruton evidently does in separating sex from erotic love; and I am tempted to believe that sexual experiences that stop short of deep love are, even as sex, deficient. But Scruton's argument (unlike his argument for the Intentionality Thesis) does not persuade me to think of these intuitions as more than pieces of my idiosyncratic history – not rare, perhaps, but surely not necessary, brought about, perhaps, by seeing too many operas at an impressionable age. I am sure we should hesitate to condemn people whose experience of desire is different from this; and Scruton gives us no reason at all to cast off that hesitation.[6]

With respect to the Character Thesis, Nussbaum sounds a similar note: "[L]ike many readers of romantic stories ... I am drawn to the idea that desire, love, and lifelong marriage just naturally go together. I would accept hardly any evidence to the contrary ... Still, I know that this is just one (powerfully appealing) account of love, and hardly a universal truth. None of it, surely, follows from the far more generally persuasive intentionality argument with which the book began."[7] As these passages indicate, Nussbaum has no problem with Scruton's claim that the ideal or pure model of sexual desire he presents is unobjectionable in principle. Her difficulty is with his suggestion that this is the only unobjectionable model of sexual desire, and that all other models represent corruptions or perversions of the ideal. Indeed, Nussbaum has occasionally been prepared to (gently) hint that Scruton's romantic model of sex may well be the ideal, even as she insists that less romantic models of sex do not corrupt or degrade their participants – or, at any rate, that they do not undermine their capacity for intimacy to such an extent that they should be criminalized.[8]

So far, though, I have argued only in the negative. I have suggested that Nussbaum has not, and need not, reject all of Scruton's conclusions. But we can go further than that: many of the arguments Scruton raises either are endorsed by Nussbaum, or seem to shed light on aspects of her objectification framework.

We have already seen that Nussbaum positively endorsed Scruton's Intentionality Thesis. This alone goes some distance in explaining why, in her view, sexual desire and touching are not invariably objectifying in a morally problematic way. Other aspects of Scruton's account of sexual desire, though, look similarly revealing. In Nussbaum's framework, the central question is whether or not one person has instrumentalized another. That, however, begs the question: is it possible to engage in sexual touching of another without treating his or her body as a thing to be used? Nussbaum, of course, suggests that instrumentalization is only per se problematic when it amounts to mere use; she is less clear about instances where the touching takes place with mixed motives, some instrumentalizing and some not. But that hardly resolves the difficulty, since we are no more enlightened as to when sexual touching might be anything other than mere use. It is, moreover, discomfiting to suppose that all sexual touching is in some sense tainted; that the question is not whether it is bad, but only how bad it is.[9] Maybe that is true. It is, however, in tension not only with contemporary attitudes about sex – that it is a practice which, in some of its forms at least, deserves to be celebrated and not only tolerated – but with Nussbaum's own remarks that sex can be objectifying in ways that are benign or positive.[10]

We can unravel this problem by looking to Scruton's distinction between the use of another's body as an instrument and the treatment of another's body as a constitutive part of her embodied personality. This aspect of his argument is critical to the Romantic Thesis. That, though, is not a reason to reject it. Nussbaum dismisses the Romantic Thesis insofar as Scruton wants to say that "desire is superficial and second-rate if it does not aim at *a lasting and deep relationship that involves the entire spiritual being of both parties*."[11] If we suppose that it is possible to treat the other's body as a constitutive part of her embodied personality without being committed to deep intimacy, then there is no contradiction in accepting Scruton's distinction between the body as instrument and the body as constitutive.

Two other aspects of Scruton's analysis look encouraging. First, his emphasis on mutual intentionality, as well as his suggestion that sex can be directed at the sharing of a way of life, provide insight into what it might mean to treat the other's body as constitutive rather than instrumental. Indeed, Nussbaum alludes to the significance of mutuality on a number of occasions in "Objectification." Second, Scruton's Particularity Thesis, as well as his Romantic and Character theses, suggest that questions of fungibility are as central to his analysis of sexual desire as they are to Nussbaum's analysis of objectification. Though it is too stark to conclude, as he does, that any sexual relationship in which one is uncommitted to one's partner is base and corrupt, we can nonetheless find in his study a basis for concluding that certain sexual acts do not treat one's partner as unacceptably fungible. That is only a first step, but it is a start.

In spite of Nussbaum's vigorous disagreement with Scruton on many points in *Sexual Desire*, then, the story he tells about sexual desire has some resonance for both. In this spirit, she praised the work for its sensitivity in capturing what *can* be wonderful about sexual desire.[12]

NOTES

INTRODUCTION

1 *R. v. Ewanchuk*, [1999] 1 SCR 330 [*Ewanchuk*].

2 See *R. v. Wilcox*, 2014 QCCA 321 at para. 96, aff'd 2014 SCC 75 [*Wilcox*]. For one early analysis of the ruling, see Maciej Lipinski, "Consent Is Neither Implied Nor Retroactive: *R v Wilcox*" *Court Blog* (24 December 2014), http://www.thecourt.ca/2014/12/24/consent-is-neither-implied-nor-retroactive-r-v-wilcox/ (emphasizing this aspect of the ruling).

3 In this book, I use "intimate relationships" in an expansive sense. It can encompass spousal relationships, dating relationships, and more casual sexual arrangements. At the same time, as I note in chapter 8, we should not assume that a marriage amounts to an intimate relationship. People may get or stay married for any number of reasons. What matters is the particular set of normative sexual arrangements the parties themselves craft – not some privileged conception of what a marriage (or other kind of relationship) must be.

4 For a discussion, see Margo Kaplan, "Sex-Positive Law" (2014) 89 NYU L. Rev. 89.

5 Given that sexual assault is a gendered offence, I will tend to use feminine pronouns to refer to (proto-)complainants, and masculine pronouns to refer to (proto-)defendants. This means, in effect, that I generally use feminine pronouns to refer to recipients of sexual touching, and masculine pronouns to refer to deliverers of sexual touching.

6 *Ewanchuk* at paras. 26–27.

7 Ibid. See also *R. v. J.A.*, [2011] 2 SCR 440 [*J.A.*].

8 *Ewanchuk* at para. 51.

9 Ibid.

10 Ibid. at paras. 24, 28, 66.

11 *R. v. Flaviano*, 2014 SCC 14. In my discussion of the facts, I draw mainly upon the Respondent's (far more extensive) version, which the trial judge generally accepted. Factum of the Respondent, http://www.scc-csc.gc.ca/factums-memoires/35488/FM040_Respondent_Her-Majesty-the-Queen.pdf.

12 *Flaviano*, Factum of the Respondent at para. 9.

13 Ibid. at para. 11.
14 Ibid. at para. 12.
15 Ibid. at para. 13.
16 Ibid.
17 Ibid.
18 Ibid. at para. 14.
19 Ibid. at para. 15.
20 Ibid. at para. 16.
21 Ibid.
22 Ibid. at para. 17.
23 Ibid.
24 Ibid. at paras. 18–19.
25 Ibid. at para. 20.
26 *Flaviano*, Factum of the Appellant, http://www.scc-csc.gc.ca/WebDocuments-DocumentsWeb/35488/FM030_Appellant_Vittoria-Thomas-Flaviano.pdf, at paras. 7–12.
27 *Flaviano*.
28 See Janine Benedet, "Sexual Assault Cases at the Alberta Court of Appeal: The Roots of *Ewanchuk* and the Unfinished Revolution" (2014) 52 Alta. L. Rev. 127 at 142–43.
29 *Ewanchuk* at paras. 2–3.
30 Ibid. at para. 3.
31 Ibid.
32 Ibid. at para. 4.
33 Ibid.
34 Ibid. at para. 5.
35 Ibid.
36 Ibid. at para. 6.
37 Ibid.
38 Ibid. at para. 7.
39 Ibid.
40 Ibid.
41 Ibid. at para. 8.
42 Ibid.
43 Ibid.
44 Ibid. at para. 10. In the reasons for acquittal, this exchange preceded the alleged touching. See *R. v. Ewanchuk*, 1998 ABCA 52 at para. 2, http://www.canlii.org/en/ab/abca/doc/1998/1998abca52/1998abca52.html.
45 *Ewanchuk*, 1998 ABCA 52 at para. 11
46 See *R. v. V. (R.)* (2004), 20 CR (6th) 346 at para. 10 (Ont. SCJ)
47 *J.A.*
48 Ibid. at para. 4.
49 Ibid. at para. 5.
50 Ibid.

51 Ibid. at para. 6.

52 Ibid. at paras. 6–7.

53 Ibid. at para. 8.

54 *Ewanchuk* at para. 31.

55 Ibid.

56 Ibid. at para. 26, emphasis added.

57 *J.A.*

58 Ibid. at para. 46. See also at para. 53.

59 Ibid. at para. 47.

60 Ibid. at para. 48.

61 The academic literature on this question is surprisingly sparse. For four relatively recent examples, see Melanie Randall, "Sexual Assault in Spousal Relationships, 'Continuous Consent,' and the Law: Honest but Mistaken Judicial Beliefs" (2008) 32 Manitoba LJ at 144; Ruthy Lazar, "Negotiating Sex: The Legal Construct of Consent in Cases of Wife Rape in Ontario, Canada" (2010) 22 CJWL at 329; Elaine Craig, "Ten Years after *Ewanchuk* the Art of Seduction Is Alive and Well: An Examination of the Mistaken Belief in Consent Defence" (2009) 13 Can. Crim. L. Rev. 247 at 259–69; Christine Boyle, "Sexual Assault as Foreplay: Does Ewanchuk Apply to Spouses?" (2004) 20 CR (6th) at 359.

62 *J.A.* at para. 47.

63 Ibid. at para. 46.

64 Ibid. at para. 58.

65 It is, therefore, quite wrong to suggest that I have raised a purely hypothetical problem, for there is nothing hypothetical about a scenario that arises every day for many couples. It would only be hypothetical to suppose that a prosecution would result from any of the situations I have posited. For reasons given below, the fact that prosecution may arise only hypothetically is not a problem for my argument. But see Janine Benedet, *"J.A.:* Consent to Sexual Activity Cannot Be Irrevocable" (2011) 84 CR (6th) 35 at 36.

66 Martha C. Nussbaum, *Women and Human Development: The Capabilities Approach* (Cambridge: Cambridge University Press, 2000) at ch. 2; Martha Nussbaum, "Rage and Reason" in *Sex and Social Justice* (Oxford: Oxford University Press, 1999) at ch. 9; Amartya Sen, *Development as Freedom* (New York: Anchor Books, 1999) at 62–63.

67 Nussbaum, *Women and Human Development* at 146–47.

68 Ibid.; Serene J. Khader, *Adaptive Preferences and Women's Empowerment* (Oxford: Oxford University Press, 2011).

69 *J.A.* at para. 64.

70 Ibid. at para. 65.

71 Ibid.

72 See also *R. v. Malmo-Levine*, [2003] 3 SCR 571. The point has been criticized by Alan Young, "Done Nothing Wrong: Fundamental Justice and the Minimum Content of Criminal Law" (2008) 40 SCLR (2d) 441.

73 I will sometimes refer to "discretely contemporaneous consent," sometimes
to "ordinary consent," and sometimes to *Ewanchuk* consent." For the most
part, and for the sake of readability, I will use the shorthand "contemporaneous consent."

74 See the discussion by Hamish Stewart, "Parents, Children, and the Law of
Assault" (2009) 32 Dal. LJ 1.

75 See Simon R. Crouch, Elizabeth Waters, Ruth McNair, Jennifer Power, and
Elise Davis, "Parent-Reported Measures of Child Health and Well-Being
in Same-Sex Parent Families: A Cross-Sectional Survey" (2014) 14 BMC
Public Health 635, http://www.biomedcentral.com/content/pdf/1471-2458-
14-635.pdf at 2/12 ("Regardless of gender however it is becoming clear that
same-sex attracted parents construct their parenting roles more equit-
ably than heterosexual parents and this may be of benefit to family functioning."); A. Perlesz, J. Power, R. Brown, R. McNair, M. Schofield, M. Pitts,
Barrett, and A. Bickerdike, "Organising Work and Home in Same-Sex Parented Families: Findings from the Work Love Play Study" (2010) 31 Aust.
NZ Fam. Therapy 374; Lawrence A. Kurdek, "The Allocation of Household
Labor by Parents in Gay and Lesbian Couples" (2007) 28 *J. Family Issues*
132; Ulrich Beck and Elisabeth Beck-Gernsheim, *Distant Love* (Cambridge:
Polity Press, 2014), 55.

76 Consider the expert evidence that was excluded (in part because its relevance depended on the legal availability of implied consent) in *Wilcox*.

CHAPTER ONE

1 I will sometimes refer to this as the criminal law's expressive function,
sometimes as its guidance function, and sometimes as its educative function. For my purposes here, I use the terms interchangeably.

2 Don Stuart, "*Ewanchuk*: Asserting 'No Means No' at the Expense of Fault
and Proportionality Principles" (1999) 22 CR (5th) 39. See also Deborah R.
Hatch, "Culpability and Capitulation: Sexual Assault and Consent in the
Wake of *R. v. Ewanchuk*" (1999) 43 CLQ 51.

3 See, e.g., Link Byfield, "Casanova Outlawed," *Alberta Report* (29 March
1999); Marjaleena Repo, "The Ewanchuk Ruling Is No Reason to Rejoice,"
Globe and Mail (4 March 1999). See also Patrick Brode, *Courted and Abandoned: Seduction in Canadian Law* (Toronto: Osgoode Society, 2002) at
201–02, 207.

4 For an analysis, see Craig, "Ten Years after *Ewanchuk*."

5 See *Ewanchuk* at para. 51, emphasis added.

6 Craig, "Ten Years after *Ewanchuk*" at 252–54.

7 Ibid. at 253.

8 Ibid. at 254.

9 *J.A.* at paras. 64–65.

10 See Lynda Holmstrom and Ann Burgess, *The Victim of Rape: Institutional Reactions* (New York: John Wiley, 1983); Lorenne M.G. Clark and Debra J. Lewis, *Rape: The Price of Coercive Sexuality* (Toronto: The Women's Press, 1977).

11 See Holly Johnson, *Dangerous Domains: Violence against Women in Canada* (Toronto: Nelson Canada, 1996) at 142–46.

12 See Lazar, "Negotiating Sex," which is quite critical of lawyers' "common sense" attitudes toward non-contemporaneous sexual touching in intimate relationships.

13 For the classic statement, see H.L.A. Hart, *The Concept of Law*, 3rd ed. (New York: Oxford University Press, 2012). See also Meir Dan-Cohen, "Decision Rules and Conduct Rules: Acoustic Separation in the Criminal Law" (1984) 94 Harv. L. Rev. 625.

14 See Dan-Cohen, "Decision Rules and Conduct Rules."

15 We may want some measure of overbreadth in order to prevent proto-defendants from trying to game the law. For reasons I explore later, any such overbreadth should be accomplished through the use of legal presumptions and not simply through an over-inclusive substantive definition of the offence.

16 Much of this section is reproduced from my paper, "The Challenge of the Bad Man" (2013) 58 McGill LJ 451.

17 Hart, *The Concept of Law* at ch. 2, 39.

18 Ibid. at ch. 2.

19 Hart's analysis has recently been subjected to sustained criticism: see Frederick Schauer, *The Force of Law* (Cambridge: Harvard University Press, 2015). See also Richard H. McAdams, *The Expressive Powers of Law* (Cambridge: Harvard University Press, 2015) at ch. 1 (noting that specific claims about law's expressive function tend not to be satisfactorily grounded or fleshed out).

20 I use "citizen" as shorthand for "members of the public." Obviously, the substantive criminal law is meant to guide everyone within a country's borders, not only citizens in the strict sense.

21 See John Kleinig, "Criminally Harming Others" (1986) 5 Crim. Just. Ethics 3; Hart, *The Concept of Law* at 38–39; Douglas Husak, *Overcriminalization: The Limits of the Criminal Law* (Oxford: Oxford University Press, 2008) (hinting that the use of punishment is a signal that the criminal law has failed to some extent).

22 There is, of course, a vast literature on the moral limits of the criminal law. See, e.g., Joel Feinberg, *The Moral Limits of the Criminal Law*, 4 vols. (New York: Oxford University Press, 1984); H.L.A. Hart, *Law, Liberty, and Morality* (Oxford: Clarendon, 1965); William Wilson, *Central Issues in Criminal Law Theory* (Oxford: Hart, 2002) at ch. 1; Ronald Dworkin, "Lord Devlin and the Enforcement of Morals" (1966) 75 Yale LJ 986; R.A. Duff, *Answering*

for *Crime: Responsibility and Liability in the Criminal Law* (Oxford: Hart, 2007) at ch. 6; Husak, *Overcriminalization*.

23 *R. v. Mabior*, [2012] 2 SCR 584 [*Mabior*].

24 Cf. James Chalmers and Fiona Leverick, "Fair Labelling in Criminal Law" (2008) 71 Mod. L. Rev. 217 (implicitly rejecting the expressive value of fair labelling). For discussion of that paper, see Plaxton, "The Challenge of the Bad Man" at 468–73.

25 Andrew Ashworth, *Principles of Criminal Law*, 5th ed. (New York: Oxford University Press, 2006) at 88.

26 See Vera Bergelson, *Victims' Rights and Victims' Wrongs: Comparative Liability in Criminal Law* (Stanford: Stanford University Press, 2009) at 50.

27 Douglas Husak, "The Costs to Criminal Theory in Supposing that Intentions Are Irrelevant to Permissibility" (2009) 3 Crim. L. & Phil. 51 at 64.

28 Stuart P. Green, *Thirteen Ways to Steal a Bicycle: Theft Law in the Information Age* (Harvard University Press, 2012). See also C.M.V. Clarkson, "Theft and Fair Labelling" (1993) 56 Mod. L. Rev. 554; Stephen Shute and Jeremy Horder, "Thieving and Deceiving: What Is the Difference?" (1993) 56 Mod. L. Rev. 548; P.R. Glazebrook, "Thief or Swindler: Who Cares?" (1991) 50 Cambridge LJ 389.

29 Green, *Thirteen Ways to Steal a Bicycle* at 53.

30 See Tom Tyler, *Why People Obey the Law* (New Haven: Yale, 1990).

31 Paul Robinson and John Darley, "Intuitions of Justice: Implications for Criminal Law and Justice Policy" (2007) 81 S. Calif. L. Rev. 1 at 21.

32 See Dirk Meissner, "Sexting BC Teen Found Guilty of Child Pornography" *CTV News Online* (10 January 2014), http://bc.ctvnews.ca/sexting-b-c-teen-found-guilty-of-child-pornography-1.1633678.

33 Carissima Mathen "Crowdsourcing Sexual Objectification" (2014) Laws 3:3 at 529, http://www.mdpi.com/2075-471X/3/3/529; Diane Keats Citron and Mary Anne Franks, "Criminalizing Revenge Porn" (2014) 49 Wake Forest L. Rev. 345, http://papers.ssrn.com/sol3/papers.cfm?abstract_id=2368946.

34 *R. v. Sharpe*, 2001 SCC 2.

35 Ibid. at para. 34.

36 See Chalmers and Leverick, "Fair Labelling in Criminal Law." For a discussion of their argument, see my "Challenge of the Bad Man" at 468–73.

37 CCSO Cybercrime Working Group, *Report to the Federal/Provincial/Territorial Ministers Responsible for Justice and Public Safety: Cyberbullying and the Non-consensual Distribution of Intimate Images* (June 2013), http://www.justice.gc.ca/eng/rp-pr/other-autre/cndii-cdncii/pdf/cndii-cdncii-eng.pdf [Cybercrime Working Group Report]. The offence would later be included as part of Bill C-13, *Protecting Canadians from Online Crime Act*, 2nd Sess., 41st Parl., 2013, http://www.parl.gc.ca/House Publications/Publication.aspx?Language=E&Mode=1&DocId=6311444.

38 Cybercrime Working Group Report at 18.

39 See Husak, *Overcriminalization.*

40 None of this, of course, takes issue with the need for prosecutorial discretion – or for some open texture in the formulation of criminal statutes.
Anglo-American criminal justice systems could not function without some
exercise of discretion: see Rachel E. Barkow, "The Ascent of the Administrative State and the Demise of Mercy" (2008) 121 Harv. L. Rev. 1332; Benjamin Berger, "The Abiding Presence of Conscience: Criminal Justice against
the Law and the Modern Constitutional Imagination" (2011) 61 UTLJ 579. I
argue only that there are limits to the responsible exercise of prosecutorial
discretion. On the rule of law problems with unlimited Crown discretion,
see Husak, *Overcriminalization* at 17–33. The Supreme Court has spoken
with a forked tongue on prosecutorial discretion. On one hand, it has
made charging decisions all but unreviewable: for a particularly stunning
example, see *R. v. Power,* [1994] 1 SCR 601 (strongly suggesting that the
Crown not publish a list of factors it will consider when deciding whether
to exercise its discretion to charge). See also Kent Roach, "Developments in
Criminal Procedure: The 1993–94 Term" (1995) 6 SCLR (2d) 281 at 337–40;
Kent Roach, "The Attorney General and the Charter of Rights Revisited"
(2000) 50 UTLJ 1. On the other hand, it has also denied that prosecutorial
discretion can save an otherwise unconstitutional criminal prohibition: see
R. v. Hess; R. v. Nguyen, [1990] 2 SCR 906 at 924; *Canadian Foundation for
Children, Youth, and the Law v. Canada (Attorney General),* [2004] 1 SCR
76 at para. 63 *[Canadian Foundation].* See also *R. v. Nur,* 2015 SCC 15.

41 Cybercrime Working Group Report at 18.

42 *R. v. Vaillancourt,* [1987] 2 SCR 636 *[Vaillancourt].*

43 Ibid. at para. 28.

44 Green, *Thirteen Ways to Steal a Bicycle.*

45 *Vaillancourt* at para. 51.

46 But see also the opinion of L'Heureux-Dubé J. in *R. v. Martineau,* [1990] 2
SCR 633 at 677–81 *[Martineau].*

47 Ibid. at 645.

48 Ibid.

49 Ibid.

50 Ibid. at 646, citing Rupert Cross, "The Mental Element in Crime" (1967) 83
LQR 215; Andrew Ashworth, "The Elasticity of *Mens Rea*" in Colin Tapper,
ed., *Crime, Proof and Punishment* (London: Butterworths, 1981); Glanville
Williams, *The Mental Element in Crime* (Jerusalem: Magnes Press, 1965);
Glanville Williams, "Convictions and Fair Labelling" (1983) 42 Cambridge LJ
85.

51 Paul H. Robinson refers to the role of mens rea in rule articulation: see
"Should the Criminal Law Abandon the *Actus Reus-Mens Rea* Distinction?"
in Stephen Shute, John Gardner, and Jeremy Horder, eds., *Action and Value
in Criminal Law* (Oxford: Clarendon Press, 1993). See also Stephen Shute,

John Gardner, and Jeremy Horder, "Introduction: The Logic of Criminal Law" in the same volume.

52 Shute, Gardner, and Horder, "Introduction" at 14. Cf. William Wilson, "Murder and the Structure of Homicide" in Andrew Ashworth and Barry Mitchell, eds., *Rethinking English Homicide Law* (Oxford: Oxford University Press, 2000).

53 Shute, Gardner, and Horder, "Introduction" at 13.

54 On the ordinary language of attempts, see R.A. Duff, *Criminal Attempts* (Oxford: Clarendon Press, 1996) at 20–21.

55 *Martineau* at 645.

56 *R. v. Darrach* (1998), 38 OR (3d) 1 (CA), aff'd [2000] 2 SCR 449.

57 Ibid. at para. 86. See also Don Stuart, *Charter Justice and Canadian Criminal Law*, 2nd ed. (Toronto: Carswell, 1996) at 74; Peter W. Hogg, *Constitutional Law of Canada*, 3rd ed., vol 2 (Toronto: Carswell, 1992) (looseleaf) at 44–35; Rosemary Cairns Way, "Constitutionalizing Subjectivism: Another View" (1990) 79 CR (3d) 260 at 262–63; Isabel Grant and Christine Boyle, "Equality, Harm and Vulnerability: Homicide and Sexual Assault Post-*Creighton*" (1993) 23 CR (4th) 252 at 258.

58 See Eric Colvin and Sanjeev Anand, *Principles of Criminal Law*, 3rd ed. (Toronto: Carswell, 2007) at 56, 103.

59 The definition of terrorism is hotly contested: see, e.g., *R. v. Khawaja*, 2012 SCC 69 (on the motive requirement in the Canadian Criminal Code's treatment). See also Kent Roach, *The 9/11 Effect: Comparative Counter-Terrorism* (Cambridge: Cambridge University Press, 2011) at 180–82, 255–57, 377–78.

60 Husak, "The Costs to Criminal Theory" at 64.

61 George Orwell, "Politics and the English Language: An Essay on Style" Horizon (April 1946).

62 To take a hypothetical example that James Chalmers has burned into my mind.

63 Chalmers and Leverick, "Fair Labelling in Criminal Law" at 235–37; W. Loh, "What Has Reform of Rape Legislation Wrought? A Truth in Criminal Labelling" (1981) 31 J. Social Issues 28 at 37.

64 On the wrongfulness of this kind of shaming, see Martha C. Nussbaum, *Hiding from Humanity: Disgust, Shame and the Law* (Princeton: Princeton University Press, 2004).

65 See Victor Tadros, "The Distinctiveness of Domestic Abuse: A Freedom-Based Account" (2005) 65 La. L. Rev. 989.

66 See Carissima Mathen and Michael Plaxton, "HIV, Consent, and Criminal Wrongs" (2011) 57 CLQ 464.

67 *The Reward* (1818), 2 Dods. 265, 165 ER 1482.

68 *Canadian Foundation* at para. 132.

69 *R. v. Hinchey* (1996), 111 CCC (3d) 353 (SCC).

70 Ibid. at para. 69.

71 *R. v. Cuerrier*, [1998] 2 SCR 371 at para. 21 [*Cuerrier*].

72 See *R. v. Kubassek* (2004) 189 OAC 339, 188 CCC (3d) 307 at paras. 17–22 [*Kubassek*].

73 *Ewanchuk* at para. 28.

74 *J.A.* at para. 63.

75 See *Canadian Foundation* at para. 204 (referring to "harmless and blameless conduct").

76 See John Gardner and Stephen Shute, "The Wrongness of Rape" in Jeremy Horder, ed., *Oxford Essays in Jurisprudence, Fourth Series* (Oxford: Oxford University Press, 2000). The paper has been reproduced in John Gardner, *Offences and Defences: Essays in the Philosophy of Criminal Law* (Oxford: Oxford University Press, 2007). All citations are to the original.

77 Douglas Husak, "Gardner on the Philosophy of Criminal Law" (2009) 29 OJLS 169 at 184–85.

78 *R. v. McDonnell*, [1997] 1 SCR 948 [*McDonnell*].

79 *Ewanchuk* at para. 28.

80 *Mabior* at para. 48.

81 See *R. v. Butler*, [1992] 1 SCR 452 [*Butler*]; *R. v. Labaye*, [2005] 3 SCR 728; Michael Plaxton, "What *Butler* Did" in Benjamin L. Berger and James Stribopoulos, eds., *Unsettled Legacy: Thirty Years of Criminal Justice under the Charter* (Markham: LexisNexis, 2012).

82 See, e.g., *R. v. Kormos* (1998), 14 CR (5th) 312 (Ont. Prov. Div.); *R. v. LePage* (1989) 74 CR (3d) 368 (Sask. QB). Even where the touching in question involved merely transitory pushing or shoving, giving rise to no injuries, it need not be regarded as de minimis: see, e.g., *Kubassek*. For a discussion, see Stewart, "Parents, Children, and the Law of Assault" at 19.

83 See the final section in chapter 4 of this book.

84 The force of this objection rests on the premise that the sexual touching in question is morally unobjectionable. In chapter 5, drawing on Nussbaum's work, I discuss the argument that sexual touching can be morally permissible even in the absence of contemporaneous consent. As I note in chapter 4, though, one can reject that argument and still maintain that the law should defer to the normative arrangements governing sexual touching in at least some intimate relationships. It may be, in other words, that sexual touching is wrongfully objectifying yet not the sort of conduct properly addressed in a criminal court.

85 See Stewart, "Parents, Children, and the Law of Assault" at 21. Stewart suggests, ostensibly following the reasoning in *Perka v. The Queen*, [1984] 2 SCR 222 at 245–46 [*Perka*], that this makes de minimis an excuse rather than a justification. Though I agree that it is not a justification, I do not agree that it is an excuse. Excuses tend to deny culpability, whereas the de minimis doctrine does not. The soundest view is that de minimis asserts

something like a limit on the jurisdiction of the court to require the defendant to answer for his wrong.

86 Stewart, "Parents, Children, and the Law of Assault" at 21.
87 Ibid.
88 *Canadian Foundation* at para. 44.

CHAPTER TWO

1 See Benedet, "Sexual Assault Cases at the Alberta Court of Appeal" at 131.
2 *R. v. Bernard*, [1988] 2 SCR 833 at para 84.
3 For the classic description of positive liberty, see Isaiah Berlin, "Two Concepts of Liberty" in *Four Essays on Liberty* (Oxford: Oxford University
Press, 1969) at 131–41.
4 Law Reform Commission of Canada, *Report on Sexual Offences* (Ottawa:
Minister of Supply and Services Canada, 1978) [*Report on Sexual Offences*].
5 Law Reform Commission of Canada, *Working Paper on Sexual Offences*
(Ottawa: Minister of Supply and Services Canada, 1978) at 16 [*Working
Paper on Sexual Offences*].
6 *Report on Sexual Offences* at 12.
7 *Working Paper on Sexual Offences* at 15–16, emphasis added.
8 See, e.g., *House of Commons Debates*, 32nd Parl., 1st Sess., vol. 10 (7 July
1981) at 11300.
9 Bill C-127.
10 Maria Łoś, "The Struggle to Redefine Rape in the Early 1980s" in Julian V.
Roberts and Renate M. Mohr, eds., *Confronting Sexual Assault: A Decade
of Legal and Social Change* (Toronto: University of Toronto Press, 1994) at
31.
11 *Report on Sexual Offences* at 15.
12 See Catharine A. MacKinnon, *Toward a Feminist Theory of the State* (Cambridge: Harvard University Press, 1989) at 133.
13 *House of Commons Debates*, 32nd Parl., 1st Sess., vol. 10 (7 July 1981) at
11300.
14 *Report on Sexual Offences*, 14.
15 Ibid.
16 Ibid. at 16. See Susan Brownmiller, *Against Our Will: Men, Women, and
Rape* (New York: Bantam, 1975) at 428–29.
17 See, e.g., Justice and Legal Affairs Committee (27 April 1982) at 78:11
(Thomson).
18 Some work on the labeling problem, inasmuch as it dwells entirely on the
effect it will have on the prosecution of offences rather than in the message
it sends to the broader community, are utterly unable to make sense of it;
see, e.g., Damian Warburton, "The Rape of a Label: Why It Would Be
Wrong to Follow Canada in Having a Single Offence of Unlawful Sexual
Assault" (2004) 68 J. Crim. L. 533.

19 Rape has sometimes been compared to torture, inasmuch as it is one of the few criminal acts that could not be justified under any circumstances. See, e.g., Gardner and Shute, "The Wrongness of Rape" at 193. See also Joel Feinberg, *The Moral Limits of the Criminal Law*, vol. 1, *Harm to Others* (New York: Oxford University Press, 1984) at 10.

20 See Rob Anders's recent proposal to restore the language of rape to the Criminal Code: Michael Plaxton, "Should We Reintroduce 'Rape'?" *Huffington Post* (24 January 2014), http://www.huffingtonpost.ca/michael-plaxton/rob-anders-rape-bill_b_4661698.html. In 2010, then-Minister of Public Safety Vic Toews made a similar proposal: Tonda MacCharles, "Tories Consider Returning the Term 'Rape' to Criminal Code" *Toronto Star* (11 May 2010), http://www.thestar.com/news/canada/2010/05/11/tories_consider_returning_the_term_rape_to_criminal_code.html.

21 Clark and Lewis, *Rape*.

22 Christine L.M. Boyle, Marie-Andrée Bertrand, Céline Lacerte-Lamontagne, and Rebecca Shamai, *A Feminist Review of Criminal Law* (Minister of Supply and Services Canada, December 1985) at 177n46. See also Christine Boyle, *Sexual Assault* (Toronto: Carswell, 1984) at 28, 64; Dianne Kinnon, *Report on Sexual Assault in Canada* (Canadian Advisory Council of the Status of Women, December 1981).

23 Clark and Lewis, *Rape* at 127.

24 Ibid. at 128.

25 Ibid.

26 Ibid. at 129.

27 Ibid. at 129–30.

28 Ibid. at 130–32.

29 On the traditional rules of evidence that reflected and reinforced these stereotypes, see Constance Backhouse, *Carnal Crimes: Sexual Assault Law in Canada, 1900–1975* (Toronto: Irwin Law, 2008). See also Benedet, "Sexual Assault Cases at the Alberta Court of Appeal" at 129, 133–35.

30 Clark and Lewis, *Rape* at 160.

31 Ibid. at 166–68.

32 Ibid. at 185–86.

33 See Kinnon, *Report on Sexual Assault in·Canada* at 53.

34 See Brownmiller, *Against Our Will*.

35 MacKinnon, *Toward a Feminist Theory of the State* at 174–75.

36 Kinnon, *Report on Sexual Assault in Canada* at 54.

37 Łoś, "The Struggle to Redefine Rape" at 32, emphasis original.

38 See Gardner and Shute, "The Wrongness of Rape" at 209–12.

39 Leah Cohen and Connie Backhouse, "Desexualizing Rape: A Dissenting View on the Proposed Rape Amendments" (1980) 2 Canadian Woman Studies 99 at 101.

40 See Gardner and Shute, "The Wrongness of Rape" at 209–12.

41 Cohen and Backhouse, "Desexualizing Rape" at 101.

42 Ibid. at 102.

43 Ibid.

44 Łoś, "The Struggle to Redefine Rape" at 33. See also MacKinnon, *Toward a Feminist Theory of the State* at 115–16.

45 MacKinnon, *Toward a Feminist Theory of the State* at 134–35.

46 Boyle et al., *A Feminist Review of Criminal Law* at 49.

47 Ibid.

48 See Plaxton, "What *Butler* Did."

49 See Gardner and Shute, "The Wrongness of Rape" at 197–98. See also Carolyn M. Shafer and Marilyn Frye, "Rape and Respect" in Mary Vetterling-Braggin, Frederick A. Elliston, and Jane English, eds., *Feminism and Philosophy* (Totowa: Littlefield, Adams & Co, 1977).

50 Ibid. at 196. For a critique, see Husak, "Gardner on the Philosophy of Criminal Law" at 184–85. See also *McDonnell*; Alan Wertheimer, *Consent to Sexual Relations* (Cambridge University Press, 2003) (arguing that the wrongness of non-consensual sexual touching is based on the victim's experiences). On the harms and risks which attend even consensual sexual intercourse, see Michelle Dempsey and Jonathan Herring, "Why Sexual Penetration Requires Justification" (2007) 27 OJLS 467 (discussing the kinds of physical injuries which may flow from sexual penetration).

51 Gardner and Shute, "The Wrongness of Rape" at 204.

52 Craig, *Troubling Sex: Towards a Legal Theory of Sexual Integrity* (Vancouver: UBC Press, 2012) at 69–70.

53 Ibid. at 72.

54 Jennifer Nedelsky, *Law's Relations: A Relational Theory of Self, Autonomy, and Law* (New York: Oxford University Press, 2011). I look more directly at Nedelsky's work in chapter 4.

55 Craig, *Troubling Sex* at 72–73.

56 Ibid. at 70.

57 This position has some affinity to two recent sex-positive approaches to US rape law: see, e.g., Kaplan, "Sex-Positive Law"; Deborah Tuerkheimer, "Slutwalking in the Shadow of the Law" (2014) 98 Minn. L. Rev. 1453.

58 Craig, *Troubling Sex* at 70.

59 *R. v. Chase*, [1987] 2 SCR 293 at 302 [*Chase*].

60 *R. v. Robicheau*, 2002 SCC 45.

61 *R. v. Robicheau* (2001), 43 CR (5th) 248 at 252 (NSCA).

62 Ibid. at 255.

63 Ibid. at 256.

64 Craig, *Troubling Sex* at 70.

65 *R. v. Litchfield*, [1993] 4 SCR 333 [*Litchfield*].

66 Ibid. at 354–55.

67 Ibid. at 355–56.

68 Craig, *Troubling Sex* at 77.

69 *Litchfield* at 357–58.

70 *R. v. Larue*, 2003 SCC 22 [*Larue*].

71 Ibid. at para. 1, quoting the dissenting opinion of Prowse J.A. in *R. v. Larue* (2002), 167 CCC (3d) 513 at paras. 2–4 (BCCA).

72 *Larue* at para. 3.

73 Craig, *Troubling Sex* at 80–81.

74 Ibid. at 81.

75 *Cuerrier*.

76 Though the touching was sexual in nature, the conduct in *Cuerrier* was prosecuted as an aggravated assault.

77 *Cuerrier*.

78 Craig, *Troubling Sex* at 78–79.

79 *Mabior*.

80 Ibid. at para. 89.

81 *R. v. Hutchinson*, 2014 SCC 19 [*Hutchinson*].

82 Ibid. at paras. 100–03.

83 Ibid. at paras. 64–74.

84 See the remarks of the concurring judges in *Hutchinson* at para. 102.

85 *Ewanchuk*.

86 Ibid. at para. 28.

87 *J.A.* at para. 57.

88 *R. v. Osolin*, [1993] 4 SCR 595 at para. 165.

89 *R. v. Seaboyer; R. v. Gayme*, [1991] 2 SCR 577 [*Seaboyer*].

90 See *Ewanchuk* at para. 51.

91 See David Archard, *Sexual Consent* (Boulder: Westview Press, 1997) at 131; *Ewanchuk* at para. 82.

92 *J.A.* at para. 3.

CHAPTER THREE

1 See *Wilcox* at para. 96.

2 *Ewanchuk* at para. 31.

3 Ibid. at para. 29, emphasis added.

4 Don Stuart, in *A Treatise in Criminal Law*, appears to proceed on the basis that this was the court's point.

5 See *R. v. Cey* (1989), 48 CCC (3d) 480 (Sask. CA) [*Cey*]; *R. v. LeClerc* (1991), 67 CCC (3d) 563 (Ont. CA).

6 Stewart, "Parents, Children, and the Law of Assault" at 7.

7 *Cey* at 488.

8 *R. v. E. (A.)* (2000), 146 CCC (3d) 449 at paras. 26 and 40 (Ont. CA).

9 *R. v. Palombi*, 2007 ONCA 486.

10 Ibid. at para. 29.

11 *R. v. D.J.W.*, 2011 BCCA 522 at para. 28, aff'd 2012 SCC 63.

12 *R. v. D.J.W.*, 2012 SCC 63.

13 *R. v. Jobidon*, [1991] 2 SCR 714 at 743 [*Jobidon*], emphasis added. Gonthier J. in fact parenthetically suggested, in the next line, that the doctrine of implied consent might not apply here. He made that observation, however, in order to show the absurdity of interpreting the law of assault in such a way that a parent could not apply this sort of force to his or her child. Certainly, he did not explain his intuition that implied consent has no application.

14 Stewart, "Parents, Children, and the Law of Assault" at 24–25.

15 I am proceeding, if only for the sake of argument, on the basis that insurance premiums should not attempt to influence behaviour, but merely track it.

16 Thus, it would be nonsensical to determine whether Alice is capable of creating legal obligations merely by asking whether others habitually obey her – i.e., whether we can predict that others will do as she demands – since that approach is as likely to reveal that she is a mob enforcer as a lawmaker. Hart, *The Concept of Law* at 19–20, 22–24. But see Schauer, *The Force of Law* at 136–37, 159–61.

17 See Stewart, "Parents, Children, and the Law of Assault" at 27 (noting that the complainant "does not actually consent to each individual application of force").

18 Consider a passage from Walter Tevis's novel, *The Queen's Gambit*. The narrator, a young chess prodigy, describes a game in which she and her opponent engage in a series of moves – compared to a dance – where neither acquires any advantage over the other. In spite of the enjoyment the narrator experiences from this dance, she feels obliged to seize the advantage when an opportunity presents itself.

19 One might reply that, since the officer has a warrant, it does not matter whether there is consent or not. But that misses the point: the fact that we would not describe this intrusion as consensual tells us something significant about what consent is not – namely resignation or fatalistic acquiescence.

20 *Cey* at 490.

21 Special considerations arise when the participants in a social practice are children and, therefore, not free to opt out. See J.S. Russell, "The Moral Ambiguity of Coaching Youth Sport" in Alun R. Hardman and Carwyn Jones, eds., *The Ethics of Sports Coaching* (London: Routledge, 2011).

22 W. Bradley Wendel, "Lawyers, Citizens, and the Internal Point of View" (2005) 75 Fordham L. Rev. 1473 at 1478.

23 Cf. Ronald Dworkin, *Taking Rights Seriously*, rev. ed. (Cambridge: Harvard University Press, 1978) at 102–03 (discussing Tal's smile at Fischer); Frederick Schauer, *Playing by the Rules: A Philosophical Examination of Rule-Based Decision-Making in Law and in Life* (Oxford: Clarendon Press, 1982) at 224n25.

24 See Alasdair MacIntyre, *After Virtue*, 3rd ed. (Notre Dame, 2007) at 187–88.

25 This is not to say that a game of hockey must be intended to challenge participants in this way. In many instances the use of physical force is actively discouraged. By the same token, a sport ordinarily regarded as non-contact – e.g., basketball – may be played by idiosyncratic rules by the participants' agreement.

26 Reasonable people will disagree about whether and the extent to which hockey is meant to challenge participants in this way. Compare, for example, the views of someone like Don Cherry to those of Ken Dryden. See Ken Dryden, "Ken Dryden on Hockey Violence: How Could We Be so Stupid?" *Globe and Mail* (11 March 2011), http://www.theglobeandmail.com/sports/hockey/ken-dryden-on-hockey-violence-how-could-we-be-so-stupid/article623061/?page=all.

27 See Harry Brighouse and Adam Swift, *Family Values: The Ethics of Parent-Child Relationships* (Princeton: Princeton University Press, 2014) at ch. 4.

28 The extent to which one can legitimately use parental force to discipline or teach one's children is obviously a far more controversial question: see Mark Carter, "'Debunking' Parents' Rights in the Canadian Constitutional Context" (2007), 86 Can. Bar Rev. 479.

29 Brighouse and Swift, *Family Values* at ch. 4.

30 See *M. (K.) v. M. (H.)*, [1992] 3 SCR 6 at 61, 63. See also Evan Fox-Decent, "The Fiduciary Nature of State Legal Authority" (2005) 31 Queen's LJ 259 at 276–78.

31 Heidi Hurd, "The Moral Magic of Consent" (1996) 2 Legal Theory 121.

32 Gardner and Shute, "The Wrongness of Rape."

33 See Arthur Ripstein, *Equality, Responsibility, and the Law* (Cambridge: Cambridge University Press, 1999) at 208.

34 This is not to suggest, of course, that we necessarily treat each other as mere ends – a point that is significant when we look ahead to Nussbaum's understanding of instrumentalization. See Martha Nussbaum, "Objectification" (1995) 24 Phil. & Pub. Affairs 249 at 265.

35 See Stewart, "Parents, Children, and the Law of Assault" at 7.

36 Ibid.

37 See Ripstein, *Equality, Responsibility, and the Law* at 208.

38 See supra n9 and accompanying quotation.

39 Brighouse and Swift, *Family Values* at ch. 4.

40 The parenting context raises unique concerns. In the adult sporting context, contemporaneous consent is possible but logically inconsistent with the participants' understanding of the social practice in which they are engaged. In the case of infants and small children, it is doubtful that meaningful consent – at least, of a sort that the law could regard as worthy of recognition – is possible at all. This distinction, though interesting, does not interfere with my broader argument that the law is flexible in what can

constitute legally valid consent – that it can shift away from *Ewanchuk*-like demands for the sake of preserving valuable social practices.

41 Wendel, "Lawyers, Citizens, and the Internal Point of View" at 1478.

42 Dryden, "Ken Dryden on Hockey Violence."

43 See Andrew O'Hehir, "Football's Death Spiral," *Salon* (3 February 2013), http://www.salon.com/2013/02/03/footballs_death_spiral/.

44 See *Canadian Foundation*.

45 See ibid. at para. 40 (holding that sec. 43 of the Criminal Code does not permit certain uses of corrective force on children).

46 See supra n2 and accompanying quotation.

47 See the introduction to this book, n29 and accompanying text.

48 I emphasize that this is a particularly charitable reading of Ewanchuk's attitudes and thinking at the time, one that reflects the defence he used at trial. The more likely possibility may be that he simply thought he could get away with pushing around a vulnerable seventeen-year-old woman.

49 *Ewanchuk* at para. 82.

50 Ibid. at para. 87.

51 Lucinda Vandervort, "Mistake of Law and Sexual Assault: Consent and Mens Rea" (1987–88) 2 CJWL 233; John McInnes and Christine Boyle, "Judging Sexual Assault Law against a Standard of Equality" (1995) 29 UBC L. Rev. 341 at 374–75.

52 *R. v. Ewanchuk*, 1998 ABCA 52 at para. 87.

53 LEAF Factum, para. 31.

54 See Cheryl Hanna, "Sex Is Not a Sport: Consent and Violence in Criminal Law" (2001) 42 Boston College L. Rev. at 239.

55 The need for context is a frequent refrain of lawyers interviewed in Lazar, "Negotiating Sex." This does not, of course, mean that the interviewees have in mind appropriate contextual factors.

56 Cf. *Hutchinson*, which some commentators take to be an implicit rolling back of the principles articulated in *Ewanchuk*.

CHAPTER FOUR

1 *Hutchinson*.

2 *Ewanchuk* at para. 26.

3 Don Stuart, *Canadian Criminal Law: A Treatise*, 3rd ed. (Toronto: Carswell, 1995) at 513.

4 *R. v. Jensen* (1996), 106 CCC (3d) 430 (Ont. CA) at 437–38, aff'd [1997] 1 SCR 304 [*Jensen*].

5 *R. v. Park*, [1995] 2 SCR 836 at 850 [*Park*].

6 Stuart, *Canadian Criminal Law*, 513, citing *Donovan*, [1934] 2 KB 498 (Eng. CA).

7 *Jensen* at 437, aff'd [1997] 1 SCR 304.

8 Ibid.

9   Ibid. at 437–38.

10 *R. v. Jensen*, [1997] 1 SCR 304 at para. 1.

11 *Park* at 850, para. 16.

12 Stuart, *Canadian Criminal Law* at 513–15.

13 Ibid. at 515.

14 Ibid.

15 On the distinction between justification and excuse, see *Perka* at 245–46; *R. v. Ryan*, 2013 SCC 3; George Fletcher, *Rethinking Criminal Law* (Boston: Little, Brown, & Co, 1978).

16 On the bindingness of *obiter* remarks made by the Supreme Court, see *R. v. Henry*, 2005 SCC 76; *R. v. Prokofiew*, 2010 ONCA 423, aff'd 2012 SCC 49.

17 See Sheila McIntyre, "Redefining Reformism: The Consultations that Shaped Bill C-49" in Roberts and Mohr, *Confronting Sexual Assault* at 306. On the consultation process, see also Kent Roach, *Due Process and Victims' Rights: The New Law and Politics of Criminal Justice* (Toronto: University of Toronto Press, 1999) at 172; Robert Martin, "Bill C-49: A Victory for Interest Group Politics" (1993) 42 UNB LJ 357.

18 *Ewanchuk* at para. 26.

19 Ibid. at para. 28.

20 *Hutchinson*.

21 *Park* at para. 42.

22 See *Ewanchuk* at para. 75

23 But see Jed Rubenfeld, "The Riddle of Rape-by-Deception and the Myth of Sexual Autonomy" (2013) 122 Yale LJ 1372 (though note that he proceeds on the basis of a narrow conception of sexual autonomy) and Deborah Tuerkheimer, "Sex without Consent" (2013) 23 Yale LJ Online 335.

24 See Richard H. Thaler and Cass R. Sunstein, *Nudge: Improving Decisions about Health, Wealth, and Happiness*, rev. ed. (New York: Penguin, 2009) at ch. 2.

25 Michael E. Bratman, *Shared Agency: A Planning Theory of Acting Together* (New York: Oxford University Press, 2014) at 15–25; Bratman, *Intention, Plans, and Practical Reason* (Cambridge: Harvard University Press, 1987; repr. CSLI Publications, 1999.); Bratman, *Faces of Intention: Selected Essays on Intention and Agency* (New York: Cambridge University Press, 1999) at 2–3. See also Scott J. Shapiro, *Legality* (Cambridge: Harvard University Press, 2011) at 121–23.

26 Bratman, *Intention, Plans, and Practical Reason* at 8; Bratman, *Faces of Intention* at 2–3.

27 Bratman, *Faces of Intention* at 15–18 (on "norms of intention rationality"); Shapiro, *Legality* at 127.

28 Meghan Daum alludes to the binding and liberating nature of plans in *The Unspeakable and Other Subjects of Discussion* (New York: Farrar, Straus, and Giroux, 2014) at 88.

29 Bratman, *Faces of Intention*.

30 Bratman, *Intention, Plans, and Practical Reason* at 2.

31 Ibid.

32 Ripstein, *Equality, Responsibility, and the Law* at 208.

33 Hanna, "Sex Is Not a Sport."

34 See the discussion in chapter 2.

35 See chapter 6, discussing Clare Chambers's *Sex, Culture, and Justice: The Limits of Choice* (University Park: Pennsylvania State University Press, 2007).

36 See Archard, *Sexual Consent* at 25–26. Because of the many concerns that arise, I cannot agree with Archard's suggestion that those in intimate relationships are "beyond consent."

37 Nedelsky, *Law's Relations* at 218–21.

38 Ibid.

39 Ibid. at 39–41.

40 See Berlin, "Two Concepts of Liberty."

41 Nedelsky, *Law's Relations* at 216–17.

42 Ibid.

43 Ibid. at 217–18.

44 Ibid. at 218–21.

45 Ibid. at 136–37.

46 Tuerkheimer, "Sex Without Consent" at 335. The paper is a response to Rubenfeld, "The Riddle of Rape-by-Deception and the Myth of Sexual Autonomy." See also Deborah Tuerkheimer, "Slutwalking in the Shadow of the Law" (2014) 98 Minn. L. Rev. 1453.

47 Joel Feinberg, "Autonomy" in John Christman, ed., *The Inner Citadel: Essays on Individual Autonomy* (Brattleboro: Echo Point, 2014 [1989]) at 32. See also Kathryn Abrams, "From Autonomy to Agency: Feminist Perspectives on Self-Direction" (1999) 40 Wm. & Mary L. Rev. 805 at 810.

48 Tuerkheimer, "Sex without Consent" at 338.

49 Turkheimer is clear that agency, so far as she is concerned, is essentially equivalent to relational autonomy: "Sex Without Consent" at 346.

50 Ibid. at 339.

51 Robin West, "Sex, Law, and Consent" in Franklin G. Miller and Alan Wertheimer, eds., *The Ethics of Consent: Theory and Practice* (Oxford: Oxford University Press, 2009) at 246.

52 Tuerkheimer, "Sex without Consent" at 342; Tuerkheimer, "Slutwalking in the Shadow of the Law" at 1490.

53 Ibid.

54 Tuerkheimer, "Sex without Consent" at 345.

55 Martha C. Nussbaum, *Upheavals of Thought: The Moral Intelligence of Emotions* (Cambridge: Cambridge University Press, 1999).

56 Nedelsky, *Law's Relations* at ch. 7.

57 Nussbaum, *Upheavals of Thought* at 135–36.

58 Ibid.

59 Ibid. at 217.

60 Ibid. at 227.

61 Ibid.

62 Ibid.

63 Ibid. at 98, 215.

64 Ibid. at 135.

65 On this point, it is worth looking at Corey Brettschneider, *When the State Speaks, What Should It Say? How Democracies Can Protect Expression and Promote Equality* (Princeton: Princeton University Press, 2014).

66 Nedelsky, *Law's Relations* at 77.

67 Joseph Raz, *The Morality of Freedom* (Oxford: Clarendon Press, 1985) at 417.

68 Ibid.

69 Nedelsky, *Law's Relations* at 216–17.

70 Ibid. at 217.

71 Ibid.

72 Hurd, "The Moral Magic of Consent."

73 See John Gardner, "Justification under Authority" (2010) 23:1 Can. J.L. & Jur. 71 at 75–83. See also François Tanguay-Renaud, "Individual Emergencies and the Rule of Criminal Law" in François Tanguay-Renaud and James Stribopolous, eds., *Rethinking Criminal Law: New Canadian Perspectives in the Philosophy of Domestic, Transnational, and International Criminal Law* (Oxford: Hart, 2012) at 42n52.

74 Thus, in "The Wrongness of Rape," Gardner and Shute argue that the law should recognize the prostitute's consent, even assuming it is a clear-cut case of instrumentalization.

75 Daniel Kahneman, *Thinking Fast and Slow* (Toronto: Doubleday, 2011) at ch. 31.

CHAPTER FIVE

1 Langton suggests several additions, but does not take serious issue with Nussbaum's list: Rae Langton, *Sexual Solipsism: Philosophical Essays on Pornography and Objectification* (Oxford: Oxford University Press, 2009) at ch. 10. See also the discussion in Ann J. Cahill, *Overcoming Objectification* (New York: Routledge, 2011) at ch. 1.

2 Nussbaum, "Objectification" at 257.

3 Ibid. at 261–62.

4 Ibid. at 261.

5 Ibid. at 264.

6 Ibid. at 263. See also Hannah Arendt, *The Human Condition* (Chicago: University of Chicago Press, 1958).

7 Nussbaum, "Objectification" at 271.

8 Importantly, Nussbaum makes it clear that her concern with instrumental-ization is with the treatment of a person as a *mere* use: "what is problematic is not instrumentalization per se, but treating someone primarily or merely as an instrument." Nussbaum, "Objectification" at 265. John Stanton-Ife, in a critique of Gardner and Shute's account of the wrongfulness of rape, has taken issue with their reliance on Nussbaum's conception of instru-mentalization: John Stanton-Ife, "Horrific Crimes" in Duff et al., eds., *The Boundaries of the Criminal Law* (Toronto: Oxford, 2010). See also Gardner and Shute, "The Wrongness of Rape."

9 Nussbaum, "Objectification" at 265. Even the wrongfulness of instrumen-talization is regarded by Nussbaum as somewhat dependent on context. In an increasingly famous passage, she suggests that the use of a lover's body as a pillow, through instrumentalizing, is not morally troubling so long as there is consent. Importantly, though, Nussbaum does not suggest that consent always or even usually has this cleansing effect. For the most part, she treats instrumentalization as per se wrongful.

10 Nussbaum, "Objectification" at 274, referring to Cass R. Sunstein, review of *Defending Pornography: Free Speech, Sex, and the Fight for Women's Rights*, by Nadine Strossen, *New Republic* (9 January 1995).

11 Roger Scruton, in his analysis of sexual desire, attempts to distinguish the human experience of sexual desire from that of animals. Nussbaum, who emphasizes that both human beings and animals have emotions with cog-nitive content, does not think it necessary to draw such hard-and-fast dis-tinctions between their sexual experiences. For the purposes of this book, I set aside the question. See Roger Scruton, *Sexual Desire: A Moral Philoso-phy of the Erotic* (New York: Free Press, 1986); Nussbaum, "Objectification" at 276–77n44; Martha C. Nussbaum, review of *Sexual Desire*, by Roger Scruton, *New York Review of Books* (18 December 1986), reprinted in *Philo-sophical Interventions: Reviews – 1986–2011* (New York: Oxford University Press, 2012) at 28. All citations are to the reprint. See also Nussbaum, *Up-heavals of Thought* at ch. 2.

12 Consider the analysis by Barbara Herman, "Could It Be Worth Thinking about Kant on Sex and Marriage?" in Louise Antony and Charlotte Witt, eds., *A Mind of One's Own: Feminist Essays on Reason and Objectivity* (Boulder: Westview, 1993); Nussbaum, "Objectification" at 266–67; Simon Blackburn, *Lust* (New York: Oxford University Press, 2004) at 94–95.

13 Nussbaum, "Objectification" at 267.

14 Scruton, *Sexual Desire* at 17.

15 See Paul Voice, "Martha's Pillow: Nussbaum on Justice and Sex" (2002) 15 Social Just. Res. 185 at 198.

16 Scruton, *Sexual Desire* at 18.

17 Ibid. at 17–18.

18 Ibid. at 18.

19 Nussbaum, "Objectification" at 260.

20 Blackburn, *Lust* at 88.

21 Ibid.

22 Gardner and Shute, "The Wrongness of Rape" at 199–203. See, for a benign example of this tendency, Oliver Sacks, *The Man Who Mistook His Wife for a Hat* (London: Picador, 2011 [1986]) at 47 (speaking of proprioception, a term which itself evokes notions of property, as the experience of owning one's body).

23 Gardner and Shute, "The Wrongness of Rape" at 201–02. See, for examples of this kind of thinking, Richard Posner, "An Economic Theory of the Criminal Law" (1985) 1193 at 1199; Donald. A. Dripps, "Beyond Rape: An Essay on the Difference between the Presence of Force and the Absence of Consent" (1992) 92 Columbia L. Rev. 1780; Guido Calabresi and Douglas Melamed, "Property Rules, Liability Rules, and Inalienability: One View of the Cathedral" (1972) 85 Harv. L. Rev. 1089 at 1100–01, 1125–27; and the discussion in Margaret Jane Radin, "Market-Inalienability" (1987) 100 Harv. L. Rev. 1849 at 1879–81.

24 Gardner and Shute, "The Wrongness of Rape" at 204.

25 Ibid. at 203.

26 See Robin West, "Legitimating the Illegitimate: A Comment on 'Beyond Rape'" (1993) 92 Columbia L. Rev. 1442 at 1451; Radin, "Market-Inalienability" at 1880.

27 Scruton, *Sexual Desire* at 251.

28 Blackburn, *Lust* at 88–89. See also Thomas Nagel, "Sexual Perversion" in *Mortal Questions* (Cambridge: Cambridge University Press, 1979) at 50.

29 Blackburn, *Lust* at 61.

30 See Nussbaum, *Upheavals of Thought*.

31 Scruton, *Sexual Desire* at 64.

32 Ibid. at 65.

33 Ibid. at 67, 70.

34 Ibid. at 92.

35 On the relationship between autonomy, self-governance, and "permeability" or "violability," see Sarah Buss, "Valuing Autonomy and Respecting Persons: Manipulation, Seduction, and the Basis of Moral Constraints" (2005) 115 Ethics 195 at 195–96.

36 See Nussbaum, *Upheavals of Thought*.

37 See Nussbaum, *Hiding from Humanity*. See also Nussbaum, *Upheavals of Thought*; Nussbaum, *From Disgust to Humanity: Sexual Orientation and Constitutional Law* (Oxford: Oxford University Press, 2010) at esp. ch. 6; Nussbaum, *Not for Profit: Why Democracy Needs the Humanities* (Princeton: Princeton University Press, 2010) at 38–40.

38 Scruton, *Sexual Desire* at 251.

39 Nussbaum, "Objectification" at 277–78.

40 Ibid. at 276–77.

41 Consider this passage from the preface to Robert Greene's popular *The Art of Seduction* (Toronto: Penguin, 2003) at xxii: "Seducers have a warrior's outlook on life. They see each person as a kind of walled castle to which they are laying siege. Seduction is a process of penetration: initially penetrating the target's mind, their first point of defense. Once seducers have penetrated the mind, making the target fantasize about them, it is easy to lower resistance and create physical surrender. Seducers do not improvise; they do not leave this process to chance. Like any good general, they plan and strategize, aiming at the target's particular weaknesses." Consider also Neil Strauss's insider account of the pick-up artist community in *The Game* (New York: Harper Collins, 2005).

42 Ovid, *Ars Amatoria I*, A.S. Hollis, ed. (Oxford: Oxford University Press, 1977), esp. at lines 439–40, 611–16; Molly Myerowitz, *Ovid's Games of Love* (Detroit: Wayne State University Press, 1985) at 142 ("The words must be familiar and coaxing and the tone one of naturalness and immediacy."); Scruton, *Sexual Desire* at 25.

43 Scruton, *Sexual Desire* at 25.

44 Ibid. at 30.

45 Indeed, many speak of "maintenance sex" or couples putting their sex life on "project status." See Brenda Cossman, *Sexual Citizenship: The Legal and Cultural Regulation of Sex and Belonging* (Stanford: Stanford University Press, 2007) at 81–82. Amy Poehler's autobiography was an object of controversy as a result of comments that "You have to have sex with your husband occasionally even though you are exhausted. Sorry." *Yes Please* (Toronto: Harper Avenue, 2014) at 154. See also Tracy Moore, "How to Have Maintenance Sex" *Jezebel* (1 January 2015), http://jezebel.com/how-to-have-maintenance-sex-1677160234.

46 D.H. Lawrence, *The Rainbow* (Toronto: Penguin, 1995 [1915]).

47 Nussbaum, "Objectification" at 275.

48 Ibid. at 275n42.

49 Ibid.

50 Ibid. at 275.

51 For the record, I am *not* suggesting that every exchange of sexual services for money amounts to a desperate bargain, or that the circumstances under which such exchanges take place make no difference to the moral analysis. For a discussion of the impact that technology can make, see Scott R. Peppet, "Prostitution 3.0?" (2013) 98 Iowa L. Rev. 1989.

52 See Elizabeth Bernstein, *Temporarily Yours: Intimacy, Authenticity, and the Commerce of Sex* (Chicago: University of Chicago Press, 2007).

53 See Gardner and Shute, "The Wrongness of Rape" at 206–07.

54 Martha Nussbaum, "'Whether from Reason or Prejudice': Taking Money for Bodily Services" in *Sex and Social Justice* ("Bodily Services").

55 Gardner and Shute, "The Wrongness of Rape" at 207n25.

56 It is in this sense that the work of Catharine MacKinnon and Andrea Dworkin has particular resonance. They are right to argue that a culture of objectification can taint sexual relationships between men and women. See Andrea Dworkin, *Intercourse* (New York: Free Press, 1987) at 140–41; Catharine MacKinnon, *Only Words* (Cambridge: Harvard University Press, 1993). See also the reasoning in *Butler*. MacKinnon contributed to the submissions by LEAF, which influenced the court. MacKinnon and Dworkin qualifiedly endorsed the ruling: Catharine MacKinnon and Andrea Dworkin, eds., *In Harm's Way: The Pornography Civil Rights Hearings* (Cambridge: Harvard University Press, 1997) at 387.

57 Nussbaum, "Objectification" at 265.

58 See the submissions of the defendant in *J.A.* at para. 58.

59 See Raz, *The Morality of Freedom* at ch. 12.

60 On loyalty, see Raz, *The Morality of Freedom* at ch. 12; Scruton, *Sexual Desire* at 241–42.

61 See Scruton, *Sexual Desire* at 248.

62 Ibid. at 247. See also Archard, *Sexual Consent* at 31–32.

63 See Fox-Decent, "The Fiduciary Nature of State Legal Authority"; Evan Fox-Decent, "Is the Rule of Law Really Indifferent to Human Rights?" (2008) 27 Law & Phil. 533.

64 Lorianna de Giorgio, "Is Bad Bedside Manner a Conscious Decision on the Doctor's Part?" *Toronto Star* (12 May 2012), http://www.thestar.com/news/world/article/1176448--is-bad-bedside-manner-a-conscious-decision-on-the-doctor-s-part.

65 Consider the discussion by Annalise Acorn, "Responsibility, Self-Respect and the Ethics of Self-pathologization" in Francois Tanguay-Renaud and James Stribopolous, eds., *Rethinking Criminal Law Theory* (Oxford: Hart, 2012), in which she distinguishes between old and new approaches to psychiatry.

66 See *Norberg v. Wynrib*, [1992] 2 SCR 226; *Strother v. 3464920 Canada Inc.*, [2007] 2 SCR 177.

67 See Federation of Law Societies of Canada, *Model Code of Professional Conduct* (2011) at r. 2.03.

68 See David Sussman, "What's Wrong with Torture?" (2005) 33 Phil. & Public Affairs 1 at 26–28.

CHAPTER SIX

1 Chambers, *Sex, Culture, and Justice* at ch. 5.

2 Ibid. at 162.

3 Ibid. at 162–63.

4 See John Rawls, *Political Liberalism* (New York: Columbia University Press, 1996) at 77–78; Nussbaum, *Women and Human Development* at 74–75. For

Nussbaum's critique of Rawls's contractarian argument for political liberalism, see *Frontiers of Justice* (Cambridge: Harvard University Press, 2006).

5 Chambers, *Sex, Culture, and Justice* at 165.

6 Nussbaum, *Frontiers of Justice* at 184–86; Nussbaum, *Women and Human Development* at 146–47; Amartya Sen, *The Idea of Justice* (Toronto: Allen Lane, 2009) at 238.

7 Sen, *The Idea of Justice* at 236–37.

8 *Marathon Man*, John Schlesinger, dir. (1976), http://www.imdb.com/title/tt0074860.

9 See Peter de Marneffe, *Liberalism and Prostitution* (New York: Oxford University Press, 2010) at 70–71.

10 Nussbaum, "Objectification" at 265.

11 Chambers, *Sex, Culture, and Justice* at 130.

12 Ibid. at 172.

13 Ibid. at 172–73.

14 See Ruthann Robson, *Dressing Constitutionally: Hierarchy, Sexuality, and Democracy from Our Hairstyles to Our Shoes* (Cambridge: Cambridge University Press, 2013).

15 D. Wendy Greene, "Title VII: What's Hair (and Other Race-Based Characteristics) Got to Do with It?" (2008) 79 U. Colorado L. Rev. 1355; Wendy Greene, "Identity Performance as a Bottleneck to Employment Opportunity" *Concurring Opinions* (10 March 2014), http://www.concurring opinions.com/archives/2014/03/identity-performance-as-a-bottleneck-to-employment-opportunity.html.

16 See Amanda Marcotte, "'Stand up and Be a Man': What the NFL Bullying Scandal Tells Us about Masculinity" *Slate* (11 November 2013), http://www.slate.com/blogs/xx_factor/2013/11/11/nfl_bullying_scandal_what_the_richie_incognito_jonathan_martin_episode_tells.html; Emily Bazelon and Joshua Levin, "NFL Bullies" *Slate* (4 November 2013), http://www.slate.com/articles/sports/sports_nut/2013/11/richie_incognito_suspended_how_the_nfl_abets_locker_room_bullies.html.

17 See Arlie Russell Hochschild, *The Time Bind: When Work Becomes Home and Home Becomes Work* (New York: Holt, 1997).

18 Chambers, *Sex, Culture, and Justice* at 173.

19 See Sally Haslanger, "On Being Objective and Being Objectified" in *Resisting Reality: Social Construction and Social Critique* (New York: Oxford University Press, 2012).

20 Haslanger, "On Being Objective and Being Objectified" at 74–75. See also Chambers, *Sex, Culture, and Justice* at 193.

21 Chambers, *Sex, Culture, and Justice* at 176–200.

22 Ibid. at 224–27.

23 Ibid. at 173.

24 See John Stuart Mill, *On Liberty* (Toronto: Penguin Classics, 1985 [1859]).

25 Chambers, *Sex, Culture, and Justice* at 198.

26 Ibid.

27 Joel Feinberg, *The Moral Limits of the Criminal Law*, vol. 2, *Offense to Others* and vol. 3, *Harm to Self* (Oxford: Oxford University Press, 1985, 1986); *Butler*. See also Chambers, *Sex, Culture, and Justice* at 212.

28 Chambers, *Sex, Culture, and Justice* at 198.

29 See Nussbaum, *Women and Human Development* at 94; Martha Nussbaum, "Judging Other Cultures: The Case of Genital Mutilation" in *Sex and Social Justice*.

30 Ibid.; Nussbaum, "Judging Other Cultures" at 123–24; Chambers, *Sex, Culture, and Justice* at 177.

31 Chambers, *Sex, Culture, and Justice* at 191.

32 Ibid. at 190.

33 See Nussbaum, *Women and Human Development* at 174–75n16. There, Nussbaum notes her disagreement with Susan Moller Okin's theoretical approach in "Is Multiculturalism Bad for Women?" in Joshua Cohen, Matthew Howard, and Martha C. Nussbaum, eds., *Is Multiculturalism Bad for Women?* (Princeton: Princeton University Press, 1999). Nonetheless, she observes that Okin's focus on "genuinely egregious violation[s] of women's capabilities" means that their "practical conclusions are not very dissimilar."

34 Chambers, *Sex, Culture, and Justice* at 120.

35 Ibid. at 123.

36 Ibid. at 124. See also Nedelsky, *Law's Relations*.

37 Chambers, *Sex, Culture, and Justice* at 121.

38 Ibid.

39 See Albert O. Hirschman, *Exit, Voice, and Loyalty: Responses to Decline in Firms, Organizations, and States* (Cambridge: Harvard University Press, 1970).

40 Leslie Green, "Rights of Exit" (1998) 4 Legal Theory 165 at 171.

41 Ibid.

42 Ibid.

43 Ibid. at 176–77.

44 See, e.g., Jeff Spinner-Halev, "Autonomy, Association, and Pluralism" in Avigail Eisenberg and Jeff Spinner-Halev, eds., *Minorities within Minorities: Equality, Rights and Diversity* (Cambridge University Press, 2005) at 57; Susan Moller Okin, "'Mistresses of Their Own Destiny': Group Rights, Gender, and Realistic Rights of Exit" (2002) 112 Ethics 205 ["Group Rights"]; Ayelet Shachar, "The Paradox of Multicultural Vulnerability" in C. Jopke and S. Lukes, eds., *Multicultural Questions* (Oxford: Oxford University Press, 1999).

45 See Nussbaum, *Women and Human Development* at 36–42; Nussbaum, "Rage and Reason"; Sen, *Development as Freedom* at 62–63.

46 Shachar, "The Paradox of Multicultural Vulnerability" at 100.

47 Hirschman, *Exit, Voice, and Loyalty* at 4.
48 Ibid. at 33.
49 Ibid. See also Okin, "Group Rights" at 229.
50 Hirschman, *Exit, Voice, and Loyalty* at ch. 3.
51 Ibid. at 37; Dwight Newman, *Community and Collective Rights: A Theoretical Framework for Rights Held by Groups* (Oxford: Hart, 2011) at 157.
52 Green, "Rights of Exit" at 171.
53 Ibid.
54 See Ayelet Shachar, *Multicultural Jurisdictions: Cultural Differences and Women's Rights* (Cambridge: Cambridge University Press, 2001) at 125, 143.
55 Hirschman, *Exit, Voice, and Loyalty* at 82.
56 Newman, *Community and Collective Rights* at 157.
57 Green, "Rights of Exit" at 171.
58 Hirschman, *Exit, Voice, and Loyalty* at ch. 7.
59 Chambers, *Sex, Culture, and Justice* at 136.
60 Ibid.
61 Ibid.
62 Ibid.
63 Ibid. at 136–37.
64 Ibid. at 137.
65 Hirschman, *Exit, Voice, and Loyalty* at 37.
66 Ibid.
67 Chambers, *Sex, Culture, and Justice* at 173.
68 Ibid. at 198.
69 Ibid. at 121.
70 Ibid.
71 Ibid. at 210.
72 See *Butler*. On the expressive significance of micro-aggressions, see Samantha Brennan, "Feminist Ethics and Everyday Inequalities" (2009) 24 Hypatia 141 at 154–55.
73 Chambers, *Sex, Culture, and Justice* at 186.
74 Ibid. at 187.
75 Ibid. at 187–90.
76 Ibid. at 121–22, emphasis original.
77 Ibid. at 178.
78 Newman, *Community and Collective Rights* at 157.
79 As that suggests, there is a sense in which the decision to enter into an intimate relationship can be a first- rather than second-order decision.
80 See Scruton, *Sexual Desire*; John Finnis, "Law, Morality, and Sexual Orientation" (1994) 69 Notre Dame L. Rev. 1049; Finnis, "The Good of Marriage and the Morality of Sexual Relations: Some Philosophical and Historical Observations" (1997) 42 Am. J. Jurisprudence 97; Sherif Girgis, Robert P. George, and Ryan T. Anderson, "What Is Marriage?" (2010) 34 Harv. JLPP 245.

81 See Barbara Ehrenreich, *Re-making Love: The Feminization of Sex* (New York: Anchor Books, 1986).

82 See Stephanie Coontz, *Marriage, a History: How Love Conquered Marriage* (Toronto: Penguin, 2005).

83 See Brenda Cossman, *Sexual Citizenship: The Legal and Cultural Regulation of Sex and Belonging* (Stanford: Stanford University Press, 2007) at 81–82.

84 This point is frequently raised in current debates over "female Viagra": see, e.g., Katherine Angel, "The History of 'Female Sexual Dysfunction' as a Mental Disorder in the 20th Century" (2010) 23 Curr. Opin. Psychiatry 536, http://www.ncbi.nlm.nih.gov/pmc/articles/PMC2978945/; Jacoba Urist, "Do Women Need Their Own Viagra?" *Atlantic* (18 December 2014), http://www.theatlantic.com/health/archive/2014/12/do-women-need-their-own-viagra/383720/.

85 MacKinnon, *Toward a Feminist Theory of the State* at 133.

86 See Abella J.'s discussion in *Quebec v. A.*, 2013 SCC 6; *Moge v. Moge*, [1992] 3 SCR 813.

87 See *R. v. Lavallee*, [1990] 1 SCR 852.

88 Hirschman, *Exit, Voice, and Loyalty* at 43.

89 I borrow this phrase from American First Amendment case law. See, e.g., *Grayned v. City of Rockford*, 408 US 104 (1972).

90 This raises interesting questions about the significance of age to the analysis. Mark Regnerus and Jeremy Uecker observe that young Americans find it difficult to talk openly about sexual matters. See *Premarital Sex in America: How Young Americans Meet, Mate, and Think About Marrying* (Oxford: Oxford University Press, 2011) at 74–76.

91 Joseph Fishkin, *Bottlenecks: A New Theory of Equal Opportunity* (New York: Oxford University Press, 2014) at 220–22.

92 Amartya Sen, *The Idea of Justice* (London: Allen Lane, 2009) at 18.

93 That we make decisions as though our past and future selves were different people is a point much remarked upon in behavioural economics and social psychology. See, e.g., Daniel Kahneman, *Thinking Fast and Slow* (Doubleday Canada, 2011) at chs. 35–38.

94 Fishkin, *Bottlenecks* at 220–24.

95 Ibid. at 221.

96 Ibid. at 196.

97 On this point, it is worth reading the majority opinion in *Moge v. Moge*, [1992] 3 SCR 813.

98 Chambers, *Sex, Culture, and Justice* at 137.

99 Ibid.

100 See Lynn Jamieson, "Intimacy Transformed? A Critical Look at the 'Pure Relationship'" (1999) 33 Sociology 477 at 486 ("The couples have applied a reflexive awareness of the malleability of the world and themselves to creating a framework of rules.").

101 Ibid. at 162.

102 See Gerald Dworkin, *The Theory and Practice of Autonomy* (Cambridge: Cambridge University Press, 1988) at 20; Sarah Conly, *Against Autonomy: Justifying Coercive Paternalism* (Cambridge: Cambridge University Press, 2013) at 82.

103 Marcel Proust, *Swann's Way* in *Remembrance of Things Past*, vol. 1 (Penguin Classics, 1985) at 85–86. See also 390: "Like many other men, Swann had a naturally lazy mind and lacked imagination. He knew perfectly well as a general truth that human life is full of contrasts, but in the case of each individual human being he imagined all that part of his or her life with which he was not familiar as being identical with the part with which he was."

104 P.F. Strawson, *Freedom and Resentment and Other Essays* (London: Methuen & Co., 1974) at 9. See also Christine M. Korsgaard, *Creating the Kingdom of Ends* (Cambridge: Cambridge University Press, 1996) at ch. 7. This point underpins much of the exasperation directed at the Quebec Charter of Values expressed by women who are part of religious communities; see, e.g., Lysiane Gagnon, "In Quebec, a Feminist Rift over Secularism" *Globe and Mail* (2 October 2013), http://www.theglobeandmail.com/globe-debate/in-quebec-a-feminist-rift-over-secularism/article14639735/; Toula Foscolos, "Quebec's White, Privileged Feminists Don't Speak for Me" *Huffington Post* (17 October 2013), http://www.huffingtonpost.ca/toula-foscolos/quebec-charter-janettes_b_4115601.html. See also L.G. Beaman, "Overdressed and Underexposed or Underdressed and Overexposed?" (2013) 3 Oñati Socio-Legal Series 1136–57, http://ssrn.com/abstract=2356817.

105 Chambers, *Sex, Culture, and Justice* at 124.

106 Martha C. Nussbaum, *Liberty of Conscience: In Defense of America's Tradition of Religious Equality* (New York: Basic Books, 2008) at ch. 5.

107 Beck and Beck-Gernsheim, *Distant Love*; Anthony Giddens, *The Transformation of Intimacy* (Redwood City: Stanford University Press, 1992) at 154–55.

108 I need to acknowledge, here, the Supreme Court's decision in *Jobidon*, in which the majority held that individuals cannot consent to the intentional infliction of bodily harm in the context of public brawls and fist fights. See also *R. v. Paice*, 2005 SCC 22 (CanLII), [2005] 1 SCR 339. That ruling can be read as prohibiting individuals from engaging in certain kinds of sexual practices, even where the participants purport to consent and are conscious throughout. For a discussion of the implications of *Jobidon* and *Paice* for sexual assault, see *R. v. Zhao*, 2013 ONCA 293 (CanLII); *R. v. Welch* (1995), 101 CCC (3d) 214 (Ont. CA); *R. v. Quashie* (2005), 2005 CanLII 23208 (ON CA), 198 CCC (3d) 337 (Ont. CA); *R. v. Robinson* (2001), 2001 CanLII 24059 (ON CA), 53 OR (3d) 448; *R. v. Amos*, 1998 CanLII 2814 (ON CA), [1998] OJ No. 3047 (CA). See also Ummni Khan, *Vicarious Kinks: S/M in the Sociolegal Imaginary* (Toronto: University of Toronto Press, 2014); Maneesha

Deckha, "Pain, Pleasure, and Consenting Women: Exploring Feminist Response to S/M and Its Legal Regulation in Canada through Jelinek's *The Piano Teacher*" (2007) 30 Harv. JL & Gender 425; David Tanovich, "Criminalizing Sex at the Margins" (2010) 74 CR (6th) 86.

109 See *J.A.*
110 Chambers, *Sex, Culture, and Justice* at 198.
111 Nussbaum, "Objectification" at 275.
112 Ibid. at 275n42.
113 D.H. Lawrence, *The Rainbow* (Toronto: Penguin, 1995 [1915]) at 50.
114 Ibid. at 49.
115 Ibid.
116 Ibid. at ch. 1.
117 Ibid. at 53.
118 Ibid. at 88–89.
119 Ibid. at ch. 2.
120 Ibid. at 90–91.
121 Langton, *Sexual Solipsism* at 229.
122 Catharine MacKinnon, *Feminism Unmodified* (Cambridge: Harvard University Press, 1987) at 182.
123 Strawson, *Freedom and Resentment* at 9.
124 Nussbaum, "Objectification" at 265.
125 Ibid.
126 Gardner and Shute, "The Wrongness of Rape."
127 Robert Flannigan, "Fiduciary Regulation of Sexual Exploitation" (2000) 79 CBR 301.
128 Law Society of Upper Canada, *Rules of Professional Conduct* (1 October 2014) at rule 2.01(1)(d), http://www.lsuc.on.ca/lawyer-conduct-rules/.
129 Canadian Medical Association, *Code of Ethics* (2004), http://policybase.cma.ca/dbtw-wpd/PolicyPDF/PD04-06.pdf at rule 2.
130 This is, obviously, a rough shorthand. The term could be said to highlight the voice aspects of Chambers's and Nussbaum's respective analyses, while playing down the significance of harm. To be clear, both deserve attention.

CHAPTER SEVEN

1 See Jessica Valenti, *The Purity Myth: How America's Obsession with Virginity Is Hurting Young Women* (Berkeley: Seal, 2010).
2 *Ewanchuk* at para. 103.
3 Archard, *Sexual Consent* at 131.
4 *Ewanchuk* at para. 82.
5 *Seaboyer* at 650. L'Heureux-Dubé J. drew upon a number of scholarly works, most notably Holmstrom and Burgess, *The Victim of Rape*; Clark and

Lewis, *Rape* (discussed in ch. 2); Vandervort, "Mistake of Law and Sexual Assault."

6 *Seaboyer* at 630.

7 Ibid. at para 27.

8 Lawrence Blum, "Stereotypes and Stereotyping: A Moral Analysis" (2004) 33 Philosophical Papers 251 at 255–56.

9 Ibid. at 261.

10 Ibid.

11 Ibid. at 265.

12 Ibid. at 266–67.

13 Ibid. at 266.

14 Ibid. See also Diana T. Meyers, *Subjection and Subjectivity: Psychoanalytic Feminism and Moral Philosophy* (Routledge, 1994) at 53.

15 Blum, "Stereotypes and Stereotyping."

16 Ibid.

17 Ibid.

18 Ibid. at 253.

19 Ibid.

20 Ibid. at 254.

21 See K. Anthony Appiah, "Stereotypes and the Shaping of Identity" (2000) 88 Calif. L. Rev. 41 at 48 (discussing normative stereotypes).

22 Hart, *The Concept of Law*. As Joseph Raz points out, the practice theory of rules by itself does not explain all rules, and does not explain what gives rules their normative force: see Raz, *Practical Reason and Norms* (Oxford, 1975) at 53–58. See also Dworkin, *Taking Rights Seriously* at 48–58; G.J. Warnock, *The Object of Morality* (Methuen, 1971) at 45–46. Since I am mainly concerned with social rules, however, and am not interested in defending these norms, Hart's analysis provides a convenient point of departure.

23 Hart, *The Concept of Law* at 55.

24 Ibid., emphasis original.

25 Ibid. at 56.

26 Ibid. at 57.

27 Ibid. at 55. The example is Hart's.

28 See Raz, *Practical Reason and Norms* at 53.

29 Hart, *The Concept of Law* at 257.

30 See Andrei Marmor, *Social Conventions: From Language to Law* (Princeton: Princeton University Press, 2009) at 8–9 (on the arbitrariness of conventions); David Lewis, *Convention: A Philosophical Study* (Hoboken: Blackwell, 2002 [1969]) at 70.

31 See Hart, *The Concept of Law* at 257; Dworkin, *Taking Rights Seriously* at 53.

32 See Edna Ullman-Margalit, *The Emergence of Norms* (Oxford: Clarendon Press, 1977) at 83–89; Lewis, *Convention*.

33 Sometimes, as with games, the conventions in question do not resolve what could be described as a coordination problem but instead *constitute* a social practice. As Marmor notes, it seems strange to suppose that the conventions constituting chess resolve a coordination problem between two people who want to play chess. In the absence of those conventions, there simply is no game of chess to *play*. Marmor, *Social Conventions* at ch. 2.

34 On the relationship between social norms and beliefs, see Lewis, *Convention* at 118–21 (distinguishing conventional behaviour from imitative behaviour); Cass R. Sunstein, "Social Norms and Social Roles" (1996) 96 Colum. L. Rev. 903. See also Patrick S. Shin, "Is There a Unitary Concept of Discrimination?" in Deborah Hellman and Sophia Moreau, eds., *Philosophical Foundations of Discrimination Law* (New York: Oxford University Press, 2013) at 173–74.

35 See Judith Jarvis Thomson, *Normativity* (Chicago: Open Court, 2008) at 204 (on epistemic oughts).

36 Blum, "Stereotypes and Stereotyping" at 261–62.

37 Ibid. at 261.

38 See the classic discussion in Erving Goffman, *Stigma: Notes on the Management of Spoiled Identity* (Toronto: Touchstone, 1986 [1968]).

39 Haslanger, "On Being Objective and Being Objectified" at 41.

40 Ibid.

41 MacKinnon, *Toward a Feminist Theory of the State* at 113.

42 Haslanger, "On Being Objective and Being Objectified" at 59.

43 Ibid.

44 Ibid. at 61.

45 Ibid. at 60–61.

46 MacKinnon, *Feminism Unmodified* at 50.

47 Langton, *Sexual Solipsism* at 278.

48 Ibid.

49 Haslanger, "On Being Objective and Being Objectified" at 65, emphasis added.

50 See Neil MacCormick, *H.L.A. Hart* (Stanford: Stanford University Press, 1981) at 34–40; Brian Z. Tamanaha, "The Internal/External Distinction and the Notion of a 'Practice' in Legal Theory Sociolegal Studies" (1996) 30 L. & Society Rev. 163 at 187–88.

51 Haslanger, "On Being Objective and Being Objectified" at 65, emphasis original.

52 Ibid. at 65–67.

53 Ibid. at 67, emphasis original.

54 Nussbaum, "Objectification" at 256.

55 Haslanger, "On Being Objective and Being Objectified" at 68–69.

56 Ibid. at 70.

57 Ibid.

58 Ibid. at 70–71.

59 See Langton, *Sexual Solipsism* at ch. 11.

60 Ibid.

61 Blum, "Stereotypes and Stereotyping" at 271.

62 See Strawson, *Freedom and Resentment* at 9. See also Korsgaard, *Creating the Kingdom of Ends* at ch. 7.

63 Blum, "Stereotypes and Stereotyping" at 271–72, emphasis added.

64 *Quebec v. A.*, 2013 SCC 6 at para. 202.

65 Denise G. Réaume, "Discrimination and Dignity" (2003) 63 La. L. Rev. 645 at 681–82.

66 See Nussbaum, "Objectification" at 261.

67 Blum, "Stereotypes and Stereotyping" at 272.

68 See Frederick Schauer, *Profiles, Probabilities, and Stereotypes* (Cambridge: Harvard University Press, 2003).

69 Ibid. See also Nussbaum, "'Whether from Reason or Prejudice.'" There has been an explosion of literature on the sorts of exchanges that should be blocked. It is worth noting, however, that these discussions generally take as their starting point that many goods and services *can* be treated as tradable commodities: see, e.g., Michael Walzer, *Spheres of Justice: A Defense of Pluralism and Equality* (New York: Basic Books, 1983); Michael Sandel, *What Money Can't Buy: The Moral Limits of Markets* (Toronto: Allen Lane, 2012); Debra Satz, *Why Some Things Should Not Be for Sale: The Moral Limits of Markets* (Oxford: Oxford University Press, 2010) at 81–82.

70 See Walzer, *Spheres of Justice*.

71 Much of this analysis, which places the focus on respect for autonomy rather than on any supposed evils of generalization, is consistent with Benjamin Eidelson, "Treating People as Individuals" in Hellman and Moreau, *Philosophical Foundations of Discrimination Law*.

72 MacKinnon, *Feminism Unmodified* at 182. See also chapter 6.

73 Langton, *Sexual Solipsism* at 228–29.

74 Ibid. at 229.

75 Ibid. at 256.

76 Haslanger, "On Being Objective and Being Objectified" at 70.

77 Consider the (in)famous "Cool Girl" passage in Gillian Flynn's *Gone Girl* (London: Phoenix, 2013) at 251: "Men actually believe this girl exists. Maybe they're fooled because so many women are willing to pretend to be this girl."

78 Ibid. at 74–75.

79 MacKinnon, *Only Words*.

80 *Butler*.

81 Report on Pornography by the Standing Committee on Justice and Legal Affairs (MacGuigan Report) (1978) at 18:4.

82 Jeremy Waldron, *The Harm in Hate Speech* (Cambridge: Harvard University Press, 2012).

83 Ibid. at 93–96.

84 Admittedly, something like this argument is sometimes raised in debates about prostitution, in suggestions that sex workers are "collaborators" in the oppression of women insofar as they reinforce pernicious gender norms. See Melissa Gira Grant, *Playing the Whore: The Work of Sex Work* (New York: Verso, 2014) at ch. 8. See also Khan, *Vicarious Kinks* at ch. 2.

85 But see *Reference re: Section 293 of the Criminal Code of Canada*, 2011 BCSC 1588 at para. 1197: "I question whether the capable consenting spouse is a 'victim.' To the contrary, she can be seen to be facilitating an arrangement which Parliament views as harmful to society generally." See also the discussion by Carissima Mathen, "Reflecting Culture: Polygamy and the Charter" (2012) 57 SCLR (2d) 357 at 368.

86 *Butler* at 479. See also *Little Sisters Book and Art Emporium v. Canada (Minister of Justice)*, [2000] 2 SCR 1120 at para. 60.

CHAPTER EIGHT

1 Boyle, *Sexual Assault* at 72.

2 Christine Boyle, "Sexual Assault as Foreplay: Does *Ewanchuk* Apply to Spouses?" (2004) 20 CR (6th) 359 at 365.

3 See Susan Moller Okin, *Justice, Gender, and the Family* (New York: Basic Books, 1989).

4 In what follows in this and the next section, it is worth considering David Archard's qualifications on his argument that some relationships are "beyond consent": *Sexual Consent* (Boulder: Westview Press, 1998) at 27:

> [T]he idea of a loving couple who are "beyond consent" is an ideal. That is not to deny that some couples may exemplify the ideal. But three cautions are in order. First, one must be careful to be sure that the behaviour of a couple is evidence of the ideal rather than something very different. In particular mutual trust and understanding should be distinguished from habits of acquiescence and passivity which might pass for the ideal. When nothing is or needs to be said between two people, that can just as easily spring from an exhaustion of the desire or capacity for dialogue as it can from a transcendence, through mutual understanding, of the need for it. This is true in sexual interaction as it is in many other areas. Second, relationships can and do change their character. What was once ideal can become less so. Because there was a time when there was no need of consent, it does not follow that now, under altered circumstances, the need does not press. Indeed, it may

press all the more strongly since the suspicion and uncertainty that follow from a loss of trust and love can be all the stronger for arising from the failure of the ideal. Third, even within a loving couple one partner can initiate a new kind of sexual activity which it would be unwise to presume the other is agreed to. Even the most trusting of lovers may, on occasion, need to assure each other that what they are about to engage in is agreeable to both.

My starting-point is that relationships should not be presumed to be ideal in Archard's sense, for these very reasons.

5 See Beck and Beck-Gernsheim, *Distant Love* at 58–66.

6 See Coontz, *Marriage, a History.*

7 For my purposes, I do not need to pass judgment on whether those arrangements are corruptions or abuses of the institution of marriage. On this point, see Finnis, "Law, Morality, and Sexual Orientation"; Finnis, "The Good of Marriage"; Girgis, George, and Anderson, "What Is Marriage?"

8 Beck and Beck-Gernsheim, *Distant Love* at 47–50.

9 I am not sure how grave an objection this would be: if we accept that the law should sometimes defer to normative arrangements governing intimate relationships, and that this principle should be reflected in the law of sexual consent, I am not sure that it much matters what we call the defence.

10 This is, I confess, a hypothetical scenario drawn from personal experience.

11 See *R. v. McSorley*, 2000 BCPC 116.

12 See *R. v. D.J.W.*, 2011 BCCA 522, aff'd 2012 SCC 63.

13 See Criminal Code, sec. 216.

14 Flannigan, "Fiduciary Regulation of Sexual Exploitation."

15 See, in the parenting context, Brighouse and Swift, *Family Values* at ch. 4.

16 See, in particular, Hochschild, *The Time Bind*; Arlie Russell Hochschild, *The Commercialization of Intimate Life* (California: University of California Press, 2003); Jan E. Dizard and Howard Gadlin, *The Minimal Family* (Amherst: University of Massachusetts Press, 1990); Bernstein, *Temporarily Yours.*

17 The decision is discussed at length in Randall, "Sexual Assault in Spousal Relationships." See also Craig, "Ten Years after *Ewanchuk*" at 259–69.

18 *R. v. V. (R.),* 2001 CarswellOnt 4565 (Ont. CJ).

19 *R. v. V. (R.)* (2004), 20 CR (6th) 346 at para. 10 (Ont. SCJ).

20 Ibid. at para. 11.

21 Ibid. at paras. 37–38.

22 *R. v. V. (R.)* (14 December 2004), Doc. CA C41566 (Ont. CA), http://www.ontariocourts.ca/decisions/2004/december/C41566.htm.

23 *R. v. V. (R.),* 2001 CarswellOnt 4565 at para. 14 (Ont. CJ).

24 *V.(R.)* (Ont. SCJ) at para. 4.

25 Archard, *Sexual Consent* at 27.

26 *R. v. T. (W.A.)* (2011), 86 CR (6th) 125 at para. 102 (Alta. QB).

27 Ibid. at para. 101, emphasis original.

28 Ibid. at para. 102 (Alta QB).

29 Janine Benedet, Annotation to *R. v. T. (W.A.)* (2011) 86 CR (6th) 126 at 126, implicitly referring to *T. (W.A.)*, at para. 72.

30 *House of Commons Debates*, 34th Parl, 3rd Sess, vol. 13 (8 April 1992) at 9504 [*House of Commons Debates*].

31 Ibid. at 9504.

32 Ibid.

33 Ibid. at 9506. See also *House of Commons Debates* (15 June 1992) at 12026.

34 *House of Commons Debates* (8 April 1992) at 9506.

35 Ibid. at 9507.

36 *Act to Amend the Criminal Code (Sexual Assault)*, Bill C-49, 3rd Sess., 34th Parl., 1991 (assented to 23 June 1992), SC 1992, c. 38, preamble.

37 *House of Commons Debates* (8 April 1992) at 9505.

38 Ibid. at 9507.

39 Ibid. at 9515–16.

40 Ibid. at 9516.

41 Standing Committee on Justice and Human Rights (20 May 1992) at 4:57.

42 Ibid.

43 Ibid.

44 Ibid. ("I really think you're taking this to a level that's just not happening, and not going to happen.")

45 Standing Committee on Justice and Human Rights (20 May 1992) at 4:58.

46 *House of Commons Debates* (8 April 1992) at 9522.

47 Ibid. at 9515–16.

48 Standing Committee on Justice and Human Rights (20 May 1992) at 4:57.

49 See, e.g., *House of Commons Debates* (8 April 1992) at 9532, 9535 (Hunter).

50 Standing Committee on Justice and Human Rights (4 June 1992) at 7:24 (MacLellan).

51 Ibid. at 7:30; *House of Commons Debates* (15 June 1992) at 12000–05.

52 Standing Committee on Justice and Human Rights (4 June 1992) at 7:24–25 (Nicholson).

53 Ibid. at 7:25 (Nicholson).

54 Ibid. at 7:30.

55 Ibid.

56 *House of Commons Debates* (8 April 1992) at 9520.

57 Ibid.

58 See, e.g., Standing Committee on Justice and Human Rights (19 May 1992) at 2:23–24, 2:26 (Lemieux); Standing Committee on Justice and Human Rights (20 May 1992) at 3:36–37 (Jaffer); Standing Committee on Justice and Human Rights (20 May 1992) at 4:48 (Bryden). This leaves aside the submission of REAL Women of Canada, which took the view that the legislation was indeed attempting to institutionalize new values into the law,

but opposed those views, and wanted to preserve a space for "cultural diversity": Standing Committee on Justice and Human Rights (19 May 1992) at 2:47.

59 *House of Commons Debates* (8 April 1992) at 9526 (Waddell).

60 See Standing Committee on Justice and Human Rights (20 May 1992) at 3:19 (Lakeman), 3:31 (Ford); Standing Committee on Justice and Human Rights (20 May 1992) at 4:28–29, 4:42 (Tellier).

61 Standing Committee on Justice and Human Rights (2 June 1992) at 6:43 (Campbell).

62 *House of Commons Debates* (15 June 1992) at 12027.

63 Ibid. at 12040 (Clancy).

64 Bill C-49, first reading.

65 See, e.g., Standing Committee on Justice and Human Rights (19 May 1992) at 2:10, 2:13, 2:33, 2:35–36, 2:44–45, 2:50, 2A:79; Standing Committee on Justice and Human Rights (20 May 1992) 4:51, 4A:25; Standing Committee on Justice and Human Rights (21 May 1992) at 5:12–13, 5A:5–6.

66 Standing Committee on Justice and Human Rights (20 May 1992) at 3:19 (Lakeman).

67 See Standing Committee on Justice and Human Rights (2 June 1992) at 6:21–36, 6A:20–27.

68 Ibid.

69 Ibid. at 6:46–47, 6:66; Standing Committee on Justice and Human Rights (4 June 1992) at 7:3.

70 Standing Committee on Justice and Human Rights (2 June 1992) at 6:31–32.

71 Ibid. at 6:47–48.

72 Boyle, *Sexual Assault* at 71–72.

73 Ibid. at 72.

74 There is a similar sort of hedging elsewhere. The Women's Legal Education and Action Fund, for example, argued in its submissions to the Supreme Court in *Ewanchuk* that even "minor" sexual touching without active consent amounts to a sexual assault: See LEAF Intervenors' Factum at para. 29. It is clear from the rest of the passage that the concern was with the use of one sexual assault "to explore the possibility of further sexual contact." But, more to the point, once LEAF turned to the scenario of "the loving intimate partner who touches his partner in a sexual manner without her prior communicated consent," it observed only that such a case was unlikely to be prosecuted: ibid. at para. 30. It did not explicitly say that such touching must be, or usually would be, criminally wrongful in the first place. That, as I argued in chapter 1, is not a question that can be ignored.

75 McInnes and Boyle, "Judging Sexual Assault Law" at 374–75.

76 Ibid. at 370n68.

77 Ibid. at emphasis added.

78 Boyle, *Sexual Assault* at 364.

79 Ibid.

80 Ibid. at 365.

81 *Chase.*

82 Where it has arisen, the courts have tended to find that the touching was indeed sexual. See, e.g., *R. v. V (K.B.),* [1993] 2 SCR 857.

83 See *S.W. v. United Kingdom,* 22 November 1995, European Court of Human Rights, No. 47/1994/494/576.

84 See Vera Bergelson, *Victims' Rights and Victims' Wrongs: Comparative Liability in Criminal Law* (Stanford: Stanford University Press, 2009) at 41–43.

85 See *R. v. V. (R.),* 2001 CarswellOnt 4565 at para. 10 (Ont. CJ). See also *R. v. Went* (2004), 25 CR (6th) 350 at para. 22 (BCSC).

86 See many of the judicial remarks reported in Randall, "Sexual Assault in Spousal Relationships," as well as the remarks of lawyers reported in Lazar, "Negotiating Sex."

87 Johnson, *Dangerous Domains* at 142–46; Diana E.H. Russell, *Rape in Marriage,* 2nd ed. (Bloomington: Indiana University Press, 1990); David Finkelhor and Kersti Yllo, *License to Rape: Sexual Abuse of Wives* (New York: Free Press, 1985).

CHAPTER NINE

1 See Dan-Cohen, "Decision Rules and Conduct Rules." The phenomenon of quasi-justificatory drift is also suggestive: Simon Gardner, "Instrumentalism and Necessity" (1986) 6 OJLS 431 at 433.

2 Much of this section is reproduced from my review essay, "Public Hostility" *Literary Review of Canada* (January/February 2013).

3 Rawls, *Political Liberalism.*

4 Ibid. at 35.

5 Waldron, *The Harm in Hate Speech.*

6 See MacKinnon, *Only Words* at 74–75.

7 *Butler.*

8 Ibid. at 485.

9 Waldron, *The Harm in Hate Speech* at 80–81.

10 John Rawls, *A Theory of Justice,* rev. ed. (Cambridge: Harvard University Press, 1999) at 211.

11 Waldron, *The Harm in Hate Speech* at 80–81.

12 Ibid.

13 Martha C. Nussbaum, *Political Emotions: Why Love Matters for Justice* (Cambridge: Harvard University Press, 2013).

14 Ibid. at 131–32, 164.

15 See Jeremy Waldron, "When Justice Replaces Affection: The Need for Rights" in *Liberal Rights: Collected Papers 1981–1991* (Cambridge: Cambridge University Press, 1993).

16 Berlin, "Two Concepts of Liberty" at 122–31.

17 But see Vincent Chiao, "Equality, Assurance, and Criminalization" (2014) 27 CJLJ, http://papers.ssrn.com/sol3/papers.cfm?abstract_id=2403074; Robert Mark Simpson, "Dignity, Harm, and Hate Speech" (2013) 32 L. & Philosophy 701.

18 Alan Brudner, *Punishment and Freedom: A Liberal Theory of Penal Justice* (Oxford: Oxford University Press, 2009) at 23–48.

19 Ibid. at 5.

20 Ibid. at 297–99.

21 Ibid. at 138.

22 Ibid.

23 Ibid.

24 Berlin, "Two Concepts of Liberty" at 131–41.

25 Brudner, *Punishment and Freedom* at 28–29.

26 See Alan Brudner, "Owning Outcomes: On Intervening Causes, Thin Skulls, and Fault-Undifferentiated Crimes" (1998) 11 CJLJ 89.

27 Raz, *The Morality of Freedom* at 374.

28 Ibid.

29 Ibid. at 204.

30 Ibid. at 204–05.

31 Ibid. at 205.

32 Ibid. at 203.

33 For various discussions of public goods generally, see J.E. Stiglitz, *Economics*, 2nd ed. (New York: W.W. Norton, 1997) at 157; Hirschman, *Exit, Voice, and Loyalty* at 101; Richard Cornes and Todd Sandler, *The Theory of Externalities, Public Goods, and Club Goods*, 2nd ed. (Cambridge: Cambridge University Press, 1996). For discussions of the extent to which Raz's understanding of public goods diverges from that of economists, compare Denise Réaume, "Individuals, Groups, and Rights to Public Goods" (1988) 38 UTLJ 1 at 3 and Newman, *Community and Collective Rights* at 67n.

34 Raz, *The Morality of Freedom* at 199.

35 See Peter Ramsay, *The Insecurity State: Vulnerable Autonomy and the Right to Security in the Criminal Law* (Oxford: Oxford University Press, 2012) at 206.

36 Ibid.

37 Waldron, *The Harm in Hate Speech* at 92–93.

38 Ibid. at 93.

39 A roughly similar point is made by Lina Papadaki, "What Is Objectification?" (2010) 7 J. Moral Phil. 16 (noting that Nussbaum's objectification inquiry is too broad and open-ended to be practically useful in moral arguments).

40. Indeed, the Supreme Court in *Chase* at 302 rejected a motive-centred interpretation of "sexual touching" in part because doing so would "defeat[] the obvious purpose" of the sexual assault provisions.

41 Cheryl Hanna, "Sex Is Not a Sport: Consent and Violence in Criminal Law" (2001) 42 Boston College L. Rev. 239.

42 Ibid. at 250.

43 Ibid.

44 Ibid. at 256.

45 Ibid. at 255.

46 Ibid. at 255–56.

47 Ibid. at 256.

48 Ibid.

49 Ibid. at 268.

50 Ibid. at 270.

51 Ibid. at 269–70.

52 Elaine Craig, "Capacity to Consent to Sexual Risk" (2014) 17 New Crim. L. Rev. 103.

53 See Khan, *Vicarious Kinks*.

54 See chapter 1, n76 and accompanying text.

55 See Gardner and Shute, "The Wrongness of Rape" at 215–16. See also Gardner, *Offences and Defences* at 118–20 (also discussing the harm principle); Joseph Raz, "Autonomy, Toleration, and the Harm Principle" in Ruth Gavison, ed., *Issues in Contemporary Legal Philosophy: The Influence of HLA Hart* (Oxford: Clarendon Press, 1987).

56 Ibid.

57 See Samuel Buell, "The Upside of Overbreadth" (2008) 83 NYU L. Rev. 1491.

58 For discussion, see Michael Plaxton, "The Challenge of the Bad Man" (2013) 58 McGill LJ 451 at 465.

59 See Buell, "The Upside of Overbreadth" at 1497–506 (discussing the distinction).

60 Hart, *The Concept of Law* at 40.

61 See the discussion in Frederick Schauer, "Was Austin Right after All? On the Role of Sanctions in a Theory of Law" (2010) 12 Ratio Juris 1 at 12–14; Scott J. Shapiro, "The Bad Man and the Internal Point of View" in Steven J. Burton, ed., *The Path of the Law and Its Influence: The Legacy of Oliver Wendell Holmes, Jr.* (Cambridge: Cambridge University Press, 2000) at 198–200.

62 Conduct rules are expected to guide everyone in the community – not only citizens in the strict sense. I use "citizens" to refer to members of the public generally.

63 See Schauer, "Was Austin Right after All?"

64 Dan-Cohen, "Decision Rules and Conduct Rules."

65 Ibid. at 673–77.

66 But see Bert I. Huang, "Shallow Signals" (2013) 126 Harvard L. Rev. 2227.

CHAPTER TEN

1 Buell, "The Upside of Overbreadth."
2 Kathleen M. Sullivan, "The Justices of Rules and Standards" (1992) 106 Harv. L. Rev. 22 at 91; Schauer, *Playing by the Rules*.
3 Buell, "The Upside of Overbreadth" at 1492.
4 See Gardner and Shute, "The Wrongness of Rape."
5 Buell, "The Upside of Overbreadth" at 1512–13.
6 There is a third possibility: that members of the public should take their guidance not only from the language of statutes, but from the enforcement practices of police and prosecutors. That seems to be the working assumption underpinning Huang, "Shallow Signals" and, more obviously, Kenneth Culp Davis, *Police Discretion* (St Paul: West Publishing, 1975). This is, however, a deeply problematic conclusion, from the perspective of the rule of law, unless one assumes (as Davis does) that there are mechanisms by which police and prosecutors can be held publicly accountable for their enforcement policies.
7 I do not necessarily reject the suggestion that it should be a positive defence in the context of assault simpliciter as well.
8 Duff, *Answering for Crime*.
9 *R. v. City of Sault Ste Marie*, [1978] 2 SCR 1299.
10 Duff, *Answering for Crime* at 243.
11 Ibid. at 243–44.
12 Ibid.
13 Ibid. at 248.
14 Ibid. at 248–49.
15 Ibid. at 247–48, emphasis added.
16 Ibid. at 249.
17 Ibid. at 249n67.
18 Ibid. at 249.
19 See the discussion in chapter 4 of this book.
20 Duff, *Answering for Crime* at 209; Victor Tadros, *Criminal Responsibility* (New York: Oxford University Press, 2005) at 105–06. See also John Gardner, "Justification under Authority" (2010) 23:1 Can. JL & Jur. 71 (taking issue with the position adopted in Michelle Dempsey and Jonathan Herring, "Why Sexual Penetration Requires Justification" (2007) 27 OJLS 467).
21 On the public relevance of family life, see Brettschneider, *When the States Speaks*. See also Okin, *Justice, Gender, and the Family*.
22 See Gardner, "Justification under Authority" at 75–83.
23 See *Canada (Attorney General) v. Bedford* [2013] 3 SCR 1101.
24 Criminal Code, sec. 212(3).
25 *R. v. Downey*, [1992] 2 SCR 10.
26 Ibid. at 37, 39.

27 Ibid. at 30. See also Michael Plaxton, "Offence Definitions, Conclusive Presumptions, and Slot Machines" (2010) 48 Osgoode Hall LJ 145; *Bedford* at paras. 141–42.

28 See the reasoning in *R. v. Audet*, [1996] 2 SCR 171. The core question in *Audet* was whether it was acceptable for the court to create a legal presumption. For my purposes, I can set that problem aside.

29 See *Bedford* at para. 101. See also *R. v. Heywood*, [1994] 3 SCR 761; *R. v. Demers*, 2004 SCC 46.

30 *Canada v. Bedford*. at para. 113.

31 See the discussion in chapter 9 of this book.

32 See *R. v. Oakes*, [1986] 1 SCR 103.

33 See *R. v. Whyte*, [1988] 2 SCR 3.

34 In principle, sec. 7 of the Charter is also engaged. Since all legal presumption cases have been analyzed as sec. 11(d) infringements, I proceed in a similar fashion.

35 It is theoretically possible that, in describing the objective, one could instead appeal to the aims of the offence of sexual assault. The Supreme Court in *Oakes* took this sort of approach: *Oakes* at para. 73. In that case, the objective would be to facilitate the conviction of those who engage in the instrumentalizing sexual touching of others. Put in those terms, the connection is more tenuous. Since the presence or absence of implied consent is relevant to whether the touching in question is instrumentalizing, the objective and the means adopted are arguably at cross-purposes. (This was the thrust of the court's reasoning in *Oakes*.) It is, however, worth remembering that this approach to rational connection in sec. 11(d) cases has been all but abandoned by the Supreme Court since *Oakes*. Those factors are more properly raised at the minimal impairment stage.

36 See *R. v. Chaulk*, [1990] 3 SCR 1303.

37 See *Seaboyer*.

CONCLUSION

1 Rebecca Solnit, *Men Explain Things to Me* (Dispatch Books, 2014).

2 Ibid. at 1–4.

3 I am painfully aware of the irony of a man writing an explanation of mansplaining in a book about sexual assault law.

4 But see Susan Cain, *Quiet: The Power of Introverts in a World that Can't Stop Talking* (Crown, 2012).

5 Solnit, *Men Explain Things to Me* at 4–5.

6 The comments are by Barbara Kay, available at http://www.press progress.ca/en/post/raw-video-national-post-columnist-offensive-comments-rape-misogyny-anorexia-female-journalists; George F. Will, "Colleges become the Victims of Progressivism," *Washington Post* (6 June

2014), http://www.washingtonpost.com/opinions/george-will-college-become-the-victims-of-progressivism/2014/06/06/e90e73b4-eb50-11e3-9f5c-9075d5508f0a_story.html.

7 Solnit, *Men Explain Things to Me* at 16.

APPENDIX

1 Scruton, *Sexual Desire.*
2 Nussbaum, review of *Sexual Desire.*
3 Dante, *The Divine Comedy: Hell*, trans. Dorothy L. Sayers (Markham: Penguin, 1978) at circle II, canto V.
4 Nussbaum, review of *Sexual Desire* at 31.
5 Ibid. at 31–32.
6 Ibid. at 30.
7 Ibid. at 31.
8 Ibid. at 30; Nussbaum, "'Whether from Reason or Prejudice'" at 283 ("It may also be that prostitution is always a cheap form of an activity that has a higher better form.").
9 See Cahill's insightful discussion in *Overcoming Objectification* at ch. 1.
10 Nussbaum, "Objectification" at 274.
11 Nussbaum, review of *Sexual Desire* at 30, emphasis added.
12 Nussbaum, "Objectification" at 261.

INDEX

disadvantage and harm, 24, 126–7, 131–3, 138–40

Duff, Antony, 208–13

exit, 128–9, 130, 131, 133–5

expressive function of law, 5, 30–2, 144, 241–3; and fair labelling, 32–5

fair labelling, 32–40, 47–8; and Canadian law, 35–40; and the expressive function of criminal law, 32–5, 38–40

Feinberg, Joel, 126

Fishkin, Joseph, 136

Gardner, John, 42, 56, 77–8, 111, 117, 142, 202–3, 206–7

Green, Leslie, 128–30

Green, Stuart, 32–3

Hanna, Cheryl, 77, 94, 199–201, 205, 206

Hart, H.L.A., 30–2, 150–1, 203–4

Haslanger, Sally, 6, 148, 153–7, 161, 162

heteronormativity, 21

Hirschman, Albert O., 128, 129, 130, 131

Husak, Douglas, 32

implied consent: as a defence to assault, 18–19, 64, 70–1; discussed in *R. v. Cey*, 70–1, 75; discussed in *R. v. J.A.*, 64; distinguished from advance consent, 19–21; distinguished from ordinary consent, 73–7; as a justification, 44; and parenting, 71–2; rationale, 18, 23, 69–70, 77–81; rejected as a defence to sexual assault, 14, 19, 67, 68–9; and sports, 70–1

influence, 18, 127–8, 128–31, 133–8

instrumentalization, 22, 23, 104, 108, 176; and objectification, 104; and sexual desire, 108; as the wrong of sexual assault, 22

intimate relationships: moral and legal significance of, 169–72, 172–7; plasticity of, 169–72

Kant, Immanuel, 107–8, 110

Kinnon, Dianne, 53

Langton, Rae, 141–2, 148, 154, 161, 162

Lawrence, D.H., 116, 140–1; *Lady Chatterley's Lover*, 116, 140–1; *The Rainbow*, 116, 140

legal presumptions, 25, 207; as an alternative to overbreadth, 25, 214–15; constitutionality of, 213–16; justification of, 211–13

Lewis, Debra J., 50–2

Łoś, Maria, 53, 55

loyalty, 120–1, 130, 142–3, 165, 176

MacKinnon, Catharine, 55, 96, 132, 141, 148, 153–4, 156, 157, 161, 162, 163, 193–4, 210

mansplaining, 218–19

marriage, 169–72, 188–9

McInnes, John, 186

McIntyre, Sheila, 89–90

mutuality, 2, 23, 24, 104, 111–21, 122, 143–4 165, 176, 190; definition of, 143–4; forms of, 104, 111–21; and instrumentalization, 111–21; and loyalty, 120–1; moral significance of, 23, 104, 111–21, 122

Nedelsky, Jennifer, 6, 23, 57, 95–100, 197, 205, 208, 210; on the reasonable steps requirement, 95–6, 100, 210; on relational autonomy, 23, 57, 95–6

Newman, Dwight, 134

non-consensual distribution of intimate images, 35

norms: governing sexual intimacy, 15–16, 138–40, 188–9; stereotypes, 24, 145–7. *See also* adaptive preferences; influence

Nussbaum, Martha, 6, 24, 59, 98, 102, 103, 104, 105–7, 109, 113–14, 116, 117–18, 121, 122, 127, 133, 138, 140–3, 156, 161, 176, 190, 194–5, 198, 221–5; and Clare Chambers, 24, 122, 133, 142; discussing portrayals of mutuality in works of D.H. Lawrence, 116, 140–1; and instrumentalization, 107, 117–18; on objectification, 105–7, 140–1, 161; on prostitution, 116; and Roger Scruton, 105, 221–5

objectification, 50–6, 104; as the wrong of sexual assault, 56, 65, 147–8; forms of, 105–7, 140–1, 161; and objectivity, 153–7; and silencing, 140–1, 161

overbreadth, 5, 25, 189, 197–205, 206–7

Ovid, 115

prosecutorial discretion, 5, 28–30, 42, 180–1, 182, 198–9, 207

Proust, Marcel, 137–8

R. v. A. (J.), 4, 11–12, 13–14, 15, 16, 17, 19, 29, 41, 42, 64, 65; facts of, 11–12; on implied consent as a defence to assault, 64; on sexual consent as subjective and contemporaneous, 13–14, 19; on sexual consent in intimate relationships, 15, 16; and voice, 12

R. v. E. (A.), 71

R. v. Bernard, 46

R. v. Butler, 43, 126, 163, 164–5

R. v. Cey, 70–1, 75, 88

R. v. Chase, 47, 57, 58, 59, 60, 61, 186, 187; defining sexual activity, 59, 60, 61, 186, 187; and sexual integrity, 47, 57, 58, 186

R. v. Cuerrier, 40–1, 62–3

R. v. W. (D.J.), 71

R. v. Darrach, 38–9

R. v. Downey, 213

R. v. Ewanchuk, 3, 6, 8–9, 10, 11, 12, 13, 14, 17, 18–19, 20, 22, 27, 28, 41, 43, 63–4, 65, 67, 68–9, 75, 81–4, 85, 90, 101, 102, 145–6, 148, 187, 189; facts of, 8–9, 67–8; on honest but mistaken belief in consent, 6, 14, 28, 65; on implied consent, 13, 14, 22, 64, 67, 68–9, 148; on sexual consent as subjective and contemporaneous, 6, 13, 90; on sexual integrity, 63–4, 90; and voice, 9

R. v. Flaviano, 7–8, 9, 10, 11, 12, 17; facts of, 7–8; and voice, 8

R. v. Hinchey, 40

R. v. Hutchinson, 63, 85, 90, 146, 147–8

R. v. Jensen, 85–7, 89

R. v. Labaye, 43

R. v. Larue, 62

R. v. Litchfield, 60–2

R. v. Mabior, 32, 43, 63

R. v. Martineau, 37–8

R. v. McDonnell, 42

R. v. Oakes, 214, 216

R. v. Osolin, 64–5

R. v. Palombi, 71, 80

R. v. Park, 85, 87, 89, 90

R. v. Robicheau, 59–60

R. v. Seaboyer, 65, 146–7, 177–8

R. v. Sharpe, 34

R. v. T. (W.A.), 175–7

R. v. V. (R.), 11, 173–5, 186–7, 189

R. v. Vaillancourt, 36–7

R. v. *Whyte*, 215
Ramsay, Peter, 197, 208
rape: abolition of the offence of, 46, 47, 48; as a crime of sexual objectification, 52–3, 54, 55–6, 94–5; as a crime of violence, 47–8, 52, 53–4; focus on penetration, 48–9; marital rape exemption, 24–5, 49, 167–8, 182, 188; the significance of sex to, 53–4; stigma of, 47–8, 51, 54–5
Rawls, John: on political liberalism, 123; on the well-ordered society, 191–2, 194–5
Raz, Joseph, 99–100, 196–7, 208
reasonable steps requirement, 11, 95–6, 100, 147–8, 172–7, 210, 211
Réaume, Denise, 159
Ripstein, Arthur, 78
Robinson, Paul, 33

Schauer, Frederick, 160
Scruton, Roger, 105, 108, 111, 112–13, 114, 115, 221–5; and Martha Nussbaum, 221–5; on sexual desire, 108, 112–13, 114
sexual desire, 107–15; and instrumentalization, 107–10, 114–15; as an intentional pleasure, 108–9; social construction of, 97–8
sexual integrity, 57, 90; and the offence of sexual assault, 57, 90; and sexual autonomy, 17–18, 57, 58, 90
sexual assault: as a crime of violence, 46; as a crime of sexual objectification, 56, 65, 147–8; as directed at all forms of non-consensual sexual

touching, 49–50; as a gendered offence, 21, 47, 56; legislative debates on, 48–50, 168–9, 177–85; the offence of, 46, 48–50; as protecting sexual autonomy, 58, 90, 177–9; as protecting sexual integrity, 46–7, 57–8, 65, 90; replacing the offence of rape, 22, 46; the wrongness of 22, 46–7, 56, 161–5
Shachar, Ayelet, 129
Shute, Stephen, 42, 56, 111, 117, 142, 202–3, 206–7
silencing, 8, 9, 12; as form of objectification, 140–1, 161
Solnit, Rebecca, 218–19
stereotypes, 23–4, 148–9, 152–3, 157–61
Stewart, Hamish, 44
Strawson, P.W., 138
Stuart, Donald R., 28, 85–8, 184; on *Ewanchuk*, 28; on implied consent, 85–8; on negligent sexual assault, 184
Sussman, David, 121

torture, 121
Tuerkheimer, Deborah, 97–8, 100

voice, 8, 9, 12, 129–31, 135–8, 139, 141–3, 219–20
voluntariness, 23, 89–93, 166; and planning agency, 91–3

Waldron, Jeremy, 132, 163, 192–3, 194–5, 210
West, Robin, 97–8